*Critical Essays on
Honoré de Balzac*

Critical Essays on
World Literature

Robert Lecker, General Editor
McGill University

Critical Essays on Honoré de Balzac

Martin Kanes

G.K. Hall & Co. ● Boston, Massachusetts

First published 1990
10 9 8 7 6 5 4 3 2 1

Library of Congress Cataloging-in-Publication Data

Critical essays on Honoré de Balzac / [edited by] Martin Kanes.
    p. cm. — (Critical essays on world literature)
   Includes bibliographical references.
   ISBN 0-8161-8845-9 (alk. paper)
   1. Balzac, Honoré de. 1799–1850—Criticism and interpretation.
I. Kanes, Martin. II. Series.
PQ2181.C75 1990
843'.7—dc20   89-39239
                                              CIP

This publication is printed on permanent/durable acid-free paper
MANUFACTURED IN THE UNITED STATES OF AMERICA

*To my wife, meticulous reader; to
André and Mireille de Moura, ever-patient
Parisians*

CONTENTS

The Modern Period: 1950–Present

INTRODUCTION

—Balzac to Mme. de Pommereul: "Not a word of truth in it: it's pure Balzac."

—Balzac in *Le Père Goriot:* "All is true."

Few writers have generated as much commentary as Honoré de Balzac. Born in 1799 and dead by 1850, he lived a life and produced a body of work that have aroused uninterrupted attention. Part of Balzac's reputation has to do simply with the quantity of his output: in twenty years he created about ninety-seven works under the collective title of *La Comédie humaine*—as well as juvenilia, plays, articles, an enormous correspondence, the *Contes drolatiques* (Droll Stories), and of course the vast mass of rewritten and transformed copy beneath the texts as they are currently read. A library of commentary has grown up around this nearly superhuman existence; to sum it all up in a single volume would be impossible. Consequently, this essay and its accompanying material will focus principally on the *Comédie humaine*—the heart of Balzac's production.[1]

No matter what approach we take as readers, Balzac's works appear as a complex, interconnected, incomplete structure. His device of using reappearing characters, his habit of carrying plots over from one novel to the next, his compulsive return to characteristic themes creating a single enormous work of which each novel would be a smallish panel—all this draws the reader into a world from which it is difficult to escape. The power of this attraction is perhaps most sharply expressed in the legends of the author's own entrapment in the world of the *Comédie humaine*. Who but Balzac could have called on his deathbed for his own fictional Dr. Bianchon?

Balzac was the subject of hundreds of anecdotes, of satirical sketches, of gossip about his excursions into the theater and about his disastrously mismanaged ventures into business. People wondered which were his favorite restaurants. "Was he elegant?" the critic Jules Bertaut asked as late as 1923.[2] The irrepressible medical man of letters Dr. Auguste Cabanès wrote a series of articles dealing with topics ranging from the portraits of doctors in the *Comédie humaine* to Balzac's own "ambulatory mania," his "megalomania," and—amazingly—his "chastity."[3] Entire volumes have been devoted to his

1

dealings with publishers and to his activities in the Société des gens de lettres.[4] Political and artistic turmoil surrounded Rodin's "scandalous" proposal for a statue to his memory.

His most striking characteristic was his headlong, heedless plunging through life. His conversation was torrential; his love affairs endless and frequently overlapping.[5] He alternated periods of frantic public activity with periods of nearly total seclusion; he consumed legendary quantities of coffee; he lived his entire adult life with a crushing debt and yet was a profligate spender to the end. He fancied himself politically adroit; he quite illegitimately adopted the coat of arms (and the nobiliary particle "de") belonging to the Balzac d'Entragues family—his own name having derived from the peasant Italian name "Balssa." Caricaturists could hardly have asked for more. The artist Gavarni, who respected Balzac's work, described him rather cruelly but with typical fascination as "impossible to make respectable, opening wide eyes at everything you said to him, at once naive and astonishing in what he did not know . . . dirty, unkempt, wearing ridiculous white waistcoats . . . eating like a pig, stupid and ignorant in his private life."[6] Clearly there was plenty of room for anecdote.[7]

It is true that where biographical investigation was concerned with the relationships between Balzac's life and his writing, it produced work of real interest,[8] especially the many studies by the great scholar and bibliophile Marcel Bouteron.[9] Nevertheless, as time passed biography seemed increasingly inadequate to account for many qualities of Balzac's work. Indeed, the *Comédie humaine* presents the critical reader with more than the usual problems of interpretation. Was the master storyteller a brilliant social analyst? A philosophical thinker? A political commentator? A historian? A cultural anthropologist of sorts? Was he a realist? A romantic? A visionary? A pre-Marxist Marxist? A pre-Freudian Freudian? All these interpretations have been advanced and have inspired the endless debates that have regularly emerged on "Balzacian" occasions: at the moment of his death, at the dedication of Falguière's statue of him in Paris, at the sesquicentennial of his birth and the centenary of his death. They still dominate Balzac scholarship.

One discusses with passion only that which is of fundamental interest. And the *Comédie humaine* interests us on several levels. For one thing, it raises the vexed question of genre: what is a novel? Some of Balzac's texts are in fact short stories; some are recognizable as "novels"; some are really multiple constructions that break down into novel-length parts.[10] But to be recognizable as a novel, a text must satisfy expectations other than those of length: we traditionally look for unity of characterization, for consistent development of plot and milieu, and above all a certain relationship to perceived reality. In this sense, some of Balzac's works are archetypical novels—*Eugénie Grandet*, for example, or *Le Père Goriot* (Old Goriot)—which perhaps accounts for the great popularity they enjoy over other parts of the *Comédie humaine*. But not all of Balzac's novels are "traditional" in any sense: some are reworkings of old myths (Melmoth, or Don Juan); some, like *Séraphîta*, are philosophical treatises; some are sociological disquisitions like *Le Médecin de campagne;* some are sheer fantasy, for example *La Peau de chagrin*.

Whatever we may choose to call these works (here they will all be called novels), they touch on the deepest and most urgent human concerns. Beneath the fantastic tale of a magic skin lie troubling questions about the nature of desire and knowledge; englobed in the recital of greed and avarice on a great provincial property is a vivid portrait of France's transformation from an estate society to a bourgeois society; embodied in the story of an obsessed painter is a pained account of artistic creativity. It is easy to see why the *Comédie humaine* became a platform from which widely divergent theses have been promulgated about human beings and the cultures they create. Like the Bible, it brings multiple answers to every question it raises.

Nor were Balzac's novels produced in a vacuum. The issues he raised were the overriding concerns of his day. As his works provoked criticism, Balzac often incorporated his reactions into his further writing, especially the polemical prefaces of which he was so fond. In sum, his work can be read as one half of a dialogue he conducted with his century; the other half is incorporated in the vast body of critical writing that was devoted to his every word.

The general principle in the unfolding of his work was the initial composition of a half-dozen novels, the notion of linking them together as "scenes" of contemporary life, the addition of further novels that tended to grow organically out of previous work and the overall conception, and finally the establishment of a set of categories and subcategories in terms of which he organized the whole. These steps were not strictly sequential, of course. New novels were added as earlier ones were being revised; new categories suggested further novels, and vice versa.

From the very beginning Balzac was concerned with presenting his work to the public as a coherent whole. But his search for formal unity should not blind us to the complexity of relationships within the work, or to the confusion and paradox that reign on many levels. The consistency of reappearing characters is often belied by gaps and contradictions; the significance of plot sometimes stands in stark contradiction to the authorial pronouncements that accompany it; the realism of description is frequently doubled by a hallucinatory tone that undercuts its mimetic function.

The organization of the *Comédie humaine* is a reflection of the scientific debate about the original unity of the cosmos then being vigorously conducted by Georges Cuvier and Geoffroy Saint-Hilaire. Balzac opted for an original "unity of composition" and conceived of a series of derivative "social species" analogous to biological species, with each human social type existing in a characteristic milieu. To describe French society, therefore, Balzac had to deal with the mores of the real world (the first section of the *Comédie humaine*—"Etudes de moeurs"), then rise to a description of the causes behind those customs (the second section—"Etudes philosophiques"), and finally conclude with an exposition of the principles governing the causes (the third section—"Etudes analytiques"). This progression also reflected his optimistic assumption that science and metaphysics were but two sides of one coin and that he could use the thought of such mystical philosophers as Emmanuel Swedenborg and Louis-Claude Saint-Martin without contradicting his scientific biases.

Although Balzac could see many theoretical subdivisions of his three great primary categories, only the first was actually so divided. The reason is easy to see: the progression went from the concrete to the abstract, and the further the work moved in that direction, the more difficult it was to conceptualize and express. And so in the final version, the "Etudes de moeurs" contains six subdivisions with seventy-three titles, the "Etudes philosophiques" contains twenty-three titles without subdivisions, and the "Etudes analytiques" contains a mere three works that are not at all abstract.[11]

Clearly the operational level, for both writer and reader, is that of "Scenes." It was the first grouping that Balzac thought of, and it remains an important unifying device, since the location of a novel in a given Scene inevitably colors the way we read it—although we are of course constantly solicited to listen to more distant echoes from other wings of the vast edifice. Even so, the plan was not easy to manage. Working in broad categories (some of the Scenes themselves had become quite large) and in an ever-developing matrix, Balzac found himself continually reorganizing and relocating his material.

La Messe de l'athée (The Atheist's Mass), for example, began in the "Etudes philosophiques"; it was then shifted to the "Etudes de moeurs," where it was placed in the "Scènes de la vie parisienne" before being moved to the "Scènes de la vie privée," where it now resides. One can see why this story of the conflict between religion and atheism might be thought of as "philosophical," and also why it might count as a study of social mores. But the shift from "Parisian Life" to "Private Life" is a more delicate matter, changing the light in which we read the tale. This final displacement makes religion a private rather than public matter—a not inconsiderable issue in nineteenth-century France—and underscores the notion of religious faith as a mystery.

Some distinctions, on the other hand, are not so obvious. The difference between country scenes (*la vie de campagne*) and provincial scenes (*la vie de province*) ostensibly reflects the difference between rural and small-town life; in fact, Balzac said that the former was intended to be more edifying and moralistic than the latter (as indeed it is). In a word, the difference is conceptual, not sociological as the titles would imply; this leaves the sometimes perplexed reader to regret the incompleteness of the overall design that was Balzac's dream. It is quite clear, however, that the divisions of the *Comédie humaine* have nothing to do with a literal description of society; they spring from Balzac's artistic purposes and the very complex processes of conceptualization.[12]

This compositional framework went hand in hand with a theory of art. As a good vitalist, Balzac saw human life as the expenditure of a reservoir of life energy in a search for intellectual or material power. This is the energizing force that drives his dark heroes and heroines, and his artists as well—all of whom confront the choice between living "rapidly" and enacting great deeds and works, or living "prudently" and producing nothing over a long lifetime.[13]

It cannot be sufficiently stressed that these theoretical structures were not conceived a priori; they developed along with his subject: a study of the July Monarchy in France, with a few excursions back to historical events that Balzac considered to be the source of contemporary issues.[14] But if his execution was episodic, his intentions were profound. Above all, he was supremely self-confident. When we hear of his enthusiastic exclamation to his sister in 1833 that he was "on the point of becoming a genius" because he had stumbled upon the key notion of reappearing characters, we are not entitled to smile. He knew whereof he spoke.[15]

When Balzac's life came to an end in 1850, the great scheme was unfinished. In the end an annotated copy of the Furne edition of his *Oeuvres complètes* bound in red leather was his literary testament.[16] Over the years, of course, there have been many reeditions of the *Comédie humaine*. They reflect a variety of approaches, ranging from scrupulous respect for the state in which he left it to various rearrangements according to the chronology of composition or the chronology of plots.[17] Things being as they are, none is entirely satisfactory.

The *Comédie humaine* has been translated into many languages. The first complete English translation appeared in 1895, under the auspices of George Saintsbury.[18] It is a Victorian version, somewhat stiff and proper in its renditions. Even today, however, no other complete English translation exists. Present-day anglophone readers will be much more likely to read modern translations of individual novels, of which there are many.

Such a massive work inevitably required detailed bibliographical analysis as a basis for reliable critical appraisal, and the first two members of the great quartet of Balzac scholars (Belgian Viscount Charles Spoelberch de Lovenjoul, the American W. H. Royce, Marcel Bouteron, and Jean Pommier) provided it with spectacular success. During a lifetime of collecting, Lovenjoul put together a superb collection of Balzaciana, which eventually came into the custody of the Institut de France and which, as of 1914, became the world mecca of all Balzacians.[19] In the course of his work, Lovenjoul produced an indispensable first history of Balzac's works and their commentators, including a bibliography of criticism up to the date of its appearance.[20]

A half-century later, W. H. Royce produced a bibliography containing no less than 4,010 items.[21] An additional 6,000 items were intended for a

Supplement, which unfortunately never appeared; the entire mass of Royce's material eventually went to Syracuse University.[22]

The purpose of all criticism is to arrive at an interpretation that knowledgeable readers of a text, at any given moment, recognize as adequate. The notion of "adequacy"—in various degrees and modes, to be sure—rather than of "correctness" is essential if any map of Balzac scholarship is to make sense. The approaches are not only complex but often mutually exclusive and run through four characteristic periods of scholarship, covering a century and a half of critical writing.

The first period of serious criticism began as soon as Balzac published under his own name, and continued with considerable vigor during his lifetime. At the time of his death his position as a major writer was not firmly fixed; although he was highly appreciated by sophisticated readers such as Stendhal and Hugo, his sales, if that is a criterion, were actually not very good.[23] Much of the early criticism was anecdotal and biographical, a mixture of personal and literary polemic that Balzac himself was not above exploiting.

At the same time, however, several serious critical attitudes could be discerned. The first assumed that Balzac was a realist, concerned with being a great historian and sociologist. Most critics who took this stance based themselves on Balzac's own remark that he was merely the "secretary of society." This group included hostile critics concerned with Balzac's supposed offenses against middle-class standards of morality and was led by Sainte-Beuve, who did not hesitate to use the term "dung-heap" to describe Balzac's work.[24]

The second type was based on the assumption that Balzac was really a philosopher, whose fiction was merely the vehicle by which he expressed a metaphysical view of man and the world. The words "philosophical" and "metaphysical" here generally meant little more than "not mimetic." This view was heavily implied, if not actually articulated, by Philarète Chasles, who used the words "fantastical" and "magic circle" in an early review of *La Peau de chagrin,* [25] and the word "visionary" in the *Journal des Débats* on 24 August 1850.

The next period, extending from Balzac's death in 1850 to about the turn of the century, was that of the "Great Debate," when Balzac's position as one of France's greatest novelists was argued and finally consolidated.[26]

The Great Debate was opened by two leading critics, Théophile Gautier and Hippolyte Taine,[27] whose sympathetic and far-ranging studies confirmed Balzac's place as a major writer and positioned him to become the paternal figure for the emerging group of "realist" novelists.[28] But it was always clear that Balzac was not a passive observer, and that even a "secretaryship to society" had political implications. Those who saw him this way quickly divided into the political Left (who could legitimize their position with the favorable comments of Marx and Engels)[29] and the Right (whose position derived largely from certain comments by Philarète Chasles).[30]

And yet almost at the same moment, the epithet "visionary" was relaunched by Baudelaire and a somewhat repentant Sainte-Beuve. Among critics taking this attitude, however, there were also variations of opinion, ranging from those who saw him as an adept of the hermetic philosophers Swedenborg and Saint-Martin, to those who preferred to read him as an orthodox Catholic. Proponents of these two views have been locked in debate for a very long time, and opinions are vehement on both sides.

The third period, extending from the turn of the century to the centenary of Balzac's death in 1950, might be called that of politics and high scholarship. Balzac made his entry into academic precincts where his work was studied for its conformity to accepted literary standards[31] and frequently for its accuracy as a mimetic transcription of reality.[32]

But at the same time, philosophical interpretation flourished, rooted in the insights of a previous era. Downplaying questions of biography, mimesis, politics, or textual characteristics, it was concerned with the theoretical view of human nature to be found in the *Comédie humaine* taken as a finished product. Undoubtedly the best-known exponents of this approach were and remain Albert Béguin and Ernst-Robert Curtius, who see the work primarily as a metaphysical analysis concerned, according to Curtius, with the search for "knowledge" or, according to Béguin, with the drive toward "power."[33]

Moralistic criticism continued,[34] but at a lower level, with much of it now becoming frankly political. This was a curious reversal. Whereas earlier moralists had seen Balzac as a producer of gutter literature, the later ones viewed him as a kind of social physician who foresaw all the ills to which the Third Republic had presumably fallen victim. Basing themselves on partial readings of the *Comédie humaine*, critics of the Right claimed him as their own.[35] Critics on the Left soon followed suit.[36] The theoretical question seemed to be whether the problems and crises of the July Monarchy—and consequently of modern France—were rooted in human nature or in the objective conditions of society. Given the turbulent course of French politics between 1900 and 1950, and the devotion of the French to a literature they consider to be a national treasure, these attempts at co-optation were more or less to be expected.

Many of these trends were summarized, so to speak, in a volume commemorating the centenary of Balzac's death, in which thirty-four scholars and critics brought their various points of view to bear on a body of writing that had acquired, by then, the status of a national monument.[37]

The centenary volume was both a closure and an overture. The last period of scholarship, our own, once again opened with a classic restatement of established positions—that of Balzac the "philosopher"[38] and of Balzac the "realist." An admirable attempt at synthesizing the positions was made by André Allemand, in a series significantly titled "Histoire des Mentalités."[39] But scholars now found themselves in the post–World War II period in which traditional issues and methodologies seemed tired and outmoded. New theories and new approaches revolutionized Balzac research. By the time this fourth period of criticism opened at midcentury, the availability of many manscripts and proofs—evidence of Balzac's complex writing and re-writing, publishing and republishing, adding and deleting—had aroused enormous interest in the analysis of the compositional process itself. This led to the systematic study of the evolution of texts from first conception to final form, in the hope that in the mass of manuscripts and proof-sheets saved by Spoelberch de Lovenjoul, some clues would be found to explain the creative process. The idea was not new; Théophile Gautier had suggested the interest of a study of Balzac's manuscripts and editions as far back as 1859, and Bernard Guyon had actually written such an analysis in the 1920s, although he did not publish his results until some thirty years later.[40]

The first really systematic, large-scale study of the manuscripts and editions was conducted at the University of Chicago in the 1930s by a group gathered around E. Preston Dargan and Bernard Weinberg,[41] but the method reached its full flowering in the group of scholars who gathered at the Chantilly archives after World War II under the presiding figure of Jean Pommier. They produced—quite apart from splendid critical editions—a remarkable series of "genetic" studies, which substituted for traditional source studies a more sensitive attempt to illuminate the stunning phenome-non of Balzac's creativity, and to do so on the basis of objective evidence.[42] Overall, the analysis of the manuscripts and editions has confirmed the accuracy of Balzac's fictional representation of historical reality, but by so doing has paradoxically tended to undermine our notion of the causality that was so often assumed to flow from history to fiction.[43]

It should thus come as no surprise that although investigations into manuscripts, proofs, and editions revealed much about the visible forms of Balzac's composition, they ultimately left the central question of his creativ-ity untouched. It was not long, therefore, before clues and sources were sought in areas less directly tied to the manuscripts: in his juvenilia, for example, or in his reading habits.[44] Moreover, this broadening of the ques-tion led quite logically to a third strand in Balzac criticism: his "poetics." Rejecting analysis based upon simple mimesis, as well as the assumption that the essence of the creative process was inscribed on paper (although they certainly profited from the work done at Chantilly), these critics attempted to grasp the nature of Balzac's work as an esthetic object using categories that were implied to be universal. Balzac here emerged neither as a philosopher nor as an observer, but as a poet. Needless to say, this tendency is the most complicated of all. It includes critics we have come to think of as es-theticians, such as Jean-Pierre Richard and Gaëtan Picon.[45] In the event, they produced what is surely one of the richest bodies of critical writing devoted to a major French novelist.

In the last decade or two, questions have arisen regarding Balzac's narra-tive technique. These inquiries have tended to be formalist in nature and are based upon the interpretation of literature through Freudian, semiotic, lin-guistic, thematic, reader-response, feminist, deconstructionist, and similar frames.[46] They are, in fact, developments of earlier trends, which did not simply vanish at midcentury. And very recently there has been a flowering of Marxist critics who see literary meaning as a secretion of history or at the very least understandable only as a function of time.[47] Even in our day, then, the *Comédie humaine* remains a battleground of ideologies. Perhaps the most famous of these encounters occurred when Roland Barthes's *S/Z*, a collocation of various types of synchronic methodologies, brought down the wrath of the leading Marxist critic, Pierre Barbéris, whose own monumental study prompted a lengthy response by Bernard Guyon.[48]

Not surprisingly, the contradictory strands of Balzac criticism have resulted in the emergence of nothing less than metacriticism; that is, criticism and analysis of Balzac scholarship and criticism itself. We shall have occasion to return to this most interesting phenomenon.[49]

Accompanying these debates from beginning to end has been an argument over his style—indeed, over whether or not he possessed one. In a country devoted to standards of stylistic clarity and purity almost 200 years old when he began to write, Balzac was a difficult phenomenon for contemporaries to swallow. The typical pattern of his novels—long and highly detailed introductory movements (often constituting the bulk of the novel), followed by very rapid and dramatic crises—was unfamiliar. His long descriptions, his exaggerated imagery, his brusque authorial interventions, his sometimes questionable syntax—all these offended ordinary readers, not to speak of professional critics such as Sainte-Beuve, Gustave Planche, and Jules Janin. Today it is amusing to read these early articles, which, starting from prescriptive notions of genre, grammar, and style, earnestly seek to demonstrate that if Balzac was a good writer it was more or less in spite of himself. The question of Balzac's style still attracts the attention of French critics, and as late as 1968 Charles Bruneau wondered if Balzac would be the great exception to the general rule that in France, a writer becomes a "classic" only on the basis of the beauty of his form.[50]

As always, such categories can be too neat, implying a critical purity that simply does not exist in reality—or worse, one that blocks the development of interpretations that do not fit prescribed patterns. However, one of the fascinating qualities of the world of Balzac scholarship is the way in which the various approaches are symbiotically linked to each other—whether through cooperation or rejection. Had Sainte-Beuve not already in 1834 developed Chasles's insights, for example, and pointed out that Balzac's prolixity was a matter of hallucination rather than logorrhea, a whole strain of criticism might not have developed.[51] Such examples can be multiplied. In our own day, the kind of eclectic philosophical criticism practiced by Per Nykrog abolishes the frontiers between philosophy, psychology, and history.

The same is true of the more sophisticated historical methodologies, used by historians such as Louis Chevalier, who explore the complex relationships between history and artistic imagination, ultimately revealing the way in which fiction can challenge the notion of historiography itself. Interestingly, this extremely nuanced historical analysis is related to the view of the *Comédie humaine* as a purely poetic object, and tries to make room for the poetic imagination in the reconstruction of the past. The greatest commentators on Balzac had always seen, of course, that there was no contradiction between Balzac the visionary and Balzac the secretary to society; one need only invoke the name of Henry James, for whom the essential unity of the *Comédie humaine* was never in question. In the end, Balzac criticism is paradoxical and suggestive because it is a response to a body of work that is itself paradoxical and suggestive.

All of the foregoing, that large collection of critical writing that extends from about 1830 to our own day, represents only one facet of response to the *Comédie humaine*. Parallel to it—and often intimately intertwined with it— is the response of novelists, for whom the problem of Balzac presents itself deeply and powerfully in the intimacy of the process of composition. These reactions are much more difficult to pin down. Sometimes they have been worked out in lengthy essays and critical studies; sometimes they have been expressed only in short and enigmatic statements; sometimes, of course, they can only be intuited in fictional production itself.

Balzac's influence on French writers between 1850 and 1950 is so great as to be almost impossible to measure. A mere decade after his death, he had become the great patron of the emerging school of realists. Emile Zola, suffering from what we have learned to call "the anxiety of influence," went so far as to draw up a curious document he called "Differences Between Balzac and Myself";[52] and while Daudet, Maupassant, Flaubert, or the Goncourt brothers did not see themselves as quite so burdened, they could hardly have avoided confronting the massive reality of the *Comédie humaine*.[53]

But there is no question that the most profound retrospective reaction was that of Marcel Proust in the first half of our century: for him Balzac was both the major novelist of an older generation and an inhabitant of his own fictional world.[54] Moreover, the existence of the *Comédie humaine* surely had something to do with the creation of such epic series as Jules Romains's *Les Hommes de bonne volonté* (Men of good will), or Roger Martin du Gard's *Les Thibault* (*The Thibaults*), or Georges Duhamel's *Chronique des Pasquier* (The Pasquier chronicle). Later, when the so-called "new" novelists of the 1950s and 1960s called into question the conventional practices of representational prose fiction, the relationship turned more confrontational. Ideas of uniform authorial point of view, chronological time sequences, consistent characterization, and logical plot development were all challenged as the necessary conditions of prose fiction. New fiction, of a type unknown until then, tested the relationship of writing to notions of reality. Clearly, this could be read as an attack on Balzac considered as the classical practitioner of the "realistic" novel. But as is often the case, the novelists themselves—Alain Robbe-Grillet, Nathalie Sarraute, and Michel Butor, among the most prominent—were not nearly as radical in their reassessments of Balzac as the critics and reviewers who trailed after them. They were too sensitive to the complexities of Balzac's art to see him merely as a recording secretary.

Despite this, Balzac's right to a place in the international pantheon was not immediately clear to French critics. One detects a certain mild indifference, or at least a certain ambivalence in this regard. Could a writer whose style—or lack of style—so irritated some traditionalists be one of France's great representatives on the stage of world fiction? This uneasiness is reflected in the fact that the first, and really only, major study devoted by a French scholar to Balzac as a world figure did not appear until well into our century, and was concerned with Balzac's own "foreign orientations."[55] It was followed by Sophie de Korwin-Piotrowska's work on Balzac in Poland.[56] No large-scale work on Balzac as a world literary figure has appeared since.

Perhaps Balzac's fictional world seemed far too *French* for his influence abroad to be easily seen. Reading him, after all, requires a fairly detailed knowledge of French history and society. On the other hand, he deals with human motivations to be found everywhere and in every century. But even in the absence of a comprehensive study, it is not difficult to see that he has had the deepest possible influence on later generations of realists as well as, at the opposite end of the spectrum, on the work of the symbolist writers.[57] Some writers, such as the Spanish novelist Benito Pérez-Galdós, freely and frequently acknowledged the influence of Balzac; the French novelist Michel Butor claims that the contemporary novel derives in all its forms from Balzac. Undoubtedly the most interesting connections for English language readers are with Henry James, who expressed his debt to Balzac in a series of essays of great length and complexity and, more subtly, with William Faulkner.[58]

But the systematic capture of his role in the creative work of other great writers is a delicate matter. Not all their judgments took the form of set pieces. There is a vision of Balzac, often difficult to make out, buried in passing comments and inadvertent judgments. Maurice Barrès records Barbey d'Aurevilly's confession to José-Maria de Heredia that "[his] entire work derives from the forty pages of Balzac's *Le Réquisitionnaire*"; Strindberg writes to Harriet Bosse on 18 April 1906, that he "now want[s] to be Balzac"; Friedrich Nietzsche is sufficiently interested in the quarrel between Balzac and Sainte-Beuve to mention it to his friend Franz Overbeck; and Theodore Dreiser thought *Un Grand Homme de province à Paris* was "a knockout."[59] These free and "unbuttoned" comments are often among the most revealing, and deserve to be disinterred and examined.

Cases such as that of Thomas Mann are even more difficult to evaluate. Although he did not devote a major study to the French novelist, Mann was constantly reading him. The German novelist's diaries record many days spent with the novels of the *Comédie humaine*.[60] Not that he was reticent about it: in interviews through the years he returned tirelessly to the subject of Balzac;[61] on 4 August 1953, he declared to the *Svenska Dagbladet* that if there had been a Nobel Prize in the early nineteenth century, he would have liked Balzac to have received it, because "both [Balzac and Tolstoy] have meant a great deal to me."[62] How that "meaning" translated into qualities in Mann's work must surely count as one of the most subtle questions of literary criticism.

So complex is the world of the *Comédie humaine* that even the most devoted reader can easily become lost in it. Consequently, guides and compendia of every description have appeared, treating it as if it were a world of real persons, places, and things.[63] In addition, specialized periodicals have been created as vehicles for scholarship. The earliest was the *Cahiers balzaciens,* whose moving force was Marcel Bouteron; this was followed by the *Courrier balzacien,* the first series of which appeared from December 1948 to December 1950, and whose principal animator was Jean-A. Ducourneau; after that came the *Etudes balzaciennes,* which was transformed in 1960 into *L'Année balzacienne.* The earlier of these publications had something of a family air about them; the *Courrier balzacien* especially contained not only erudite articles, but also a "For Sale" and "Wanted" column for Balzaciana, odd bits of news about places and things associated with him, advertisements of books on Balzac, and wonderful sketches and caricatures. The *Etudes balzaciennes,* and especially *L'Année balzacienne,* are much more austere in their conception, and rank as major scholarly publications.

Inevitably, a work of such dimensions, surrounded by such a scaffolding of critical appraisal, encouraged groupings of those who suffered from "balzaphilia," as the *Courrier balzacien* once rather inelegantly put it. An organization known as the "Groupe d'études balzaciennes" was founded in the late 1950s; it has been succeeded by the "Groupe international de recherches balzaciennes." There is also a "Société d'études balzaciennes," devoted principally to the publication of the *Année balzacienne.* But surely the least formal, most lively assembly of all was the lunchtime group that met across the street from the Lovenjoul archives when they were located in the charming town of Chantilly to talk of Balzac over omelets and wine.

What does the future hold? Here, perhaps, an overriding wish should be expressed: it is that a new complete translation of the *Comédie humaine* into English be undertaken. The numerous excellent translations of individual novels suffer from having to be read as independent works, cut loose from the governing framework of the whole.

With respect to criticism and scholarship, future trends will surely be extensions of approaches already tried. Some, of course, will have run their course. There is not much to be anticipated from further bioliterary investigations: new proposals for prototypes of characters and places will not add anything essential to our understanding of the novels. On the other hand, the exploration of the *Comédie humaine* as an expression of its times still offers intellectual historians and critics a wealth of possibilities. In historiography itself, Balzac's work will continue to play a central role; for if, as Armand Hoog has observed, Balzac's fiction has *made* part of our reality, and if Hayden White is correct in seeing history as a form of fiction, then it follows that Balzac is the great bridge between modern France and its immediate past—the bridge over which notions of fiction and reality pass in both directions.

The "new" comparative literature and current interest in comparative hermeneutics could be focused on the *Comédie humaine* and its relationship to other fiction and to the other arts. Whereas much ink has been spilled over Balzac's debt to the visual and musical arts, very little indeed has been written about influence in the opposite direction.[64] Nor should comparative studies neglect the question of Balzac and the sciences; we have hardly begun the evaluation of Balzac's presence at a critical juncture in the evolution of biology, and the way in which he anticipated and indirectly prepared us for modern scientific concepts.

In literary theory, Balzac's work will surely continue to be at the center of recurring debates on the definition of "canon," and one can anticipate that developing theories of narratology will be applied to it. As long as novels are written and read, Balzac's work will stand as one of the few major western models against which new literary forms will be measured.

One area of investigation that should provide a wealth of insights into the *Comédie humaine* is Balzac's critical reception by his contemporaries. We have already alluded to the dynamic relationship that existed between Balzac and his critics; this whole subject needs further examination, and will undoubtedly shed a great deal of new light on many of Balzac's narrative strategies.

And Balzac abroad? Although his relationship to specific authors has been paid some attention, we still lack broad, comprehensive studies of his fortunes in many national literatures other than French.

Finally, new computer technologies for handling texts seem explicitly designed to help critics cope with the mass of the *Comédie humaine*. The growing efficiency with which large bodies of text can be digitized for computer analysis makes it almost certain that the *Comédie humaine* will sooner or later be available "on line" for sophisticated manipulations.

In all of this critical activity we are not alone. Our most illustrious colleague in the examination of Balzac criticism is Balzac himself. It has long been obvious that many of Balzac's narrative strategies were aimed at a theoretical "reader."[65] But the reading public was changing rapidly during his lifetime, and he was acutely aware of that fact.[66] It is only recently that we have realized the quite astonishing degree to which the *Comédie humaine* itself is a reaction to criticism.

This places "reception theory" on an entirely new and dynamic plane. Balzac here falls victim to his own perspicacity by immensely complicating the act of reading: to understand him fully, one must also understand his audience and read his critics. How else can one interpret narrative tactics that were aimed at contemporary readers? This is a difficult and complicated job; Balzac responded not only to major critical voices but also to many very minor ones now buried and forgotten in newspaper files. But at the very least, recent work in this direction has begun to rescue some of his fictional strategies from characterizations as crude, gross, and simplistic. Two critical moments—his emergence as a novelist between 1829 and 1832, and the years 1839–40, when he was fighting the scandals produced by *La Vieille Fille* (*The Old Maid*) and certain other works—have provided particularly rich fields for such studies.[67] But much more needs to be done. The constant interplay between creativity and reception in Balzac's mind makes the proper framing of our own perceptions an extremely important, if contentious, matter. For a very large question remains: can those who read the *Comédie humaine* as an ongoing dialogue with the nineteenth century be reconciled with those who see it as an autonomous structure rooted in, but not mirroring, its times?

The *Comédie humaine*, then, constantly raises the question of the historicity of reading. Today we are a good deal less optimistic about anything like a final "meaning" than we used to be. We have learned to live with diversity. And yet, along with the divisions that we have noted in Balzac criticism, there are some curious convergences. Who would have expected the Marxist Pierre Macherey to deny that the *Comédie humaine* is a reflection of reality, or the psychologically and esthetically oriented Bernard Guyon to have been so deeply rooted in history? Who would have expected Pierre Barbéris to find as many congenial interepretations as he did in Roland Barthes's *S/Z*? Perhaps we owe such glimmerings of tolerance to our powerful modern critical bias toward self-awareness. We have become conscious of our own stance as readers and critics because we have learned that it, too, is historical. If such an approach carries the danger of turning Balzac criticism into a set of Chinese boxes (one can imagine future critics commenting on the commentators of Balzac's critics), it also reflects Balzac's own sensitivity to what was being said and written around him. And so the Great Debate continues: discoveries and interpretations succeed each other in a never-ending process, and we must recognize that there will be no final, authoritative interpretation. The fact is that it is not necessary for us to choose among the various Balzacs that criticism has offered us. There *were* that many Balzacs.

A word on methodology. This brief overview will surely have demonstrated the impossibility of sorting out of the immense body of Balzac scholarship a small group of works that would be the "best" or the "most representative." The editor of this volume followed two obvious criteria: quality of writing and thought, and representative distribution among major streams of scholarship and criticism. A few items were regretfully set aside because of difficulties in obtaining permission to reprint. Although the distinction between creative "writers" and professional "critics" is murky, the collection presents a sampling of both, in chronological order. The aim has been to

provide sufficient echoes and counterechoes to give some sense of the ongoing vitality of this Balzacian dialogue. Unless otherwise specified, all translations are the editor's.

And if the editor could be granted a closing wish, he would urge the
reader to view the necessary gaps in these selections simply as reasons to go
back into the world of Balzac and his critics for further commentary and,
inevitably, further controversy.

MARTIN KANES

State University of New York at Albany

Notes

1. Aside from the *Comédie humaine* itself, Balzac's major literary achievement is clearly
his correspondence. Although it does not have the literary and intellectual interest of Flaubert's, nor the anguished self-portraiture of Baudelaire's, it provides us with an incredibly
detailed picture of the busy life of a midcentury literary figure. It has received careful and
detailed editing by Roger Pierrot (five volumes of *Correspondance* [Paris: Garnier, 1960–69],
and four volumes of *Lettres à Madame Hanska* [Paris: Delta, 1967–71]). The latter, in Pierrot's
words, are nothing less than "the novel of a life."

2. In *Le Gaulois*, 11 August 1923.

3. Amusing as they may appear today, these articles were taken quite seriously when they
were written; all appeared in the *Chronique médicale* between 1899 and 1901.

4. See A. Parménie and C. Bonnier de la Chapelle, *Histoire d'un éditeur et de ses
auteurs, P-J Hetzel* (Paris: Albin Michel, 1953); also Pierre Descaves, *Le Président Balzac* (Paris:
Laffont, 1950).

5. Aside from Balzac's well-known liaisons (Mme de Berny, Mme d'Abrantès, Mme de
Castries, Marie de Fresnaye, the Contessa Guidaboni-Visconti, Caroline Marbouty, Hélène de
la Valette, his housekeeper Mme Brugnol, and of course Mme Hanska, "L'Etrangère" who was
to become his wife), there are veiled allusions to other women in Balzac's correspondence. He
was especially frank with his beloved sister, Laure Surville, from whom he apparently withheld
very little in the way of intimate confessions.

6. Cited in *Les Nouvelles littéraires*, 19 May 1949, 4. It is only fair to Balzac to note that
Alfred de Vigny, who saw him in later life, remarked on his flourishing stylishness.

7. See, for example, R. Bouvier and E. Maynial, *Les Comptes dramatiques de Balzac*
(Balzac's dramatic book-keeping) (Paris: Sorlot, 1938); Léon Gozlan, *Balzac en pantoufles* (Bal-
zac in slippers) (Paris: 1865; repr. Delmas, 1949); Alphonse Séché and Jules Bertaut, *Balzac*
(Paris: Louis-Michaud, n.d.). The last appeared, appropriately enough, in a series entitled "La
Vie anecdotique et pittoresque des Grands Ecrivains."

8. Thorough inquiries into the literary consequences of Balzac's biography were hardly
possible before the accurate establishment of the chronological facts of the writer's life. This was
begun by *Les Etudes balzaciennes* in 1951 and continued by *L'Année balzacienne* when it
succeeded the earlier journal; since then, others (especially Barbéris) have attempted to breathe
new life into the old formulaic "Man and his Works" approach.

9. For an account of Bouteron's work, see Jean Pommier, "Marcel Bouteron," *Etudes
balzaciennes* (Paris: Jouve, 1954), v–xv.

10. In a general way, Balzac's texts became longer as time went on, which suggests that he

grew in his ability to handle large themes and complicated issues. More important was the conceptual and structural evolution of the Balzacian novel as circumstances and readership changed. See André Vanoncini, "Pour une critologie balzacienne," *Littérature* 42 (1981):57–65.

11. These numbers are approximate. There are certain groupings within the "Scenes" (*Illusions perdues* or *Splendeurs et misères des courtisanes*) that are in effect made up of several novels.

12. Balzac often toyed with various arrangements. The best known are the *Prospectus*, published in 1842 by his publisher Furne and Dubochet, and the *Catalogue* of 1845, which Balzac had printed privately and which was later published by Amédée Achard in *L'Assemblée nationale* for 25 August 1850. Even at this late stage in his career, there were five novels (including the masterpieces *La Cousine Bette* and *Le Cousin Pons*) that he did not anticipate writing.

13. It was only very late in his career, with the diptych of *Les Parents pauvres*, that Balzac seems to have abandoned the vitalist theory in favor of something much closer to the notion of work as defined in modern physics. Artistic creativity, as a consequence, would become not the expenditure of a life-force but the exploitation of differences in resistance to entropy. See, in this connection, William Paulson, "Le Cousin Parasite: Balzac, Serres et le Démon de Maxwell," *Stanford French Review* 9 (1985): 397–414; and Nicole Mozet, "Création et/ou Paternité dans *La Cousine Bette*," *Revue des sciences humaines* 175, no. 3 (1979): 49–60.

14. Balzac obviously thought of the French as sufficiently archetypical of human nature to call his work a "human" rather than "French" comedy. There is some uncertainty about the title itself. According to some accounts, it was suggested by his secretary, Auguste de Belloy, in 1841; there are some indications that Balzac may have thought of it a year or two earlier.

15. The story is variously told. The traditional version can be found in G. Brandes, *Main Currents in Nineteenth Century Literature* (London: Heinemann, 1904), V, 186.

16. For an older but still useful analysis of the evolution of the whole enterprise, see Brucia Dedinsky, "Development of the Scheme of the *Comédie humaine*: Distribution of the Stories," in *The Evolution of Balzac's Comédie humaine*, ed. by E. Preston Dargan and Bernard Weinberg (Chicago: University of Chicago Press, 1942), 22–187.

17. For a listing of the principal collected editions, see the bibliography.

18. *La Comédie humaine* (London: Dent, 1895). It was reprinted by various publishers (Estes, Avil, Gebbie, and Crowell) in both England and the United States, and is still the only existing complete translation. (The Boston firm of Roberts Brothers had published a seven-volume version in 1885, and Routledge & Sons in London brought out a twelve-volume version in 1886.)

19. There are many fascinating stories about Lovenjoul's adventures in rescuing Balzac's manuscripts from oblivion. An interesting portrait of him appears in Pierre Descaves, *Le Président Balzac* (Paris: Laffont, 1950). Originally housed in a former mansion in the town of Chantilly (where it was almost inaccessible and open only for a very limited number of days per year), the collection has now been moved to Paris.

20. Charles Spoelberch de Lovenjoul, *Histoire des oeuvres de H. de Balzac* (History of the works of H. de Balzac) (Paris: Calmann-Lévy, 1879). The book went through three editions; the first contained a bibliographical appendix of thirty-five books and thirty-three articles, plus references to a number of further sources. In the third edition, which appeared a mere nine years later, the number of critical items had doubled.

21. William Hobart Royce, *A Balzac Bibliography: Writings Relative to the Life and Works of Honoré de Balzac* (Chicago: University of Chicago Press, 1929). The complexity of the volume soon necessitated the publication of *Indexes to A Balzac Bibliography, Containing an Index to Periodicals and a Topical Index to Items in This Bibliography* (Chicago: University of Chicago Press, 1930).

22. The need for Royce's supplement has been removed by the appearance of annual

bibliographies in *L'Année balzacienne* and in the *Annual Bibliography* of the Modern Language Association. Assessments of Balzac criticism have also regularly appeared. The most important of these are, in chronological order: G. Pellisier, "Balzac et la critique," *La Revue*, 15 August 1906, 514–21; Charles Gould, "The Present State of Balzac Studies," *French Studies* 12 (1958): 299–323; Anthony Pugh, "Ten Years of Balzac Studies," *Modern Languages* 46 (1965):91–97; Annie L. Cosson, "Vingt Ans de bibliographie balzacienne (1948–1967)," *Dissertation Abstracts International* 31 (1970):2378A (Mo, Columbia) [to be used with caution because of frequent gaps and errors]; Maurice Ménard, "Fécondités balzaciennes (Balzacian riches): 1970–1976," *Stanford French Review* 1 (1977): 261–74; Nicole Billot, "Balzac vu par la critique (1839–1840) (Balzac seen by the critics, 1839–1840)," *L'Année balzacienne* (1984), 229–67.

23. Which is not to say that he was not widely known (Berlioz tells an amusing anecdote in his memoirs about a passionate discussion of Balzac he had with the postmaster at Tilsit in February 1847 while on his way to a concert tour in Russia). But Balzac's problems were perhaps cultural as well as personal: novelists were not admitted to the Académie française until 1858, in the person of Jules Sandeau.

24. Hippolyte Castille, a well-known critic, made a curious distinction between Balzac's *art* (excellent) and his *morality* (deplorable), and concluded that Balzac owed his popularity to his shortcomings rather than to his achievements ("M. H. de Balzac," *La Semaine*, 4 October 1846). This brand of criticism even drove Balzac to count up the number of "virtuous" as against "fallen" heroines in his stories, in an attempt to prove that he was not merely writing gutter literature.

25. Philarète Chasles, "La Peau de chagrin," *Le Messager des Chambres*, 6 August 1831.

26. The amount of commentary was enormous. An interesting summation of it all can be found in Georges Pelissier, "Balzac et la critique," *La Revue mondiale*, no. 63 (15 August 1906): 514–21.

27. Théophile Gautier, *Honoré de Balzac* (Paris: Poulet-Malassis et de Broise, 1850). Hippolyte Taine also wrote a series of articles in *Le Constitutionnel* in February and March 1858, which were collected with other materials in 1865 under the title *Nouveaux Essais de critique et d'histoire* (New essays in criticism and history).

28. For an extended analysis of Balzac's literary fortunes during this period, see David Bellos, *Balzac Criticism in France 1850–1900*. (Oxford: Oxford University Press, 1976).

29. Engels's classic statement about Balzac occurs in a letter to Margaret Harkness dated April 1888, in which he says that he considered Balzac "a far greater master of realism than all the Zolas *passés, présents et à venir . . .*" and that "[he] learned more [from Balzac] than from all the professed historians, economists and statisticians of the period together." Engels's point was that Balzac's artistic integrity made him write "against" his class interests.

30. Chasles wrote an introduction to the 1831 edition of *Romans et contes philosophiques*, which was probably inspired, if not partially written, by Balzac himself. It refers to King and Priest, who represent "the highest levels of our collapsing hierarchy"—especially the Priest, "whose thought represents the highest and greatest development of human intelligence . . ."

31. Academic criticism had, of course, begun earlier, in the 1880s with studies by Emile Faguet and Ferdinand Brunetière. It flowered, however, in the years immediately preceding and following the first World War. See André Le Breton, *Balzac l'homme et l'oeuvre* (Balzac, the man and his work) (Paris: Armand Colin, 1905) [a straightforward academic accounting]; Ferdinand Brunetière, *Honoré de Balzac* (Paris: Calmann-Lévy, 1906) [formalist and doctrinaire]; Emile Faguet, *Les Grands Ecrivains français: Balzac* (Great French writers: Balzac) (Paris: Hachette, 1913) [descriptive rather than critical]; André Bellesort, *Balzac et son oeuvre* (Balzac and his work) (Paris: Librairie académique Perrin, 1924) [esthetic criticism].

32. For example, the case of the real-life criminal-turned-policeman Vidocq as a prototype for the fictional Vautrin has been examined by Marcel Bouteron, "En Marge du Père Goriot: Balzac, Vidocq et Sanson," *La Revue* 1 (1 January 1948): 109–24; by Paul Vernière, "Balzac et la

genèse de Vautrin," *Revue d'histoire littéraire de la France* 48 (1948): 53–68; and by Jean Savant, *La Vie fabuleuse et authentique de Vidocq* (The true and fantastic life of Vidocq) (Paris: Seuil, 1950).

33. Ernst-Robert Curtius, *Balzac* (Bonn: Friedrich Cohen, 1923; tr. into French in 1933; repr. Bern: A. Franke Verlag, 1951); and Albert Béguin, *Balzac visionnaire* (Balzac the visionary) (Genève: Skira, 1946). The latter was republished, with a set of prefaces to various novels, as *Balzac lu et relu* (Balzac read and reread) (Paris: Seuil, 1965).

34. Ernest Seillière, *Balzac et la morale romantique* (Balzac and romantic morality) (Paris: Alcan, 1922); Henri Bordeaux, *Les Ecrivains et les moeurs* (Writers and mores) (Paris: Fontemoing, 1902); Jean Carrère, "Les Mauvais Maîtres: Balzac (Bad teachers: Balzac)," *La Revue hebdomadaire*, 30 August 1902.

35. For example, in an interview with *La Revue d'Europe* in September 1900, Maurice Barrès explicitly associated Balzac with the early nineteenth-century royalist theoretician de Bonald. The Comte de Gobineau also expressed his admiration for Balzac—although not on the racist grounds for which he became famous. Later, the chief conservative commentator, whose interpretations are much more sophisticated and persuasive than those of his predecessors, was surely Maurice Bardèche, whose powerful *Balzac romancier* appeared in 1940.

36. The leading Marxist commentator of this period was undoubtedly George Lukács, whose extensive analysis of *Les Paysans* (The Peasants) and *Illusions perdues* appeared in English in 1950, although it was written much earlier. See George Lukács, *Studies in European Realism* (London: Hillway, 1950).

37. J. Duron, ed., *Balzac: Le Livre du centenaire* (Balzac: The centenary studies) (Paris: Flammarion, 1952).

38. See especially Marc Eigeldinger, *La Philosophie de l'art chez Balzac* (Balzac's philosophy of art) (Geneva: Cailler, 1957); and Henri Evans, *Louis Lambert et la philosophie de Balzac* (Louis Lambert and Balzac's philosophy) (Paris: Jose Corti, 1951).

39. André Allemand, *Unité et structure de l'univers balzacien* (Unity and structure of the balzacian universe) (Paris: Plon, 1965).

40. Bernard Guyon, *La Création littéraire chez Balzac: la genèse du 'Médecin de campagne'* (Balzac's literary creativity: the genesis of *The Country Doctor*) (Paris: Armand Colin, 1951).

41. E. Preston Dargan and Bernard Weinberg, eds., *The Evolution of Balzac's Comédie Humaine* (Chicago: University of Chicago Press, 1942).

42. Three scholars especially undertook such investigations with often rich and fascinating results: Suzanne Bérard, *Illusions perdues, Le Manuscrit de la collection Spoelberch de Lovenjoul* (Paris: Armand Colin, 1959) and *La Genèse d'un roman de Balzac. Illusions perdues* (The genesis of a Balzac novel: *Lost Illusions*) (Paris: Armand Colin, 1961); Ki Wist, *Le Curé de village, Manuscrits ajoutés, 1841* (*The Village Priest*. The added manuscripts of 1841) (Bruxelles, Henriquez, 1963) and *Le Curé de Village, Le Manuscrit de premier jet* (*The Village Priest*. The initial manuscript) (Bruxelles, Henriquez, 1964); and Jacques Borel, *Le Lys dans la vallée et les sources profondes de la création balzacienne* (*The Lily In the Valley* and the deepest sources of balzacian creativity) (Paris: José Corti, 1961).

43. Jean Pommier summed up the approach in a series of lectures at the Collège de France, which were later gathered under the title of *Créations en littérature* (Creativity in literature) (Paris: Hachette, 1955).

44. Next to the great masterpieces, the juvenilia are indeed small efforts, but they have recently been recognized as the primitive forms of much that was to come later in both theme and technique. For a complete reedition in contemporary format, see the J-A Ducourneau, ed., *Romans de jeunesse* (Juvenilia), 15 vols. (Paris: Editions Bibliophile de l'Originale, 1964). Geneviève Delattre has proposed the intriguing notion of "creative reading as a source of ideas,"

and has demonstrated the role it may well have played in several episodes of the *Comédie humaine*.

45. Picon wrote a series of essays on Balzac over a period of several years; they were eventually gathered in a "Suite Balzacienne," which opens the second volume of his collected essays, *L'Usage de la lecture* (The uses of reading) (Paris: Mercure de France, 1961). J. P. Richard devoted half of his volume *Etudes sur le romantisme* (Studies in romanticism) to a series of essays entitled "Corps et décors balzaciens (Balzacian bodies and settings)." (Paris: Seuil, 1970).

46. For a narratological analysis, see Françoise Van Rossum-Guyon; for metaphorical analysis, see Lucienne Frappier-Mazur; for thematic analysis, see Martin Kanes; for semiotic analysis, see Naomi Schor and the team of Le Huenen and Perron; for deconstructionist analysis, see Samuel Weber. Marxist criticism is best represented by Pierre Barbéris, Pierre Macherey, and André Wurmser. Roland Barthes offers a rich mixture of Marxist, Freudian, and semiotic analysis.

47. Although the very conservative ideological criticism common in the late nineteenth and early twentieth centuries has faded away, it is nevertheless exaggerated to claim, as does Fredric Jameson in the article reproduced in this volume, that interest in Balzac is automatically a declaration of a critic's Marxist orientation.

48. Roland Barthes, *S/Z* (Paris: Seuil, 1970); Pierre Barbéris, "A Propos du *S/Z* de Roland Barthes," *L'Année balzacienne* (1971), 109–23; and Bernard Guyon, "Lettre à Pierre Barbéris sur *Balzac et le mal du siècle* (Letter to Pierre Barbéris on Balzac and the malady of romanticism)," *Esprit* 405 (1971): 154–65. Carol Coates has explored many of these conflicts in her article "Engagement and Purity in Balzac Criticism," *Romanic Review* 56 (1965): 277–83.

49. The most important of these assessments are, in chronological order: Coates, "Engagement and Purity in Balzac Criticism"; François Flagothier, "Propos sur Balzac," *Revue des langues vivantes* 34 (1968), 402–13; Pierre Barbéris, *Balzac: Une Mythologie réaliste* (Balzac: A realistic mythology) (Paris: Larousse, 1971); W. G. Moore, "The Changing Study of Balzac," in D. G. Charlton, Jean Gaudon, and A. R. Pugh, eds., *Balzac and the Nineteenth Century: Studies in French Literature Presented to Herbert J. Hunt by Pupils, Colleagues and Friends* (Leicester: Leicester University Press, 1972), 187–92; Jacques Georges, "Chronologie et symbolisme: Questions de méthode en recherche balzacienne (Chronology and symbolism: Questions of method in balzacian research)," *Les Lettres romanes* 28 (1974): 172–77; Josephine Ott, "Henry James, critique de Balzac," *L'Année balzacienne* (1977), 273–81; Michel van Schendel, "Balzac: de l'oeuvre au texte (Balzac: from work to text)," *University of Texas Quarterly* 51, no. 1 (Fall 1981): 112–24; André Vanoncini, "Pour une critologie balzacienne: esquisse d'une problématique ("Towards a science of balzacian criticism: outlines of a problem")," *Littérature* (Paris) 42 (May 1981): 57–65. One must also note the final section of André Wurmser's acerbic *La Comédie inhumaine* (The inhuman comedy) (Paris: Gallimard, 1964), devoted to a scorching Marxist overview of Balzac criticism.

50. Ferdinand Brunot, *Histoire de la langue française*, 12: Charles Bruneau, *L'Epoque romantique* (Paris: Armand Colin, 1968), 366–86; Mario Roques, "La Langue de Balzac," *Le Livre du centenaire* (Paris: Flammarion, 1952), 246–57; Alain, "Etude d'ensemble sur le style de Balzac," *Esprit* 18 (December 1949): 874–91. An article that pointed the way toward a number of more technical studies was that of Henri Mitterand, "A Propos du style de Balzac," *Europe* 43 année, nos. 429–30 (January–February 1965): 145–61.

51. For an analysis of these chronological linkages, see André Vanoncini, "Pour une critologie balzacienne: esquisse d'une problématique," *Littérature* (Paris) 42 (May 1981): 57–65.

52. This manuscript is now in the Bibliothèque nationale, Paris. It has been published in Henri Massis, *Comment Emile Zola composait ses romans* (How Emile Zola composed his novels) (Paris: Fasquelle, 1906), 24–26.

53. Perhaps the most curious literary response to Balzac's work among late nineteenth-century writers was Pierre Louÿs's story "La Fausse Esther," in which a supposedly true-life Esther Gobseck protests to Balzac over the usurpation of her name, but in the end is absorbed into the identity of the fictional character.

54. In the sense that Proust's Marquise de Villeparisis tells of having seen him in her youth in the salons of the July Monarchy.

55. Fernand Baldensperger, *Les Orientations étrangères chez Honoré de Balzac* (Foreign orientations in Honoré de Balzac) (Paris: Champion, 1927).

56. Sophie de Korwin-Piotrowska, *Balzac et le monde slave* (Balzac and the slavic world) (Paris: Champion, 1933); and, by the same author, *Balzac en Pologne* (Balzac in Poland) (Paris: Champion, 1933).

57. To list the writers who fell under Balzac's spell would be practically an endless task, and consequently futile. Some typical responses can be found in the section of this book entitled "Literary Vignettes and Essays."

58. In this connection one must cite Peter Brooks's excellent *The Melodramatic Imagination: an Essay on Balzac, Henry James and the Mode of Excess* (New Haven: Yale University Press, 1976). Probably the most thoroughgoing analysis of James's debt is to be found in Adeline R. Tintner's *The Book World of Henry James* (Ann Arbor: UMI Research Press, 1987).

59. Maurice Barrès, *Mes Cahiers* (Paris: Plon, 1929), 1, 157; August Strindberg, *Letters to Harriet Bosse*, ed. and trans. Arvid Paulson (New York: Nelson, 1959), 155; Friedrich Nietzsche, *Briefe Januar 1880–Dezember 1884* (Berlin: de Gruyter, 1981), 16; Theodore Dreiser, *Letters of Theodore Dreiser: A Selection* (Philadelphia: University of Pennsylvania Press, 1959), 1, 211.

60. He was reading Balzac on 15 and 19 June 1919 (*César Birotteau*, although on the 23d he gave it up); on 29 April 1920 (*La Fille aux yeux d'or*); in July 1920 (*Illusions perdues*); on 24 May 1921 (the whole afternoon spent reading *Adieu*); August 1937 (*Le Père Goriot*); on 1 May 1938 (*Le Lys dans la vallée*); in March 1940 *La Peau de chagrin*. From Thomas Mann, *Diaries 1918–1939*, trans. Richard and Clara Winston (New York: Harry N. Abrams, 1982); and Thomas Mann, *Tagebücher 1940–43* (Diaries 1940–1943), ed. Peter de Mendelssohn. (Frankfurt-am-Main: S. Fischer Verlag, 1982).

61. In August 1935 he told a reporter that "On the one hand, Balzac's work is the reflection of French society, and to a certain extent that society is Balzac's work. I too have had the experience that the Buddenbrooks's or Tonio Kröger's way of speaking have directly influenced real conversations." (*Frage und Antwort: Interviews mit Thomas Mann 1909–1955* (Questions and answers: interviews with Thomas Mann 1909–1955) (Hamburg: Albrecht Knaus, 1983), 218–19.

62. *Ibid.*, 373.

63. The most important and useful is Fernand Lotte, *Dictionnaire biographique des personnages fictifs de "La Comédie humaine"* (Biographical dictionary of fictional characters in The Human Comedy) (Paris: José Corti, 1952). This work was ultimately revised and integrated into volume 12 of the Pléiade edition. The Pléiade edition also contains three other indices pertaining to real, historical, and mythological characters, as well as literary and artistic works cited, and a short list of works produced by the fictional artists of the *Comédie humaine*. Another useful compendium is L. F. Hoffman, *Répertoire géographique de "La Comédie humaine"* (Geographical Repertory of *The Human Comedy*) 2 vols., (Paris: José Corti, 1965–68). The very old *Répertoire de "La Comédie humaine" de H. de Balzac* (Repertory of Balzac's *The Human Comedy*) by Anatole Cerfberr and Jules Christophe (Paris: Calmann-Lévy, 1887) deserves mention chiefly for historical reasons.

64. An excellent beginning is to be found in Anne Hyde Greet, "Picasso and Balzac: *Le Chef d'oeuvre inconnu*," *The Comparatist* 6, no. 1 (May 1982): 56–66. Greet provides a detailed

study of the illustrated edition of Balzac's novel produced by Picasso for Ambroise Vollard in 1931.

65. See Mary Susan McCarthy, *Balzac and His Reader* (Columbia: University of Missouri Press, 1982).

66. Christopher Prendergast, *Balzac: Fiction and Melodrama* (London: Arnold, 1978).

67. Pierre Barbéris, "L'Accueil critique aux premières grandes oeuvres de Balzac (1829–1830) ("The critical reception of Balzac's first great works [1829–1830]") *L'Année balzacienne* (1967), 51–72; Pierre Barbéris, "L'Accueil critique aux premières grandes oeuvres de Balzac (1831–1832) ("The critical reception of Balzac's first great works [1831–1832]")," *L'Année balzacienne* (1968), 165–95; Nicole Billot, "Balzac vu par la critique (1839–1840) ("Balzac seen by the critics [1839–1840]")," *L'Année balzacienne* (1984), 229–67.

LIST OF ABBREVIATIONS

Although not all ninety-seven novels of Balzac are referred to in the essays reproduced here, a complete list of the standardized abbreviations adopted by the second Pléiade edition has been provided for readers who wish to pursue their study of Balzac. A few titles of fragments and sketches have not been included. The various forms of reference used in the essays in this volume have been regularized insofar as possible according to this system. Titles of Balzac's novels have been left in the original French in the texts of the articles; English translations are provided below.

French Title	Abbreviation	English Title
Adieu	Ad	Farewell
Albert Savarus	AS	Albert Savarus
Auberge rouge, L'	AR	The Red Inn
Autre Etude de femme	AEF	Another Portrait of Lady
Bal de Sceaux, Le	BS	The Ball at Sceaux
Béatrix	B	Beatrix
Bourse, La	Bo	The Purse
Cabinet des antiques, Le	CA	The Collection of Antiques
Chef-d'oeuvre inconnu, Le	ChO	The Unknown Masterpiece
Chouans, Les	Ch	The Chouans
Colonel Chabert, Le	Col	Colonel Chabert
Comédiens sans le savoir, Les	CSS	The Unconscious Humorists
Contrat de mariage, Le	CM	The Marriage Settlement
Cousin Pons, Le	CP	Cousin Pons
Cousine Bette, La	Be	Cousin Betty
Curé de village, Le	CV	The Village Priest
Curé de Tours, Le	CT	The Vicar of Tours
Député d'Arcis, Le	DA	The Representative from Arcis

Deux Amis, Les	DxA	The Two Friends
Duchesse de Langeais, La	DL	The Duchesse de Langeais
El Verdugo	Ve	The Executioner
Election en province, L'	EP	A Provincial Election
Elixir de longue vie, L'	ELV	The Elixir of Life
Employés, Les	E	The Government Clerks
Enfant maudit, L'	EM	The Hated Son
Envers de l'histoire contemporaine, L'	EHC	The Seamy Side of History
Etude de femme	EF	Study of a Woman
Eugénie Grandet	EG	Eugenie Grandet
Facino Cane	FC	Facino Cane
Fausse Maîtresse, La	FM	The Imaginary Mistress
Femme abandonnée, La	FA	The Deserted Woman
Femme de trente ans, La	F30	A Woman of Thirty
Ferragus	F	Ferragus
Fille aux yeux d'or, La	FYO	The Girl with the Golden Eyes
Gambara	Gam	Gambara
Gaudissart II	Gau	Gaudissart II
Gobseck	Gb	Gobseck
Grenadière, La	Gr	La Grenadière
Héritiers Boirouge, Les	Boi	The Boirouge Heirs
Histoire des treize	H13	The Story of the Thirteen
Histoire de la Grandeur et de la décadence de César Birotteau	CB	The Rise and Fall of Cesar Birotteau
Honorine	H	Honorine
Illusions perdues	IP	Lost Illusions
Illustre Gaudissart, L'	IG	Gaudissart the Great
Interdiction, L'	In	The Commission in Lunacy
Jésus Christ en Flandres	JCF	Christ in Flanders
Louis Lambert	LL	Louis Lambert
Lys dans la vallée, Le	Lys	The Lily in the Valley
Madame Firmiani	Fir	Madame Firmiani
Maison Nucingen, La	MN	The Firm of Nucingen
Maison du chat-qui-pelote, La	MCP	At the Sign of The Cat and Racket
Maître Cornelius	Cor	Master Cornelius
Marana, Les	Ma	The Maranas
Massimilla Doni	Do	Massimilla Doni
Médecin de campagne, Le	MC	The Country Doctor

Melmoth réconcilié	MR	Melmoth Reconciled
Mémoires de deux jeunes mariées	MJM	Memoirs of Two Young Brides
Message, Le	Mes	The Message
Martyrs ignorés, Les	MI	The Overlooked Martyrs
Messe de l'athée, La	Ath	The Atheist's Mass
Modest Mignon	MM	Modeste Mignon
Muse du département, La	MD	The Country Muse
Paix du ménage, La	PM	Domestic Peace
Parents pauvres, Les	PP	Poor Relations
Passion dans le désert, Une	Des	A Passion in the Desert
Pathologie de la vie so-ciale	PVS	Pathology of Social Life
Paysans, Les	Pay	The Peasants
Peau de chagrin, La	PCh	The Wild Ass's Skin
Père Goriot, Le	PG	Old Goriot
Petites Misères de la vie conjugale	PMV	The Pinpricks of Married Life
Petits Bourgeois, Les	Bou	The Middle Classes
Physiologie du mariage	Phy	The Physiology of Mar-riage
Pierre Grassou	PGr	Pierre Grassou
Pierrette	P	Pierrette
Proscrits, Les	Pro	The Exiles
Rabouilleuse, La	R	A Bachelor's Establish-ment
Recherche de l'absolu, La	RA	The Quest for the Abso-lute
Réquisitionnaire, Le	Req	The Conscript
Sarrasine	S	Sarrasine
Scènes de la vie privée	SVpriv	Scenes of Private Life
Scènes de la vie de prov-ince	SVpro	Scenes of Provinical Life
Scènes de la vie parisienne	SVParis	Scenes of Parisian Life
Secrets de la princesse de Cadignan, Les	SPC	The Secrets of the Prin-cesse de Cadignan
Séraphîta	Ser	Séraphîta
Splendeurs et misères des courtisanes	SetM	Scenes from a Courtesan's Life
Sur Catherine de Médicis	Cath	About Catherine de Medi-cis
Un Début dans la vie	DV	A Start in Life
Un Drame au bord de la mer	Dr	A Seaside Tragedy

Une Double Famille	DF	A Second Home
Une Fille d'Eve	FE	A Daughter of Eve
Un épisode sous la Terreur	EpT	An Incident during the Terror
Une Ténébreuse Affaire	TA	The Gondreville Mystery
Un Homme d'affaires	HA	A Businessman
Un Grand Homme de province à Paris	GH	A Provincial Personality in Paris
Un Prince de la Bohème	PrB	A Prince of Bohemia
Ursule Mirouet	UM	Ursule Mirouet
Vendetta, La	Ven	The Vendetta
Vieille Fille, La	VF	The Old Maid
Z. Marcas	ZM	Z. Marcas

LITERARY VIGNETTES AND ESSAYS: 1837–1949

Vignettes

[A Tourist's Memoirs]   Stendhal*

I found a volume of Balzac in my room: it is *L'Abbé Birotteau*, of Tours. How I admire that author! How well he set out the unhappiness and pettiness of the provinces! I would like a simpler style, but then would provincial people buy the book? I suppose he writes his books in two stages: first sensibly, and then clothing them in a fine neological style, with "*sufferances of the soul*" and "*it is snowing in my heart*" and other choice morsels.

[Letter to His Brother, 9 August 1858]   Fyoder Dostoevsky†

Balzac is extraordinary! His characters are the creations of a universal mind. Such a development in a man's mind was prepared not by the spirit of the times, but by thousands of years and all their turmoil.

[Balzac's Universality]   Victor Hugo‡

All his books form but a single book, a living, shining, profound book, in which our whole contemporary civilization can be seen going and coming, walking and moving, with a terrible and frightening *je ne sais quoi* mixed in with reality: a marvelous book called by its maker a comedy but which he might have called a history, which assumes all shapes and styles, which goes beyond Tacitus to Suetonius, and reaches beyond Beaumarchais to Rabelais; a book that is both observation and imagination, lavish in truth, intimacy, middle-class values, triviality, materiality, and that, suddenly and occasionally, tearing these realities wide open, lets us glimpse the most somber and tragic ideal.

Mémoires d'un touriste (A Tourist's memoirs), 27 April 1837 (Paris: Le Divan, 1929) 83.
†*Pisma* (Letters) (Moscow: State Publishing House, 1928).
‡*Actes et paroles* (Deeds and Words) Paris: Club français du livre, 1968), I, 421.

[Letter to Vicomtesse du Plessis]   Alfred de Vigny*

I only saw him three times in my life, but I have always admired in him the perseverance and the obstinacy of his works, despite nature, which had given him no facility, [and] despite the public, which had disdained his first works. I first met him as a printer; and in that capacity he sent me the proofs of the second edition of *Cinq-Mars*. He was a very dirty, very thin, very talkative young man, mixing up everything he said, spitting as he talked because all the upper teeth were missing from his moist mouth. About six years ago I went to listen to the discussion of the law concerning literary property at the Chamber of Deputies. A voice, from the back of the section where I was, said to me, "Well, Monsieur de Vigny, will poets always be, as your Chatterton said, *intelligent pariahs?*" I turned around, and I saw that these words emerged from a mouth whose teeth were the best-arranged pearls in the world, from a large chest, from a round, fat body, from a chubby and quite red face. He observed to me that we were the only poets or writers present, although the matter concerned all of them.

[Conversations around the Table]   George Sand†

This very simple ensemble of stories, this uncomplicated tabulation, this multitude of fictional characters, these interiors, chateaux, garrets, these thousand aspects of the world and of the city—all this work of fantasy is, thanks to a prodigious lucidity and an extraordinary, conscious effort, a mirror in which fantasy has grasped reality. Do not look into factual history for the names of the models who passed in front of this magic mirror; the mirror has preserved only anonymous types. But you must understand that each of these types has summed up all by itself a whole variety of the human species; that is the great miracle of art. And Balzac, who so sought the absolute in a certain range of discoveries, almost found in his own work the solution of a problem unknown before him: complete reality in complete fiction.

[The Essence of Balzac]   Charles Baudelaire‡

If Balzac made something admirable, always odd and often sublime, out of this vulgar genre [of the novel], it is because he poured all his being into it.

Correspondance d'Alfred de Vigny (Paris: Calmann-Lévy, 1905), 192–93.
†*Autour de la table* (Around the dinner table) (Paris: Dentu, 1862), 200.
‡"Théophile Gautier," *L'Artiste*, 13 March 1859. Reprint, Paris: Gallimard (Editions de la Pléiade), 1954, 1037.

I have often been astonished that Balzac's great glory has been to be perceived as an observer; it always seemed to me that his principal merit was to have been a visionary, a passionate visionary. . . . He sometimes makes me think of those printmakers who are never content with the bite of the acid but who transform the main lines of the plate into ravines. Marvels emerge from this astonishing natural tendency. But this disposition is generally defined as "Balzac's faults." To put it more accurately, they are precisely his qualities. Who can boast of being as greatly gifted as he, and able to apply a method that permits him so confidently to clothe pure triviality with light and purple? Who can do that? Indeed, whoever does not do that, to tell the truth, does nothing much.

[Letter to Edmond de Goncourt, 31 December 1876]   Gustave Flaubert*

I've just read Balzac's *Correspondence*. I gather from it that he was a very good man and that I would have liked him. But what a preoccupation with money! And how little love of Art! Have you noticed that he doesn't speak of art *a single time?* He sought Glory but not Beauty. And he was Catholic, legitimist, a landowner, wanted to be a Deputy and a member of the Academy—above all he was dumb as an ox, a *provincial* down to his fingertips: luxury flabbergasted him. His greatest literary hero was Walter Scott! In a word, for me he is a huge presence, but of second quality. His death was pitiful. What an irony of fate! To die on the threshold of happiness!

[Inside Balzac]   Guy de Maupassant†

Everything in him is brain and heart. Everything happens inside; exterior things hardly interest him, and he is only vaguely attracted to plastic beauty, pure form, the meaning of things, the life with which poets endow matter; for there is very little of the poet in him, despite what he may say. . . . He is above all a dealer in ideas, a spiritualist; he says so, he affirms it and repeats it. He is much more a prodigious inventor than an observer, but he always guessed correctly. He conceived his characters all at one go; and then from the qualities he had given them, he infallibly deduced every-

---

Oeuvres complètes, vol. 4: *Correspondance* (Paris: Conard, 1935) 283.
†"Balzac seen in his correspondence," *La Nation*, 22 November 1876. Reprint, *Oeuvres complètes de Guy de Maupassant: Etudes, Chroniques et Correspondance* (Paris: Librairie de France, 1938).

thing they were to do and all the occasions of their lives. He aimed only at the soul. The object and the fact were only accessories.

[Infallible Balzac]   Algernon Swinburne*

The pure artist never asserts; he suggests and therefore his meaning is totally lost upon moralists and sciolists—is indeed irreparably wasted upon the run of men who cannot work out suggestions. Balzac asserts; and Balzac cannot blunder or lie. So profound and extensive a capacity of moral apprehension no other prose writer, no man of mere analytic faculty, ever had or can have. . . . Once consent to forget or overlook the mere *entourage* and social habiliment of Balzac's intense and illimitable intellect, you cannot fail of seeing that he of all men was fittest to grapple with all strange things and words, and compel them by divine violence of spiritual rape to bring forth flowers and fruits good for food and available for use.

[Visiting with Balzac]   Oscar Wilde†

It was said of Trollope that he increased the number of our acquaintances without adding to our visiting list; but after the *Comédie humaine* one begins to believe that the only real people are the people who have never existed. Lucien de Rubempré, le Père Goriot, Ursule Mirouet, Marguérite Claes, the Baron Hulot, Madame Marneffe, le Cousin Pons, De Marsay—all bring with them a kind of contagious illusion of life. They have a fierce vitality about them: their existence is fervent and fiery-coloured; we not merely feel for them but we see them—they dominate our fancy and defy scepticism. A steady course of Balzac reduces our living friends to shadows, and our acquaintances to the shadows of shades. Who would care to go out to an evening party to meet Tomkins, the friend of one's boyhood, when one can sit at home with Lucien de Rubempré? It is pleasanter to have the entrée to Balzac's society than to receive cards from all the duchesses in Mayfair.

*William Blake. A Critical Essay (London: John Camden Hotten, 1868), 102–103.
†"Balzac in English," Pall-Mall Gazette, 13 September 1886. Repr. in Reviews, vol. 13 of The First Collected Edition of the Works of Oscar Wilde (London: Dawson's of Pall Mall, 1969) 78–79.

[Mystical Balzac]   W. B. Yeats*

There is no evidence that Balzac knew that things exist in being perceived, or, to adopt the formula of a later idealism, that they exist in being thought; his powerful body, his imagination which saw everywhere weight and magnitude, the science of his day, made him, like Descartes, consider matter as independent of mind. What then drove him half-way back to the mediaeval hypothesis? At some time of life, probably while still at college, before or during the composition of that *Treatise upon the Will* which he attributes to Louis Lambert, he must have had, or met in others, supernormal experiences resembling those that occur again and again in the *Comédie humaine*. Passages in *Séraphîta* suggest familiarity with a state known to me in youth, a state transcending sleep when forms, often of great beauty, appear minutely articulated in brilliant light, forms that express by word or action some spiritual idea and are so moulded or tinted that they make all human flesh seem unhealthy. Then he must have known of, or had some vision of, objects distant in time or place, perhaps in the remote past like that vision seen by Lucien de Rubempré before his death. Something more profound, more rooted in the blood than mere speculation, drove him to Swedenborg, perhaps to Bonaventura and Grosseteste; constrained him to think of the human mind as capable, during some emotional crisis, or, as in the case of Louis Lambert by an accident of genius, of containing within itself all that is significant in human history and of relating that history to timeless reality.

The Lesson of Balzac   Henry James†

In reading him over, in opening him almost anywhere today, what immediately strikes us is the part assigned by him, in any picture, to the *conditions* of the creatures with whom he is concerned. . . . To Balzac's imagination that was indeed in itself an immense adventure—and nothing appealed to him more than to show *how* we all are, and how we are placed and built-in for being so. What befalls us is but another name for the way our circumstances press upon us—so that an account of what befalls us is an account of our circumstances.

Add to this, then, that the fusion of all the elements of the picture, under his hand, is complete—of what people are with what they do, of what

*"Louis Lambert," *Essays and Introductions* (New York: Macmillan, 1961), 439–40. Reprinted from *Essays and Introductions* by W. B. Yeats. © Mrs. W. B. Yeats 1961 by permission of Macmillan Publishing Company and A. P. Watt Ltd. on behalf of Michael B. Yeats and Macmillan London Ltd.
†*The Question of Our Speech* and *the Lesson of Balzac: Two Lectures by Henry James* (New York: Houghton-Mifflin, 1905), 103, 106–107.

they do with what they are, of the action with the agents, of the medium with the action, of all the parts of the drama with each other. Such a production as *Le Père Goriot* for example, or as *Eugénie Grandet*, or as *Le Curé de village* has, in respect to this fusion, a kind of inscrutable perfection. The situation sits shrouded in its circumstances, and then, by its inner expansive force, emerges from them, the action marches, to the rich rustle of this great tragic and ironic train, the embroidered heroic mantle, with an art of keeping together that makes of *Le Père Goriot* in especial a supreme case of composition, a model of that high virtue that we know as economy of effect, economy of line and touch.

[Balzac's Characters]   W. Somerset Maugham*

It is hardly too much to say that if romanticism had not existed, [Balzac] would have invented it. His observation was minute and precise, but he used it as a basis for fabrications of his fantastic imagination. The idea that every man has a ruling passion suited his instinct. It is one that has always attracted the writers of fiction, for it enables them to give a dramatic force to the creatures of their invention; these stand out vividly, and the reader, from whom nothing is demanded but to know that they are misers or lechers, harpies or saints, understands them without effort. We of to-day, largely through the works of the novelists who have sought to interest us in the psychology of their characters, no longer believe that men are all of a piece. We know that they are made up of contradictory and seemingly irreconcilable elements; it is just these discordances in them that intrigue us and, because we know them in ourselves, excite our sympathy. Balzac's greatest characters are formed on the model of those older writers who drew every man in his humour. Their ruling passion has absorbed them to the exclusion of all else. They are propensities personified; but they are presented with such wonderful power, solidity and distinctness that, even though you may not quite believe in them, you can never forget them.

[A Conversation with Steven Crane]   Joseph Conrad†

Crane then was, I believe, staying temporarily in London. But he seemed to have no care in the world; and so we resumed our tramping—east

Ten Novels and Their Authors (London: William Heinemann, 1954), 101–102. Copyright William Heinemann Limited. Reprinted by permission of William Heinemann Ltd. and A. P. Watt Ltd. on behalf of The Royal Literary Fund.
†["Introduction," in Thomas Beer, *Stephen Crane: A Study in American Letters* (London: Heinemann, 1924), 17–18. Reprinted by permission of Alfred A. Knopf, Inc.]

and north and south again, steering through uncharted mazes the streets [*sic*], forgetting to think of dinner but taking a rest here and there, till we found ourselves, standing in the middle of Piccadilly Circus, blinking at the lights like two authentic night-birds. By that time we had been (in Tottenham Court Road) joined by Balzac. How he came in I have no idea. Crane was not given to literary curiosities of that kind. Somebody he knew, or something he had read, must have attracted lately his attention to Balzac. And now suddenly at ten o'clock in the evening he demanded insistently to be told in particular detail all about the *Comédie humaine*, its contents, its scope, its plan, and its general significance, together with a critical description of Balzac's style. I told him hastily that it was just black on white; and for the rest, I said, he would have to wait until we got across to Monico and he had eaten some supper. I hoped he would forget Balzac and his *Comédie*. But not a bit of it; and I had no option but to hold forth over the remnants of a meal, in the rush of hundreds of waiters and the clatter of tons of crockery, caring not what I said (for what could Stephen want with Balzac?), in the comfortable assurance that the Monstrous Shade, even if led by some strange caprice to haunt the long room of Monico's, did not know enough English to understand a single word I said. I wonder what Crane made of it all.

[Comments at an Interview]   Paul Claudel*

Too often style and purism are confused. To write well is to say exactly what you wish to say. That's how you recognize a writer's class. And Balzac is first class. His openings are sometimes slow, involved. He needs preparation, like the musician who tries out his piano before playing a piece, or loosens his fingers with arpeggios. But then expression bursts forth. A motor can misfire. Every writer worthy of the name has his failures. Look at Saint-Simon, Shakespeare. There are so many awful passages in *Romeo and Juliet!* Balzac, after this stamping about, carries you away. To carry away the reader, that is the essence of style . . . The author is not made for the style, but the style for the author. Balzac is a writer who dominates language . . . Yes . . . And language trembles in his presence.

*Paul Claudel, interview with *Les Nouvelles littéraires*, 19 May 1949.

Essays

Weekly Chat

Emile Zola*

All our great minds have participated in the broad, democratic movement of modern times. Since the beginning of this century, our most illustrious writers have taken the people's side. In their writings they have finally killed the past and revealed the future; they have each brought their stone to the structure of future society. It is a unique spectacle: many of them were direct descendants of former privileged classes, yet they have gone over to democracy in an open and striking way. Others, more singularly and even more importantly, have tried to work at reviving old régimes, and they have done it in such a way that they have administered the final blow. The latter, these unconscious democrats, actually are making the strangest imaginable admission of the logical and final arrival of the people.

There is an excellent study to be done on these great minds who believed they were preaching a return to the past and who in reality were only hastening the arrival of the future. The century was in them, unbeknownst to them. And when their great work was done, it released a spirit of liberty, a profound love of simple people, a continual recognition of deeds accomplished, a great involuntary surge toward the twentieth century, which classifies them, despite their efforts, among the most active soldiers of free thought. The triumph of the Revolution is complete. Not only has it been proclaimed by its partisans, but its very adversaries have written in its favor without realizing it, so deeply has the breath of revolution penetrated all our souls.

I was ruminating on this as I recently paged through the splendid edition of the *Oeuvres complètes de Balzac* (Complete works of Balzac) published by Michel Lévy. This edition, which will consist of twenty-five volumes, is only one-third complete. But the published volumes already suffice to establish Balzac in all the eminence of his strange genius. The edition was revised and completed according to the notes left by the author himself. Soon, therefore, we will have before us a definitive monument, worthy of the illustrious novelist.

His is a curious case. Here is a man who during thirty years of uninter-

*Reprinted from *La Tribune*, 31 October 1869.

rupted production bowed down each day before royalism and Catholicism. Here is a man who perhaps believed when he died that he was leaving a magnificent disputation in favor of kings and priests. And today, when we read the thousands of pages that he has written, we feel in them only that strong revolutionary breath. His kneeling before thrones and altars seems to us a mania that we pardon. On his knees he burns what he adores, without even seeming to notice. He says his prayers like a man whose every prayer becomes a blasphemy. He solemnly makes a profession of Catholic and monarchist faith, and then he writes a purely democratic work, which draws conclusions that go against his *Credo*. It is the pure naiveté of genius. Intelligence carries this unknowing democrat to places where he does not wish to go. The intoxication of his high faculties draws the truth from him, the way wine makes drunkards speak. And he, moreover, does not know that he has a secret hidden in his heart; he says everything believing that he has nothing to say; he leaves to later generations a Balzac that he does not know, a Balzac who was the historian of democracy under the first Empire, the Restoration, and Louis-Philippe.

I do not have much space; I cannot give multiple examples here to show the whole *Comédie humaine* written by an unknowing democrat. But it is simple for me to prove rapidly to what extent Balzac went against all the beliefs that he enunciated so loudly.

In many passages, Balzac weeps over the former nobility. He finds it great, legitimate, useful. He is a declared opponet of the division of large properties. Everything had been fine, and he declares that we have spoiled it all. He is especially sympathetic to the principle of primogeniture. And this is the mind that wrote *Le Cabinet des antiques* (The collection of antiques). I know of no more violent satire of the former nobility. The drawing room of the d'Esgrignon family is like a menagerie in which a tribe of grotesque, aged, and foundered animals whimper, croak, and whinny. The marquis, despite the sovereign dignity that the author intends to give him, is simply an idiot in his second childhood; the chevalier de Valois stinks of the shameful court of Louis XV; the venerable ladies sitting around the great fireplace do not even have the grace and amiable generosity of their grandmothers; they are made of iron and wood, their joints grate like those of mechanical dolls. But that is nothing; that is still merely a picture in which the mocking spirit of a man of Touraine delights. You must read to the end of the novel, which seems to have no purpose other than to condemn the nobility as a whole. A young gentleman, the son of the marquis, Victurnien d'Esgrignon, after having grown up in this fossilized milieu, turns into a very pleasant knave. His father has told him so many times that the d'Esgrignons lived in a feudal heaven, quite separate from the peasants of this earth, that one fine day Victurnien commits forgery in order to run off with his mistress, without even being aware of the enormity of his crime. His education has borne its fruits; he believes himself inviolate, for the Assizes court cannot be meant for a d'Esgrignon. In any case, he doesn't even think of the court; he commits forgery the way a hundred years earlier he would have beaten a serf to death, simply because he was the master and such was his good pleasure. I would have wanted to see this young gentleman in the prisoners' dock, between two guards. Balzac preferred to save him through the excellent Chesnel, the son of a former d'Esgrignon servant, who spends the money he has earned as a notary to save the family that he still worships blindly.

Surely the great figure of this novel is neither the marquis nor Victurnien; nor is it even the aunt of the young rascal, Mademoiselle Armande, who resigns her share of an inheritance in his favor. In my opinion, it is the notary Chesnel who dominates all the other characters, that excellent son of the people, who grows with his times, who earns a fortune, and who gives it to a good-for-nothing to whom he owes nothing. I do not know what was Balzac's true intention. But I would willingly believe that he wanted above all to show how a great house can crumble in these accursed modern times. If he does not approve of Victurnien, he seems to accuse the Revolution of having upset the great territorial fortunes to the point of reducing a d'Esgrignon to committing forgeries. Sensing how ridiculous these mummies of another century appear in our times, he tries to adorn his marquis with great nobility and his Mademoiselle Armande with nun-like devotion. But in spite of his efforts, it is the former valet's son who dominates his work. Balzac obeyed a secret impulsion: he made a giant out of a secondary character. Chesnel represents the people who know their strength, who have reconquered intelligence, activity, and life; he represents the people who are called upon to regenerate society and to take precedence over their former masters; he represents the people who will take into their hands all the wealth, all the dignity, all the sovereignty of the country. And so here we have the Catholic and monarchist Balzac deifying the people. Even more: he has the people toss a last handful of alms to the dying nobility; he endows the people with goodness of heart after endowing them with the firmness and justice that emerges from intelligence.

I could have taken any other novel than *Le Cabinet des antiques*. There are few works of Balzac that do not go against the political and religious opinions of their author in this way. The Rastignacs, the de Marsays, the Maxime de Trailles, all the ironic and rotten debris of the nobility appear unimaginably shameful in the presence of the echoing tide of the people that one hears rumbling in the background of the *Comédie humaine*. Balzac seems to have continued *La Fin du monde* (The End of the world) by Diderot. He makes us witness the agony of old France, instinctively mocking and satirical, as he declares at every line his love for that dying country. But his was a platonic love. His unavowed sympathies were for the obscure martyrs of the bourgeoisie, for the Birotteaus, for the Popinots, and the other little people who rise to fortune and honor by the strength of their own limbs. Balzac loved vigor too much, he loved herculean energies too much not to admire the living strength of humanity. He, the literary giant who animated a world, could not lie as he confronted the colossal accomplishment of this century. Thus, on every page, there emerges his admiration for workers who scale the social ladder at a single bound, for peasants who inherit the earth. If he expresses grief on the tomb of the nobility, he is drawn to salute with a cry of surprise and joy the new society that is carving out its place with great hatchet blows.

One has to penetrate deeply into this mind in order to find the key to its apparent contradictions. In literature Balzac was temperamentally and by virtue of his genius an autocrat. He wanted to be the undisputed king of writers, and he also was determined to manipulate like humble, docile subjects the characters of the world he had created. Sanguine and of a rich and powerful nature, he loved willpower, domination, and order imposed at the command of a single person—a reasonable and useful despotism. Thus he had accepted monarchy and Catholicism as two excellent systems of absolute government. To his mind, priests and kings were necessary to govern men, just as he alone could guide his many subjects in the *Comédie humaine* to their true destinies. Any writer of his stature must have a political and religious dogma, failing which he will go astray and contradict himself. He chose his dogmas according to his needs; handy dogmas in which moreover he himself does not always believe and which he often contents himself with listing as simple rules of social hygiene. Such is the monarchist and Catholic Balzac. The other Balzac, the one who studied the miseries of the peasants with love, who gave the people and the bourgeoisie a passport into literature, is indeed the same man; but the same man detached from his dogmas by the blinding light of reality. He is too intelligent to be a fanatic. When the people pass, and he sees their superb rush forward, he cries out with admiration; he shows their greatness naively, because that is the way things are and he is a painter of reality. To the devil with his beliefs! He denies them, or rather he keeps them for the sake of convenience; he wraps himself in them, as in everyday clothing designed for practical use, which he continually tears apart and which he continually tries to sew together again.

If it is regrettable that a mind of this quality did not frankly work for the Revolution, there is a great consolation in the thought that he was with us all the same. On the flag on which he wrote Royalty and Catholicism, our children will read the word Republic. His whole work is there, crying out: "Don't listen to him, he is lying to himself, he worked for the future, he described the first stammerings of universal democracy."

M. de Guermantes's Balzac   Marcel Proust*

Sometimes the Marquis came to see his brother; when this happened, they were very apt to "get on to Balzac," for Balzac was much read when they

*From *Marcel Proust on Art and Literature 1896–1919*. Trans. Sylvia Townsend Warner (New York: Meridian Books, 1957), 199–209. Reprinted by permission of Chatto & Windus and Carroll & Graf Publishers, Inc.

were young and in their father's library they had read these very same volumes, which the Count had inherited and which now stood on his shelves.[1] Their taste for Balzac still unsophisticatedly reflected the preferences of readers of that time, before Balzac had become a classic and subject as such to the fluctuations of literary opinion. If someone, someone who was not an outsider, mentioned Balzac, the Count cited various titles, which were not the titles of the Balzac novels we now most admire. "Balzac! Balzac!" said he. "He takes some reading. The *Bal de Sceaux* (The Ball at Sceaux), for instance. Have you read the *Bal de Sceaux*? It's capital." It is true that he said the same thing of *Le Lys dans la Vallée:* "Mme de Mortsauf! None of you have read all that, I suppose. Charles!"—calling in his brother— "Mme de Mortsauf, *Le Lys dans la Vallée,*—capital, isn't it?" He spoke in the same way of *Le Contrat de Mariage,* which he called by its first title, *La Fleur des Pois,* and of *La Maison du Chat-qui-pelote*. On days when he had really got going on Balzac he also referred to books which to speak truth are not by Balzac but by Roger de Beauvoir or Céleste de Chabrillan. But it must be pleaded for him that the small library to which the *sirop* and the biscuits were brought up to him, and where on rainy days, if there was no one below who might catch sight of him he was saluted through the open window by the windlashed poplar tree, curtseying three times a minute, contained together with the works of Balzac, those of Alphonse Karr, Céleste de Chabrillan, Roger de Beauvoir, and Alexandre Duval, all bound alike. When one opened them, and the same thin paper printed in large type brought the heroine's name before you, exactly as if it were she herself who had come before you in this convenient portable guise, accompanied by a slight odour of glue, dust, and old age which seemed the very breath of her charm, it went against the grain to classify these books by a pseudo-literary canon, arbitrarily based on ideas that were equally foreign both to the theme of the book and the look of the volume. And to talk to you Blanche de Mortsauf and the others made use of such beguilingly clear print (the only effort required of you in order to follow them was to turn over those pages that old age had gilded and made transparent, but which were still as pliable as a fine muslin) that it was impossible not to believe the narrators had been one and the same, and that there had not been a much closer kinship between Eugénie Grandet and the Duchesse de Mers than there was between the *Eugénie Grandet* in one's hand and a Balzac novel in a shilling edition.

I must admit that I can understand M. de Guermantes, I who throughout my childhood read in the same fashion, I, for whom *Colomba* was for so long "the book where they said I must not read the story *La Vénus d'Ille*" (*they* meant you, Mamma). Those copies in which we read a book for the first time, they are like the dress a woman was wearing when we first saw her— they tell how the book came to us then, and how we came to the book. Hunting for these is my only form of bibliography. The edition in which I read a book for the first time, the edition in which it made its original impression on me, these are the only "first" editions, "original" editions, that are dear to me. Besides, all I really want to do is to recall them. Their old pages are so porous, so ready to take in a memory, that I am afraid they might absorb today's impressions too, so that I should find my impressions of the past were no longer there. I want them to open, whenever I think about them, at the page where I closed them as I sat under the lamp, or on the wickerwork garden chair, when Papa would say to me: "Sit up straight."

And there are times when I wonder whether even today my way of reading is not more like M. de Guermantes's than contemporary critics'. To me, a book is still a living entity, which I begin to know from the first line, which I listen to with deference, and which, while we remain together, I unreservedly and undemurringly agree with. When I find M. Faguet saying in his *Critical Essays* that the first volume of *Le Capitaine Fracasse* is splendid and the second volume tame, or that in *Le Père Goriot* everything to do with Goriot is first-rate and everything to do with Rastignac shoddy, I am quite as surprised as if I heard someone saying that the country round Combray is ugly on the Méséglise side, but on the Guermantes side, beautiful. When M. Faguet goes on to say that lovers of Gautier do not read beyond the first volume of *Le Capitaine Fracasse*, I, who took so much pleasure in the second, can only feel sorry for the lovers of Gautier, but when he adds that the first volume was written for the lovers and the second for schoolboys, my pity for the lovers turns to scorn of myself, since I realise how schoolboyish I still am. Finally, when he declares that Gautier wrote the second volume in a state of intense boredom, I am amazed that what was so boring to write should later on become so entertaining to read.

So, too, with Balzac, where Sainte-Beuve and Faguet pick and choose and analyse, and think that the beginning is wonderful and the end worthless.[2] The only advance I have achieved towards this outlook since my childhood, and the sole point on which, if I may say so, I claim to differ from M. de Guermantes, is that I have slightly extended the bounds of this unalterable world, this mass from which nothing can be subtracted, this quantitative reality, so that I no longer think of it in terms of single books, but as the works of an author. I see but little difference between the various books. I am as much perplexed by critics who think, as does M. Faguet, that in *Un Ménage de Garçon* Balzac wrote a masterpiece, and in *Le Lys dans la Vallée* the worst of all bad books, as I was by Mme de Guermantes when she thought that on such an evening the Duke of X . . . had been intelligent and on some other occasion stupid. My own opinion of people's intelligence may vary from time to time, but I know quite well that it is my opinion that varies, not their intelligence. Nor do I believe it true that intelligence is a variable force, which at the will of God is sometimes powerful, sometimes feeble. I believe that the mental level to which it rises is always the same, and that it is precisely on that level that it syphons into those vessels which communicate with the past and which, whether it be *Un Ménage de Garçon* or *Le Lys dans la Vallée*, are the Works of Balzac.

However, if M. de Guermantes thought the "vicissitudes," the careers of René Longueville or Félix de Vandenesse "delightful," by which he really meant, diverting and make-believe, on the other hand he often dwelt admiringly on Balzac's powers of observation: "Life in a solicitor's office, it's the very thing; I've had my dealings with people of that sort; it's the very thing. *César Birotteau* and *Les Employés!*"

A person who did not agree with him and whom I tell you about because she represents another type of Balzac reader, was the Marquise de Villeparisis. She refused to believe that Balzac's portraits were true to life. "The man says: I will show you how a solicitor talks. No solicitor ever talked like that in his life." But what, above all, she could not stomach was that he should have laid claim to describe good society. "To begin with, he never set foot in it, he was invited nowhere, what could he have known about it? Towards the end he knew Mme de Castries, but he could not have seen anything of it in her house, she was a nobody. I once saw him there, just after I married, he was a very common sort of man, with nothing in particular to say, and I wouldn't have him introduced to me. Somehow or other in the end he contrived to marry a Pole, she came of a good family, distant relations of our Czartoryski cousins. The whole family was appalled at it, and I can assure you they don't look any too pleased if one talks to them about it. Besides, it all ended very badly. He died almost immediately." Then, looking censoriously down at her knitting: "And I *have* heard some very nasty stories about that. Do you really mean to say that he ought to have been *at* the Académie?" (as one might say, *at the Opéra*). "To begin with, he hadn't the wherewithal for it. Besides, the Académie is 'a chosen few'. Sainte-Beuve, yes! Now there was a charming man, so witty, such a gentleman, he never put himself forward, and one never had to meet him unless one wanted to. Not like Balzac. And then, he had been to Champlâtreux; so he, at least, would have been able to write about society. But he took care not to, because he was a gentleman. Besides, that Balzac, he was a bad man. There's no good feeling in what he wrote, there are no nice people. It's always unpleasant reading, he always sees the seamy side of everything. It's all he ever sees. Even if he describes a poor parish priest, he has to make him unfortunate, every one's hand has to be against him." "You can't say—" said the Count before the assembled listeners, who were thrilled to be present at such an absorbing tilting-match, and dug each other in the ribs to draw attention to the Marquise "taking the bit between her teeth"—"Aunt, you can't say that the *Curé de Tours*, which is the one you mean, isn't well drawn. That country town, could anything be more like the real thing?" "Precisely," said the Marquise, proceeding to what was one of her favourite gambits, and the universal test that she applied to literary productions, "and in what way can it interest me to read a treatise about things I know quite as much about as he? People say, It's so like a country town. By all means; but I know all about that, I've lived in the country, so why should I be interested in it?" And so proud was she of this line of argument, a favourite one of hers, that a smile of arrogance brightened her eyes as she glanced towards her audience, adding, to pour oil on the troubled waters: "You may think it very silly of me, but I must admit that when I read a book, I am weak-minded enough to want to learn something new." For the next two months, it was retailed, even among the Countess's remotest cousins, that this particular At Home at the Guermantes's had been quite the most interesting affair imaginable.

For when a writer reads a book, the closeness of social observation, the slant towards pessimism or optimism, are accepted conditions which he does not dispute, which he does not even begin to see. But for "intelligent" readers the fact that something may be "untrue" or "dismal" is a defect in the author himself, which they are astonished and rather pleased to find recurring, and even being made more of, in each of his books, as if he had not been able to get the better of it, and which finally makes them see him in the disagreeable light of a person who is always wrong-headed or who has a depressing effect on one, so much so that whenever the book-seller hands them a Balzac or a George Eliot, they push it away, saying: "No, thank you! It's bound to be untrue, or gloomy, this new one will be worse than all the rest, I don't want any more of it."

As for the Countess, when the Count said: "Ah, Balzac, Balzac! He takes some reading. Have you read *La Duchesse de Mers?*" she remarked: "I don't care for Balzac myself, I think he exaggerates." In general, she disliked people who "exaggerated," and were thus an implied rebuke to those who, like herself, did not; people who gave "exaggerated" tips, which made hers look exceedingly stingy, people who felt a more than ordinary degree of sorrow at the death of a relation, people who did more than is usually done for a friend in distress, or went to an exhibition expressly to see any picture that was not a portrait of someone they knew or "the thing to see." She herself, who did not exaggerate, when someone asked her if she had seen this or that picture at an exhibition, simply replied: "If it's on show, I saw it." . . .

Of these readers of Balzac, it was the young Marquise de Cardaillec, by birth a de Forcheville, who was the most susceptible to his influence. Among her husband's properties was the old mansion of Forcheville at Alençon, with an imposing front on the town's main square, as in *Le Cabinet des Antiques*, and a garden stretching down to the Gracieuse, as in *La Vieille Fille*. The Comte de Forcheville, who saw no point in going to "bury himself" in Alençon, had abandoned it to the garden staff. But the young Marquise had it done up, and every year she spent several weeks there, finding it full of a charm which she herself described as Balzacian. She had some old furniture brought from the castle of Forcheville, where it had been stowed away in the attics as out of date, pieces that had belonged to the Comte de Forcheville's grandmother, together with various objects that were interesting historically or for reasons, at once sentimental and aristocratic, of family piety. In Paris she had in fact become one of those young women of the aristocracy who cherish their rank with a sort of artistic appreciation, and who stand in relation to the old nobility as do the shrewd hotel-keepers of Mont Saint-Michel or the "William the Conqueror" to the common people of Brittany or Normandy— young women who had realised that their charm (a charm of retrospect which they were first made aware of by literary men whom their own personal charms had attracted) rested specifically under the protection of that antiquity, a compound reflection of both literature and contemporary (though lineaged) beauty being thus thrown over this aestheticism.

In the house at Alençon photographs of the loveliest of the great ladies of today stood on bracket-tables of old oak, such as had belonged to Mlle Cormon.[3] But the ladies had posed in those old-fashioned, Book of Beauty attitudes which through masterpieces of painting and literature have become so evocative of the grace of bygone days, so the photographs only added a further artistic touch to the period effect—which in other respects, alas, from one's first sight of the servants in the lobby to the conversation of their employers in the drawing-room, was inevitably of today. So much so, that the little conjuration of Balzac in the house at Alençon worked best on people with more taste than imagination, who knew what to look for but needed to set eyes on it, and who came away in raptures. For my part, I found it rather disappointing. When I heard that at Alençon Mme de Cardaillec lived in the very house of Mlle Cormon or Mme de Bargeton, the knowledge that something I had so often pictured in my mind really existed made too deep an impression on me for it to be possible for the disparities of real life to live up to it.

I ought to say, however, before I wash my hands of Balzac, that Mme de Cardaillec did the honours of her house like a most accomplished Balzacian. "If you like, I'll take you to Forcheville tomorrow," she said to me. "You'll see what a to-do it will make in the town—like the day when Mlle Cormon had her mare harnessed for the drive to Prébaudet. Meanwhile, let us have lunch. And if you feel strong enough to stay on over Monday—I am 'at home to company' that evening—you won't leave my part of the world without having seen M. du Bousquier and Mme de Bargeton with your own eyes, and you'll see the cut-glass chandelier lit up in honour of all these good people, which Lucien de Rubempré, you remember, found so overwhelming."

Well-informed persons who witnessed this pious reconstruction of a bygone provincial aristocracy put it down to her Forcheville blood. I myself knew that it was attributable to her Swann blood, which she had forgotten about, but whose intelligence and good taste she had retained, and even a sufficiency of that intellectual detachment from the world of aristocracy (howsoever she might be attached to it for practical motives) to find in it, as in something alien, useless, and extinct, an artistic charm.

Notes

1. [Ed. note: In the course of this early essay, Proust introduces characters who will reappear in *Remembrance of Things Past*. Among them, Mme de Villeparisis will express the same opinion of Balzac that she expresses here. Théophile Gautier and C. A. Sainte-Beuve were contemporaries of Balzac. The other writers mentioned were already unread when Proust was writing and are completely forgotten today.]

2. What is rather odd and rather comforting is that Sainte-Beuve said: "Who has ever drawn the duchesses of the Restoration better than he?" M. Faguet laughs uproariously at his duchesses, and invokes M. Feuillet. Finally, M. Blum, who likes making distinctions, admires his duchesses, but not in so far as they claim to represent duchesses of the Restoration. Here, I admit, I feel inclined to say with Sainte-Beuve: "Who told you so, what do you know about it?" and "On this point I prefer to rely on persons who knew them, and" . . . above all, on Sainte-Beuve.

3. Mlle Cormon, Mme de Bargeton, M. du Bousquier and Lucien de Rubempré are all characters from the *Comédie humaine*.

"Balzac and Reality"   Michel Butor*

1

I take particular pleasure in speaking of Balzac, since he is generally used as a sort of bogey to intimidate any attempt at innovation, at invention in the contemporary novel. In simplistic fashion we contrast the so-called "Balzacian" novel with the modern novel, that is to say, with all the important works of the twentieth century; yet it is child's play to show that this "Balzacian" novel is in fact derived from only a tiny part of Balzac's work, and that the only true heirs of this great man during the past fifty years are Proust, Faulkner, etc.

Alas, the critics who brandish the name of Balzac as if it were a sort of shield, the reactionary novelists who claim to be perpetuating Balzac, evidently know his work very slightly; they have read two or three well-thumbed chapters of *La Comédie humaine*—*Eugénie Grandet*, for example, or the *Curé de Tours*—and leave it at that. Unfortunately, on occasion certain open-minded, quite advanced people allow themselves to be intimidated by this propaganda, and inform us that they long to shake off the tyranny of Balzac, to write anti-Balzac novels, thereby controverting a ridiculously inadequate idea of Balzac.

Of course, the body of work is so enormous that it is extremely difficult to get through it all; each reader selects more or less what suits him. Very rare, in fact, are those who had read all of Balzac, which is however, indispensable to a true appreciation. Fortunately one comes across fewer and fewer people who claim to judge Proust after having read two or three

*Reprinted from *Inventory*, 100–13. Trans. Remy Hall. © Editions de Minuit, 1960. Used by permission of Georges Borchardt, Inc.

volumes, but it is still quite common to hear, among relatively cultivated people, reactions such as: "Balzac, well, of course I haven't read all of Balzac." Indeed, you haven't read the juvenilia which he disowned, and probably haven't read the *Contes drolatiques,* nor the plays, but at least, since you are talking about Balzac, since you are setting Balzac up against us, or since you are setting yourself up against Balzac, have you read all the fragments of that great unfinished novel the *Comédie humaine?* "I've read at least five or six." What! And you talk about Balzac, and you have theories about Balzac: you can't be serious! Would you talk about Baudelaire after having read only five or six poems without even knowing whether they were well or badly chosen? Alas, it happens!

And when it does, the usual justification is to declare: "Of course Balzac is a very great writer, but an uneven one." Which is rather like saying that the abbey of Vézelay is a splendid building, but not all the stones composing it are of equal interest. Even today, very few readers are capable of grasping the whole or, consequently, the justification for those sections which, considered in isolation, are indeed no more fascinating than the stones assembled in the columns or the walls of Vézelay.

But this choice, within the *Comédie humaine,* which isolates two or three elements in order to discard the remainder as esthetically inferior, has been revealed, in the course of literary history during the past hundred years, as extremely contingent; the line separating the good from the bad in the *Comédie humaine* certainly did not pass through the same places for Paul Bourget, let us say, for Proust, and for Baudelaire or Albert Béguin; it is therefore high time we stop considering the work of Balzac in bits and pieces, and instead come to terms with its general movement; as for the relation between Balzac and the most audacious forms of the modern novel, one can, quite roughly, propose this formula: if one takes a novel, almost at random, from those which compose the *Comédie humaine,* it is easy enough to show what differentiates it from literature nowadays, what is dated or old-fashioned, but if one takes the work as a whole, one discovers that its richness and audacity are far from having yet been fully appreciated, and that it is, therefore, a prodigious mine of edification for us.

Balzac's work is incomparably more revolutionary than it appears to a superficial and fragmentary reading; among the novelties it affords, some have been systematically exploited in the course of the nineteenth century, others found echoes only in the most original works of the twentieth, and this fecundity is far from being exhausted.

2

Let us begin by pointing out the extent to which Balzac is deliberately and systematically an innovator, how conscious he is of his originality as a novelist, the degree to which he considered his technique and his technical invention to be open, capable of surprising developments, far from hardening into that academicism which is attributed to him as the result of a complete misunderstanding, and in which his false disciples are trapped.

We know that the *Comédie humaine* contains a whole gallery of men of genius: painters of genius, musicians of genius, criminals of genius; of course there had to be a novelist of genius. He plays a fairly unobtrusive role in this incomplete structure, but he nevertheless has the time to issue a proclamation in favor of a "new novel." His name is d'Arthez, and in the second part of *Illusions perdues*, *Un Grand Homme de province à Paris*, he meets young Lucien de Rubempré, who has just arrived from Angoulême with his sonnet sequence, *Les Marguerites*, under his arm, but also the manuscript of a historical novel, *L'Archer de Charles IX* (Charles IX's bowman). D'Arthez is the center of a group of young geniuses, of young men who are on the side of truth and who oppose the brilliant world of journalism which will tempt the young provincial to his ultimate ruin. Lucien reads his novel to d'Arthez, who makes the following pronouncement:

> "You have made a good start on the right path, but your work must be revised. You must create a different style for yourself if you do not want to ape Sir Walter Scott, for you have imitated him. You begin, like him, with long conversations to introduce your characters; once they have spoken, you follow with description and action. That antagonism, necessary to every dramatic work, comes last. Invert the terms of the problem. Instead of diffuse conversation—magnificent in Scott's work but quite colorless in your own—use the descriptions to which our language lends itself so well. Your dialogue should be the long-awaited consequence that crowns your preparations. Plunge straight into the action. Treat your subject from different points of view, sideways, backwards; finally, vary your methods so that you are never the same. . . . Every authentic reign, from Charlemagne on, calls for at least one work, and sometimes four or five, like the reigns of Louis XIV, Henri IV and François I. In this way you will create a picturesque history of France in which you will depict costumes, furniture, houses, interiors, private life, giving us the spirit of the time rather than laboriously narrating the known facts. You have it in your power to be original by challenging the popular misconceptions which disfigure most of our monarchs. Be bold enough in this first work of yours to rehabilitate the great and magnificent figure of Catherine whom you have sacrificed to the prejudices which still cloud her name. . . .

We know that Balzac himself sought to realize d'Arthez's project in the astonishing triptych, *Sur Catherine de Médicis*. It is rather amusing to discover in this text that many novels today described as Balzacian would have been regarded by him as servile imitations of Walter Scott. It is interesting to emphasize in Balzac what I shall call the principle of systematic variation and exploration of form. But Balzac's definitive victory over his great predecessor, his liberation from him, finds its expression in an extraordinary invention which will utterly transform the structure of his work, allowing him to make the novel *à la* Walter Scott into a detail or chapter of what he, Balzac, regards as *his* novel. I mean the recurrence of characters. In an admirable text which is indispensable to the reader who wants to surmount the academic concept of Balzac too often prevalent, the preface of 1842, he returns to the ideas he had attributed to d'Arthez, elaborating on them:

> Hence Walter Scott raised the novel to the philosophical value of history. . . . But, not having so much imagined a system as found his style in the fire of work or through the logic of this work, it had not occurred to him to link his compositions together in such a manner as to coordinate a complete history, each chapter of which would have been a novel, and each novel an epoch. Upon discovering this lack of a link, which incidentally does not make the Scotsman any the less great a writer, I saw at the same time the system most favorable to the execution of my work and the possibility of executing it.

In Walter Scott and in the other novelists whom he considered classic—Longus, Rabelais, Cervantes, the Abbé Prévost, Richardson, Defoe, Lesage, Macpherson whom he regards as a novelist, Rousseau, Sterne, Goethe, Chateaubriand, Mme. de Staël, Benjamin Constant, and Bernardin de Saint-Pierre—he discovers the possibility of representing a historical epoch by a character in a small novel, hence representing the whole sequence of historical epochs by a sequence of characters linked by adventures; he transposes this sequence into a simultaneity, discovering that these characters represent not only epochs but different "species." Thus, gradually discarding the project of a general history of humanity, he concentrates on the description of contemporary society, a world whose riches increasingly develop before his eyes, and whose depiction is made possible by the recurrence of characters, a technique which to begin with has the advantage of being a sort of novelistic ellipsis, a means of considerably shortening a narrative otherwise inordinately long.

He poses the problem thus: "How does one make interesting the drama for three or four thousand characters which is offered by a society?"

It is obvious, first of all, that this society consists of more than three or four thousand characters, and secondly that it would be impossible to study three or four thousand characters in detail; thus, a certain character must be representative of a whole class, and when he has been described in certain circumstances, he must also be able to function in others. If one needs, for the purpose of such a drama, a lawyer for example, it is useless to describe all over again his household, his married life; it will suffice to refer to a certain other work in which he already appears.

The principle of the recurrence of characters is therefore first of all a principle of economy, but it will have extraordinary consequences which will, one might say, fundamentally transform the very nature of novel writing.

Indeed, each individual work will lead to other works; the characters who will appear in one novel will not be restricted to it, but will return in other novels in which we shall find complementary information about them.

In each element of this whole, we will be given what is indispensable for us to know about one character or another for a superficial understanding of the adventure in question; and it will be possible for us to go further by reading the other books in which these same characters appear, so that the structure and the bearing of a particular novel change according to the number of other novels we have read; a story which seemed linear and somewhat simplistic at first reading, when we were ignorant of the Balzacian world, is later revealed as the meeting point of a whole series of themes already explored elsewhere.

Thus we find ourselves confronting a certain number of facets which are linked together and among which we can wander at our leisure.

The result is what one might call a novelistic mobile, a whole formed by a certain number of parts which we can approach in almost any order we please; each reader will follow a different trajectory through the universe of the *Comédie humaine;* it is like a sphere or an enclosure with many entrances.

Evidently the recurrence of characters or their persistence from one novel to another has in Balzac a much greater importance than in what is called the *roman fleuve, À la recherche du temps perdu (Remembrance of Things Past)*, for example, in which the various secondary units, the various volumes, follow each other in chronological order; where one picks up, in the subsequent volume, the characters at the point, at the moment in their lives, where one had left them in the preceding volume.

This chronological sequence of adventures, of fictional units, is for Balzac only a particular case of their possible combinations, a particular case magnificently illustrated in that sort of dorsal spine of the *Comédie humaine* constituted by the series: *Illusions perdues, Splendeurs et misères des courtisanes, La Dernière Incarnation de Vautrin*. But we know that in order to enjoy *Splendeurs et misères* properly, we must benefit from the oblique illumination afforded by *Le Père Goriot*, the lateral light shed by *La Maison Nucingen*.

In the writing of the *Comédie humaine*, Balzac does not for a moment follow chronological order; he gradually explores the aspects of a reality which evolves before his eyes, and, in order to do this, constantly makes use of flashbacks; as far as the reader is concerned, it is impossible to find a way of reading the *Comédie humaine* which satisfies a simple chronology; moreover, we know that in the novels taken individually, the temporal sequence always presents complexities. If one takes the principal characters of Balzac's universe, one sees that whatever the reading order adopted, their adventures will be presented according to different sequences, as d'Arthez said: "from different points of view, sideways, backward. . . ." The "Book" Mallarmé dreamed of and could not produce in the order of lyrical poetry, Balzac had already prodigiously exemplified in the order of the novel.

3

But the principle of the recurrence of characters has not only the advantage of provoking an almost automatic multiplication and exploration of novelistic structures, it almost supplies a remarkable solution to the problem of the novel's relations with reality, entirely justifying the introduction of real characters in a fictional universe.

We must see how the Balzacian characters increasingly detach themselves from real characters, how his fiction methodically constitutes itself within a study of reality.

Since he is concerned to give a description that is historically determined, it is indispensable to introduce occasionally certain characters whose individuality is closely connected with a certain nation or a certain period. Wanting to situate a particular episode, it is necessary for him to talk about Napoleon, for example, or Louis XVIII, and these are such common references, so well-known, that there is no question of replacing them. They are historical characters and their historicity is expressed by the fact that it is not only possible but inevitable to find information concerning them outside the individual novel or the fictional world of the *Comédie humaine*.

This characteristic has an enormous disadvantage for the novelist: he cannot take liberties with these characters, he cannot attribute to them or imagine adventures for them other than those which he actually knows, without finding himself contradicted by some document, and in the most serious cases be accused of lying or slander; since such characters are unique, he cannot give them other names without falsifying the situation which they must, precisely, designate.

At the other end of the social ladder, we find classes of almost interchangeable individuals: concièrges, for example, or lawyers: it is then extremely easy for the novelist to invent a lawyer who does not exist in the official records and who is nevertheless entirely probable and upon whom consequently the novelist's imagination can lavish itself in all its freedom and in all its strength.

We therefore have two poles: on the one hand, characters like the kings and emperors, irreplaceable because it is in their nature to be known as such, but about whom, as a result, the novelist cannot say much; on the other hand, the obscure characters about whom the novelist can say anything he likes precisely because it is in their nature to be replaceable, because they are always more than one and because it is perfectly natural that we should not know the name of So-and-so.

Between these two poles is to be found a particularly interesting region, that of famous people, I mean the characters whose celebrity will play a role in the narrative, for example the poets or painters; their celebrity makes them into quasi-obligatory points of reference, their plurality permits adding to their number a fictional colleague who could be the double of one among them, a character *à clef*.

Thus, when Balzac talks about the literary world of his times, he is obliged to mention Lamartine, Victor Hugo, etc., otherwise the reader would not recognize that world; but if he wants to speak of an individual poet, he cannot take Lamartine as a direct example, or in order to talk about a lady novelist he cannot take George Sand, for by attributing a specific adventure to them he risks being accused of lying, so he replaces them with representatives: Canalis or Camille Maupin.

Now, these copies, these doubles, will inevitably detach themselves more and more from their real models, the latter becoming more celebrated, their adventures better known to the public, and more distinct, obviously, from those attributed to them in the *Comédie humaine*.

One can therefore recognize three stages in the composition of such characters: first they are one example among others, a poet like the rest, an ordinary poet in the same way as we have an ordinary lawyer, but since the poet naturally possesses a recognized individuality, since the ordinary poet would be naturally a mediocre poet, it is necessary to attribute to him an originality which is modeled at first on an existing originality: Canalis-Lamartine; but once the uniqueness of the character *à clef* detaches itself from the original model, once Canalis detaches himself from Lamartine to the point when he can appear next to him in a list, he begins to represent not a living poet any longer but in fact a possibility of a poet who does not exist in reality and who should exist there; he fills a gap which he discloses in reality, and he has the characteristic of being far clearer than his real colleagues, far more revealing. Thus, in several passages of the *Comédie humaine*, Balzac will in later printings replace Lamartine by Canalis, a personality who has become even better known, a word whose signification is far more precise.

Balzac writes: "On seeing several previously created characters reappear in *Le Père Goriot*, the public has understood one of the author's boldest intentions, that of giving life and movement to a whole fictitious world whose characters will perhaps still subsist when the majority of the models will be dead and forgotten."

Thus, in one of the novels taken individually, the real characters refer us to a whole literature, a daily press, a conversation; the important imaginary characters refer us to other novels, to a much nearer literature; these two categories of characters form two concentric spheres: that of the far vaster reality in which they are extremely numerous and in which we recognize Napoleon, Louis XVIII, Lamartine and Victor Hugo, and that of the *Comédie humaine* in which all relations are in a sense shortened, in which we recognize Vautrin, Rastignac, Canalis, etc. In relation to each of the aspects of the *Études sociales* [sic], the whole constitutes, as a result, a kind of nearer reality: the relation between what one says about a fictitious character in one novel and what one says about him in the others being the same as that between what is said about a real character in the *Comédie humaine* and what one has said about him or her elsewhere.

4

These inter-novel relationships are extremely complex. The fictitious characters can represent groups of real characters only because, in reality itself, individuals and objects have relations of signification. Balzac's imaginary poets can only come to life because in reality itself, by means of fame, of celebrity, the poets represent each other; Canalis can represent and supplant Lamartine only because Lamartine already represents and supplants a whole category of poets, without mentioning the fact that he represents a large number of other men, in certain respects gives them his name.

There is therefore a whole organization of reality in relation to its representation, a whole organization which the novelist merely extends: the divisions which Balzac has introduced into the *Études sociales* [sic] are a kind of reflection or transposition of it.

Indeed, one cannot fail to be struck by the arbitrary appearance of this classification: *Scènes de la vie privée, Scènes de la vie de province, Scènes de la vie parisienne, Scènes de la vie politique, Scènes de la vie militaire, Scènes de la vie de campagne*, since we find in the *Scènes de la vie privée* certain passages situated in Paris or in the provinces, military or political episodes, etc. This is because each of these regions is obviously in communication with all the others, and because the terms used designate above all the emphasis placed on a certain type of relation which finds its best illustration in certain environments such as the provinces, Paris or the army; it is therefore easy to see that the *Scènes de la vie privée* are addressed to the reader in the simplest manner possible and that it is for this reason that Balzac has put them at the head of his work: all revolving around the theme of marriage, they have a very simple moral concern, they strive to enlighten the young and to spare them certain fatal errors.

In the work as a whole, the *Scènes de la vie privée* come closest to the daily life of the average young reader. The scene is set either in Paris or in the provinces, whichever is more appropriate to the anecdote told.

Balzac will place the emphasis on this appropriateness of setting, of geography, in the *Scènes de la vie de province*, whose goal is to put the Parisian reader in touch with a certain reality he knows little about; but this documentary aspect is accompanied by a far deeper study, for each provincial town considered is shown to be particularly characteristic of one aspect of all the others; each one is taken, consequently, both as an ordinary town and as the town appropriate to the story told, the town in which this story has—or might have—been able to assume its most significant form.

If the provincial towns are in a sense on equal footing and represent each other by each one's isolating in a particularly clear manner an aspect of their functioning, Paris stands in a privileged relation to all of them: Paris is not a city like the rest, does not have with the rest that relation of reciprocal signification, is somehow their multiplication, the concentrated image of their collective relations; the city of Paris is to the rest of France what the *Études sociales* [sic] are to reality; Paris is France's dream or its novel; Paris is in its recesses the novel of itself, the real as fiction; in these studies, therefore, extraordinary, incredible events will take place, not only extraordinary to foreigners, as the *Scènes de la vie de province* seem extraordinary to the ignorant Parisian, but extraordinary to that Parisian himself; after having recognized himself in the *Scènes de la vie privée*, he had to be disturbed, displaced, by the *Scènes de la vie de province* in order to confront the far greater displacement awaiting him in his own city.

Just as the city of Paris reflects all the provincial towns and is unique for each one of them, just as a man in the public eye represents the other men and is unique for each of them, the *Scènes de la vie politique* are therefore the necessary complement of the *Scènes de la vie parisienne* (we have already seen the kind of difficulties this part of the work encounters); and just as the city of Paris is not only the representation but also the dream of other cities, there are lives which are the dream of others, which are the release of what the others can only contain. Balzac declares: "After having depicted social life in these three books, it remained for me to show the exceptional lives which epitomize the interests of many or of all, and which are in some manner outside the common law: whence the *Scènes de la vie politique*. Did I not have to show this vast picture of a finite, completed society in its most violent state, breaking out of itself, either in self-defense or in conquest? Whence the *Scènes de la vie militaire*."

We have followed a progressive displacement from the *Scènes de la vie privée* to the *Scènes de la vie parisienne, politique, militaire;* from ordinary lives to increasingly exceptional lives, an ever-increasing social complexity; but, in the *Scènes de la vie militaire* in particular, we shall find events which strip the individual of this social complexity, which cast him back upon the naked earth; there may be, from the reader's habitual life, another displacement which will place him in a far deeper generality: instead of returning to Paris, the road which passes through the *Scènes de la vie de province* can take an even wider detour and lead us into a region in relation to which the one in which the reader lives is already a novel and a dream, a region one of whose essential characteristics will be precisely that one does not read there, a region, consequently, to which the novel cannot address itself directly, and which represents for the novel a sort of absolute "other," a wall into which he collides, for that very reason the unshakable basis of all judgments, a final reference, reality in its ultimate resistance to language, the "thing" which, close to us geographically, is farthest from us mentally, the savage we encounter not in the street of a town but on a road between the two towns: the *Scènes de la vie de campagne*.

5

Balzac, in order to make reality known, tells stories which have not taken place; in order to make us understand real people, he invents others who are like them, who are a sample of their species; but this sample can become so remarkable that it will constitute a new species, affording us a much better grasp of the functioning of groups and powers. The problem concerning individuals recurs on the level of groups, and Balzac will therefore be led to constitute imaginary groups concerning which he will have to explain, in order to give them some probability, why they are not known. Thus in the *Scènes de la vie parisienne* and the *Scènes de la vie politique*, one of his fundamental themes, or, if one prefers, one of his fundamental instruments, will be the secret society. Thus we see how the universe of the *Études sociales* [sic] increasingly detaches itself from reality in order to constitute a fantastic universe which completes and illuminates it.

In all the novels we have mentioned up until now, the departure from reality remains within certain limits. However astonishing and unlikely, however disconcerting these stories, they nevertheless remain probable, at least for Balzac, and this not only because they obey the laws of nature in general but also because they are confined within what might be the subject of conversation in a Paris salon; it is within conversation or journalism or news imparted that all these events are "inscribed." We could have heard the story from any one of our friends. It is therefore not only possible, but possible within narrow geographical confines (France and on occasion a bit of Switzerland, in *Albert Savarus*) and historical limits (by and large: since the Revolution).

But just as it is sometimes better, in order to speak of real characters, to use fictitious characters, so in order to speak of recent events it is necessary to invoke past events; in order to make comprehensible certain aspects of daily life, it is often better to give fantasy free rein. Certainly relationships which it would be extremely difficult and wearisome to describe in detail can be expressed in a striking condensation, a shortcut. Just as an invented character can represent a large number of real characters, so an obviously invented event can epitomize a whole study.

This contraction of reality which occurs in the first part of the *Comédie humaine* will continue into the second part, in the *Études philosophiques*, which all have as a common characteristic their distance, their greater departure, from daily life.

We have used the image of two concentric spheres to symbolize the relations between the universe of the *Comédie humaine* and the reality in the midst of which Balzac wrote. Inside the *Comédie humaine* the relation is reflected, and the whole of the *Études philosophiques* is a kind of third sphere inside that of the *Études sociales* [sic]; this third sphere plays, in relationship to the latter, the same role that the latter plays in relation to reality: a role of clarification and contraction.

We have seen that the imaginary characters who populate the *Études sociales* [sic] are a remarkable form of ellipsis; the fantastic or remote events which we find in the *Études philosophiques* are also ellipses, much more violent ones. The relation between the two levels of the work is particularly clear, easily understood, if one considers the characters of artists. We see very well how Frenhofer or Gambara, improbable painter and improbable musician, epitomize, and elaborate, up to a certain limit, the painters or the musicians who appear in the first part.

Since the role of the *Études philosophiques* as a reflective center at the heart of the *Comédie humaine* explains certain of the strangest and hitherto the least understood aspects of this work, I want to speak of the importance which Balzac attaches to certain sciences now considered bogus: Lavater's physiognomy, or Gall's phrenology. The Balzacian ellipsis—the fact that a whole category of characters is represented by just one, hence by just one face—strengthens the link between external appearances and function, temperament, etc. In the *Comédie humaine*, these links obey laws even simpler than reality; Gall's and Lavater's generalizations, which today strike us as utterly childish or imaginary, recover precisely their true value in Balzac's world as imaginary science, codifying certain relations internal to the novel, and whose application to reality can very well have only a figurative value. The same is true of the theory of animal magnetism, of electricity, of the material power of thought. All this possesses a different degree of application, depending on the region of the *Comédie humaine* in which we happen to be. It is quite easy to see how these imaginary sciences and Swedenborg's imaginary philosophy—which crowns the *Études philosophiques* in *Séraphîta*,—reflect the peculiarities of the Balzacian universe and constitute a provisional elucidation of its relations with reality.

For anyone interested in the theory of the novel, all this constitutes an enormous, virtually unexploited mine of examples and problems.

6

But the movement of Balzac's thought does not stop within this reflection; after the *Études philosophiques* come the *Études analytiques*. This is certainly the most neglected part of the work and for a very simple reason: it exists only in embryonic form, but it is indispensable to consider it if one wants to appreciate the Balzacian project in all its breadth.

Balzac declares in the 1842 preface: "Finally, after having sought, I don't say after having found, this motive for the social mechanism, must one not meditate upon the natural principles and see how far societies depart from or draw closer to the eternal rule, the true, the beautiful?" and further on, having once again described the *Études philosophiques*: "Above, you will find the *Études analytiques*, about which I shall say nothing, for only one of them has been published, the *Physiologie du mariage*. Sometime hence I must offer two more works in this genre. First the *Pathologie de la vie sociale*, then the *Anatomie des corps enseignants* and the *Monographie de la vertu*." In the 1845 prospectus he adds a *Dialogue philosophique et politique sur les perfections du dix-neuvième siècle*. He will publish none of these, and we have only one other *Étude analytique*: the *Petites Misères de la vie conjugale*. The titles themselves indicate that these are works quite different from what we usually call a novel. The two we have are humorous manuals with theorems and axioms, illustrated by brief scenes. They are pamphlets against contemporary mores, at the end of the inquiry into society, the effort to transform it. The movement which has led us to the *Études philoso-phiques* reverses itself, and we rediscover daily life in a polemic intent. The two books which we have are *Scènes de la vie privée,* but told in an alto-gether different tone.

To account for the presence of the *Études analytiques,* it is necessary to abandon the image of spheres, which now appears to be inadequate, for the whole of the work now begins to move, the *Études analytiques* being sup-ported by the *Scènes de la vie de campagne,* as the *Études philosophiques* are supported by the *Scènes de la vie parisienne.* They were to be the practical conclusion to the work, its point of engagement, its immediate action on the revealed sore points, and it is perfectly understandable that this section should have remained in embryonic form because of the evolution occurring in Balzac's thought while he was striving to realize this plan to which he constantly had to add new divisions. We know that Balzac's politics are at the start as reactionary as possible; his design was, as he said, "a return to the principles which are to be found in the past for the very reason that they are eternal," and he declares without ambiguity what these principles are for him: "I write in the glow of two eternal truths, religion and monarchy, two necessities which contemporary events proclaim and which every writer of good sense must try to restore to our country."

But we also know that Balzac's Christianity, tinged throughout with Swedenborg, had less and less to do with that of the Church, that the monarchy as it was appeared to him more and more unsatisfactory. The result of his enormous career of novel writing was to call more deeply into question those principles to which he had declared himself attached, and which revealed themselves to him to be increasingly farther from that truth he had set out to find. The immense movement of the work provokes a kind of plowing-up, a turning of the soil, a revolution of the image of reality which bears him, politically speaking, far beyond the goal first proposed.

Balzac's work pivots on itself, and one can say that it has carried all subsequent novels in its careening course, that we are still in its wake. It is a solid foundation, we can build upon it; there are few contemporary inven-tions that cannot find in it their precursor and their justification. There is little to read, consequently, that is more enriching for a novelist, that forms a better introduction for the reader to the problems of the contemporary novel; but let there be no misunderstanding here—I am saying: Balzac.

CRITICAL ESSAYS

Early Years: 1830–1850

Literature: *Scenes of Private Life*, published by M. de Balzac, author of *Le Dernier Chouan ou La Bretagne en 1800*

K.*

I have the misfortune of not being acquainted with *Le Dernier Chouan*, and I will probably never get to know it. A novel is like a play: you want the first fruits or you do without it. In that first work M. Balzac, they say, showed himself to be a man of talent and wit. He is therefore worthy of hearing the truth, and I will have the courage to tell it to him. He himself felt the shortcomings of his *Scènes de la vie privée;* not all of them, but several, because he wrote a preface and an epilogue to alert the critics. In the former, he modestly confesses that certain minds will object to his emphasis on apparently superfluous details; that it will be easy to accuse him of a kind of childish garrulousness; that his tableaux will seem to have all the faults of Dutch painting without any of its virtues. Less modest in the latter text, he boldy sets out literary principles in order to justify himself: "Now that in our day all possible combinations seem worn out, now that all fictional situations seem used up, now that the impossible has been tried, the author firmly believes that only *details* will constitute the merit of works improperly called *novels*." And later he adds that to undertake to paint historical periods and to amuse oneself by seeking out new fictions, is to give more importance to the framework than to the picture. But one has only to read the *Scènes de la vie privée* to be rescued from such errors; and indeed not one of the six tales offered by M. Balzac fails to refute them. If the preface judges the book, the book refutes the epilogue. My task will be accomplished when I shall have demonstrated this, and if the author is not content he will only have himself to blame; all the more since, in this little discussion, I will have occasion to prove my good will toward him with a certain amount of praise.

Let us first speak of the basis of the book. M. Balzac's intentions were good. We know private life because we have seen it, not because we have read about it. The novels and plays that aim to paint it are mostly wildly off

*Translated and reprinted from *Le Globe*, 25 June 1830, 517–18.

target. On what stage, in what book does one find a true picture of the relationships that exist between husband and wife, fathers and children, lovers and mistresses? Everywhere there is more or less the same agreed-upon falsity of circumstance, language, and feeling. It has come to such a point that when a writer happens to catch a true trait, everybody exclaims: here is an original writer.

* * *

M. Balzac has not amused himself by looking for new stories. That is truly a pity. It is always good to excite the curiosity of the reader, and to do it you might as well offer him new stories as old ones. But is a story even needed? What is a story? "A framework," M. Balzac tells us, "an accessory. If you want to portray a period, portray it; the rest is unimportant." In my opinion, the rest is very important; indeed it is the main thing. If there is no drama there is no life, and hence no effect. An action that starts up, becomes complicated, moves from incident to incident to an unforeseen or desired outcome; actors whose passions and character traits stand out everywhere in high relief: these are the necessary elements of works whose purpose is to interest us. Without this, everything languishes, everything is dead. Of what importance to me is the historical frippery in which you dress your puppets? You create no illusion for me, because you leave my heart cold. You hardly catch my attention. It is as if you reduced the action to a collection of assorted bits of information. Such compositions are monsters without springs to animate them. But have all combinations been worn out, have all situations been used up, has the impossible itself been tried? This is an excuse for those who lack imagination. I thought the excuse itself was worn out, and I am astonished to find it in M. Balzac, who could invent things if he tried—if only he didn't have the vanity of giving birth to a volume a month.

* * *

Here is his method: he sees a house, examines it from the front and the back, describes it from top to bottom and down to the very last nail. Then he goes inside, finds one, two, or three individuals whom he describes in their turn—clothing, faces, gestures, habits. He then explores their relationships under a magnifying glass—a third description, which soon leads to a fourth. Nothing is more exasperating than these immobile figures, waiting to be described. In addition, this method stops the story at every step, and one loses the thread. It's like stagnant and muddy water. The author swims around in it, plays about, gives himself airs, and manages some clever feats. Unfortunately, he wants to discover something that is not there. He has so many quirks that smell of mannerism and searching for effects; so many pretensions that end up in commonness and bad taste!

* * *

So it must be said: M. Balzac's *details* would spoil excellent stories, and the stories spoil excellent details. Nevertheless, just as I do not take as absolutes the rules of art that I have urged against his own system of composition, he himself sometimes happily departs from the route he has set himself. He never moves us; he never hides [*sic*] a lively pleasure. But in two or three of his stories, he sometimes excites interest, and agreeably soothes our minds with ingenious descriptions. In the country, when one is alone and there is nothing to do and it's raining, his book can still be a piece of good luck, because after all, it is better than a long, uninterrupted tedium. Let me cite [a] passage, so as to be forgiven my criticisms: the Young Ambitious Woman set before us by the author maintains that "if like her father, she had influence in the legislature, she would have a law passed requiring that merchants, especially dry-goods dealers, be branded on the forehead like berrichon sheep, through the third generation; or that only the nobility have the right to wear those old-style clothes that looked so good on Louis XV's courtiers; because after all it is perhaps a great misfortune for the monarchy if there is no distinction between a merchant and a French Peer." Isn't that M. de Polignac's idea—the idea of rigging out our young noblemen in apple-green? The great politician didn't even invent that. What a humiliation.[1]

Note

1. [Ed. note: Minister under Charles X, it was Polignac whose oppressive ordinances brought about the Revolution of 1830.]

Literature: *The Wild Ass's Skin, a Philosophical Novel*   Anonymous*

What role can a wild ass's skin play in a philosophical novel? That is what many people have wondered, without thinking about the current fad of giving frivolous titles to serious subjects. "The author has fooled us!" cried those readers who dislike jokes. "There is nothing philosophical in this novel." Others said that the author gives himself more importance than he merits. This wretched *Peau de chagrin* has baffled everybody. And yet there is nothing more philosophical, more serious, more dramatic.

A young man, Raphaël de Valentin, is about to drown himself; he walks toward the Seine; but the moment is ill-chosen. The water was cold and dirty, as an old woman points out to him. Moreover, he glances at the shack on which are written these words: *Help for the Drowning*. This sight reminds him of all the hideous details of this kind of suicide. He prefers to wait to die at night. He walks along toward the Quai Voltaire, and comes to the shop of a dealer in antiques and curiosities, and just to fill time lets himself be tempted into examining these old things in all their varied and bizarre forms, a résumé and history of the past. What he saw in that shop, what he

*Translated and reprinted from *Le Globe*, 20 August 1831, 928.

felt in the midst of that fantasmagoria of a world whose relics, spread around him, seemed alive and luminous, bedazzling his exalted imagination, all this must be read in M. Balzac's novel. But the most marvelous of all these marvels is a *peau de chagrin* hung from a nail, which would not have caught the young man's attention without an astonishing old man who appears expressly to tell him about its magical properties.

A mysterious and satanic intimacy soon establishes itself between the old man and the young one. The latter naively tells him about his intention to commit suicide, about his despair, and his deep and helpless poverty. "Wait," cries the old man, "I will make you richer than a constitutional monarch. Look at this *peau de chagrin* and read the mysterious words cut into it:"

> If you possess me you will possess everything;
> But your life will belong to me; God has
> Wished it so. Desire, and your desires
> Will be fulfilled. But adjust
> Your desires to your life.
> It is there. At each
> Wish I will shrink
> Like the days.
> Do you want me?
> Take me. God
> Will hear
> So be it

Oh happy young man! Hope, desire, you will possess what you wish. To possess! To enjoy! Who these days has not pronounced these words with the bitterest despair, with the bloody irony of a disappointed life from which reality incessantly escapes!

To possess! To use! It is the dream of the old man who saps himself trying to reanimate an exhausted existence and revive the joys of a patched-up existence; it is the dream of the young man whose devouring energy demands action, who needs an activity corresponding to his strength and his ardor, who sighs for the holy love of a woman who would enlighten and exalt him.

Oh! It is the dream of the starving multitudes who ask for their daily bread from society, who ask for morality, education, and hope! It is the dream of the lazy minority, fatigued with doing nothing in the midst of all the delights of luxury, that suffers, cries, and dies gorged with riches, without having satisfied a life undermined by the languor of an existence without enthusiasm, without love. To posssess! To possess totally! Today it is everyone's ungraspable shadow, everyone's dream!

There is impotence everywhere in a society incapable of giving mankind a goal to be attained or a destiny to be accomplished; the impotence of those who abandon themselves to the undefined vagueness of immense desires impossible to realize; the impotence of that multitude of beings who, for want of foresight, cannot avoid poverty, even in the narrow limits of the most ordinary life. These people wear themselves out maneuvering and working; they die in garrets, in hospitals, in prisons. As for others, they die crushed by boredom, melancholy, and spleen. Or else if they have a somewhat energetic nature, they daze and enervate themselves by indulging in debauchery, orgies, gambling, entertainments, vice, and crime; they excite and kill themselves by overindulging in the most brutal, sensual pleasures.

The impossibility of playing a satisfying role in a disorganized society, one that would correspond to one's abilities and that would fulfill heartfelt desires and legitimate ambitions—this was the martyrdom of Mirabeau, Byron, and Hoffmann; this was the cause of the disorder of their lives. This was also the inspiration for Don Juan, for Schiller's *The Brigands,* and above all for *Faust,* that terrible personification of the consequences of disharmony between man's desires and his capabilities.

Like Faust, Raphaël Valentin[1] is devoured by an unbridled need for possession and exploitation; he concludes a pact with a fatal power. This *peau de chagrin* is the measure of his life and happiness; with it he can do anything. But with each accomplished wish it shrinks and shrivels up, and its decrease is a signal of death.

No matter! Long live joy! Long live hope! Long live happiness! And long live death . . . later. One must observe with what shock this idolator, who an instant before was lost, ruined, and almost drowned, contemplates this *peau de chagrin;* with what intoxication he seizes it, touches it, clutches it! And what will he do with it?

Oh! Who among us, in childhood dreams, in oriental fairy-tales, amidst the fantastic worlds created by suffering, disappointment, and despairing helplessness, who has not believed he possessed a fairy's wand, Gygès's ring, the favor of a genie, of an Armide or of an angel; who has not imagined himself all-powerful, full of endless pleasures? But when disorder and egoism are in our hearts and all around us in society, they turn up in our dreams, and this magical power often serves only to create endless egotistical happiness and crude self-indulgence.

Through the power of the *peau de chagrin,* Raphaël is drawn into one of those debaucheries, an orgy of the senses, an orgy of the frenzied imagination, an intellectual orgy in which man, drunk with skepticism, mocks, stigmatizes, and sullies everything. This scene is described by M. de Balzac with the verve of a shameless hussy. In the middle of the night, when the participants are resting, exhausted from their excesses, Raphaël Valentin tells his story; it is common enough.

* * *

Raphaël finishes his tale just as dawn illuminates the pale and hollow faces of the men and women. As breakfast is served, a notary arrives bringing a fortune of six million francs to Raphaël. Long live *la peau de chagrin!*

Raphaël had an uncle in India who has died without direct heirs: millions always come from India. But this piece of news is a thunderbolt for the young man. The good fortune reduces his life by ten years at least: he has felt the *peau de chagrin* shrink. You should see these depraved celebrants raving ecstatically about the pleasures that these millions can produce, and Raphaël's pale despair—Raphaël, whom these joys cost a part of his life. Malediction! To have the riches of the world before one, to be able to enjoy the delights of a refined civilization and, if one touches them, to feel death pressing close, exhausting you, wearing you down!

Raphaël wants to live as long as possible, and to do so he is obliged, for fear of seeing the fatal *peau de chagrin* shrink, to remove from his life all desire, all will, all hope, all happiness, all love; he must create a shadow life for himself, the existence of a phantom flitting along, hardly touching life, withholding his sighs, controlling the beating of his heart, his fearful eyes fixed on the *peau de chagrin,* whose behavior tells him if he has had *the misfortune of being happy,* as Mme Sophie Gay would say.

This infernal idea does honor to M. de Balzac's talent; nothing has been created for a long time that expresses so well the disenchantment, the despair, the doubt, the pains of not being happy in this society, which has no future to offer, in which every joy is bought with tears, and often at the price of death not only for the happy individual but for those close to him.

We do not intend to preach Christian morality here, or to deplore the vanity of this world and the impossibility of *finding happiness in this fallen world*—these are banal expressions that have lost all meaning. But we will say that today we are paying a high price for our Christian education, which for a long time was powerful enough to make man tolerate with love the consequences of his disdain of this world because he had faith in another. But this faith now being destroyed, man is left without hope on an earth that he has learned is unable to satisfy his desires; and so he finds an immense emptiness in his heart. There is no more heaven for him, no more paradise, but only this damned and sterile earth, a true *peau de chagrin*, bringing forth only death. No more God for him, but only the Devil, who has taken control of his life in a thousand ways—through gambling, through debauchery, through all kinds of disorderly passions—and who gives man the power of satisfaction only in order to destroy him.

* * *

Raphaël Valentin believes in the fatal power of that *peau de chagrin,* which so pitilessly grants all his desires. This frightened young man, desperate to live, more or less leads the life of a vegetable. One evening, however, he wants to go to the Théâtre des Italiens,[2] and finds himself next to a woman who attracts everyone's attention with her beauty. He recognizes her: it is Pauline, the young girl of the hotel Saint-Quentin in the rue des Cordiers. It is clear that Raphaël is loved by the Pauline he had once abandoned for the Countess Foedora. It is clear that he has been regretting it and has loved her in return; and now finally they have met again! Malediction! It is happiness:

the *peau de chagrin* shrinks. But love makes Raphaël forget life, and he gives way to his happiness. He marries Pauline. Several months pass in the raptures of shared tenderness, when Pauline notices Raphaël's pallor and weakness. . . . The *peau de chagrin* is barely as large as a hundred-sou coin. Valentin leaves his wife to travel; he remains absent a long time. Pauline searches for him, and he himself suffers from the separation. They meet at last: the *peau de chagrin* can hardly be felt! Pauline learns that she is the cause of Raphaël's deadly weakness; she wants to flee. Raphaël makes a last effort to seize her and falls into her arms. The *peau de chagrin* is no more; Raphaël is dead.

Well, what do you think of this book and of this *peau de chagrin?* In the midst of so many oddities, it is impossible not to admire the wit, verve, and feverish honesty that amuse us, carry us along, and excite us. Above all, M. de Balzac's style shines with striking, blinding color. He takes pleasure in describing, in demonstrating, in mixing and spreading his colors; he is a first-class painter.

This novel, with its caprices, its illogicality, its immoralities, seems to us to be a faithful expression of our society; that is why we do not admit the distinction that M. de Balzac claims between himself and the hero of his book. It seems to us impossible for him to have drawn with such success the life of the men around us without his having experienced all the feelings that move them. We would not be surprised if M. de Balzac beieved a bit, like Raphaël Valentin, in the *peau de chagrin*.

Nobody is more superstitious than a skeptic. People never believe as much in witches, evil genies, vampires, and all those mysterious and deadly powers, as in periods of unbelief. Today's poets take their inspiration less from God than from specters, trilbys, djinns, gnomes or deadly comets: Hoffmann believed in his tales.

Notes

1. [Ed. note: The correct name of this character is Raphaël de Valentin; the review consistently drops the "particule." In this translation, the name will be left as the newspaper printed it.]

2. [Ed. note: One of the popular "boulevard" theaters, originally established by a company of Italian actors.]

The Great Debate: 1850–1900

Monday Chat

Charles-Augustin
Sainte-Beuve*

M. de Balzac prided himself on being a physiologist, and he certainly was one, although with less rigor and exactitude than he imagined; but physical nature, his and others', plays a great role and makes itself continuously felt in his descriptions of our customs. I am not blaming him for this; it is a trait that affects and characterizes all picturesque literature of our times.[1] One day, M. Villemain, still quite young, was reading to Sieyès his *In Praise of Montaigne*, that charming encomium, the first that he had composed, full of lightness and freshness.[2] When he came to the passage where he says: "But I would fear, reading Rousseau, to pause too long over guilty weaknesses, which one must always keep far from oneself . . ." Sieyès interrupted him saying, "Not at all; it's better to let them approach, so as to be able to study them close up." The physiologist, who is above all curious, here argued with the literary man, who looks for taste above all. Shall I confess it? I am like Sieyès.

This is also to say that I am a bit like M. de Balzac. But I challenge him, and myself, on two points. I like, in his style, the delicate parts, the *efflorescence* (I can find no other word) by which he gives everything a feeling of life and makes the very page tremble. But I cannot accept, under the cover of physiology, the continual abuse of that quality—that often pleasing and decomposing style, enervated, pink and striated with many colors, that style of delicious corruption, all "asiatic" as our teachers used to say, more disjointed and more flexible in certain places than the body of an antique mime. Petronius, somewhere in the midst of the scenes that he describes, misses what he calls *oratio pudica*, the *modest* style that does not give way to the *fluidity* of movement.

Another point on which I challenge the physiologist and the anatomist in M. de Balzac, is that in this genre he has imagined at least as much as he has observed. As an anatomist sensitive to manners, he has certainly found new veins to exploit; he has discovered and so to speak injected sections of lymphatic vessels unperceived until then. But he invents some too. There is

*Translated and reprinted from *Causeries du lundi* (Monday conversations) (Paris: Garnier, 1851), II, 421–29

a moment when, in his analysis, the true and real plexus ends and the illusory plexus begins, and he does not distinguish them: most of his readers, and above all his women readers, have confused them just as he has. This is not the place to insist on the points that separate us. But it is well known that M. de Balzac has a declared weakness for Swedenborgs, Van Helmonts, Mesmers, Saint-Germains, and Cagliostros of all types: that is, he is subject to illusions. In a word, to follow my physical and anatomic image, I will say: when he grasps the carotid artery of his subject, he injects it firmly, vigorously, and completely. But when he errs, he injects all the same and goes on pressing, thus creating, without really realizing it, imaginary networks.

M. de Balzac had pretensions to science, but what he actually possessed was above all a kind of physiological *intuition*. M. Chasles has put it well: "It has been often said that M. de Balzac was an observer, an analyst; but he was better, or worse: he was a *voyant*."

* * *

To present his true literary theory, we need only borrow his own words: if I take *Les Parents pauvres* for example, his last novel and one of his most vigorous, published in *Le Constitutionnel,* I find there, in connection with the Polish artist Wenceslas Steinbock, the author's favorite ideas and secrets, if he ever had any. For him, "a great artist today is a prince without a title; it is glory and fortune." But this glory is not acquired by playing or dreaming; it is the reward for obstinate work and applied effort: "You have ideas in your head? So what . . . I have ideas too . . . What does the content of our mind matter if we don't do anything with it?" That is what he thought, and as a consequence he never spared himself the relentless work of execution. To conceive, he said, is to play, it is to *puff enchanted cigarettes;* without execution everything goes up in smoke and dreams.

* * *

A true, sincere, and intelligent Aristarchus, if he could have stood him, would have been very useful to Balzac; for this rich and luxurious nature squandered itself, could not govern itself. There are three things to consider in a novel: the characters, the action, and the style. M. de Balzac excels in setting up characters; he makes them live, he sculpts them in an indelible fashion. There is exaggeration, there is infinite detail, but what does it matter? They have in themselves the material of real existence. In Balzac we sometimes make fine, gracious, coquettish, and very joyous acquaintances, and at other times we make very nasty ones; but once made, we are sure never to forget either kind. He is not content to draw his characters well; he names them in an appropriate and unusual way, which fixes them forever in our memory. He attached the greatest importance to this way of baptising his people; like Sterne he attributed to proper names a certain *occult power* in harmonious or ironic relationship to character. The *Marneffes*, the *Bixious*, the *Birotteaus*, the *Crevels*, etc., are thus named by virtue of a mysterious, confused onomatopoeia according to which the man and the name resemble each other. After the characters, the action: it is often weak in M. de Balzac,

it goes astray, it is exaggerated. He is less successful here than in the formation of characters. As for his style, it is clever, subtle, familiar, picturesque,
without any connection to tradition. I have sometimes wondered what would
be the effect of a book by M. de Balzac on an honest mind, nourished till
then on good, ordinary French prose in all its frugality; the kind of mind we
no longer have, trained in the simple, serious, and scrupulous style of Nicole
and Bourdaloue[3], *which implies more than it says,* as La Bruyère[4] observed:
such a mind would be dizzied for a month. La Bruyère also said that there is
only a *single* correct expression for any thought, and that it must be found.
M. de Balzac seems to ignore this as he writes. He has sequences of expressions that are vivid, disquieting, capricious, never definitive—*attempted*
expressions that seek themselves. His printers knew it well; when he had his
books printed, he endlessly reworked and rewrote each set of proofs. In his
case, the mold itself was in a state of continual ebullition, and the metal
couldn't take shape in it. Even when he had found the desired form, he
continued to look for it.

*   *   *

Notes

1. [Ed. note: This article, which first appeared in *Le Constitutionnel* on 2 September
1850, marks Sainte-Beuve's reconciliation with Balzac—although after the latter's death. Its
friendly tone contrasts sharply with the hostile and usually vindictive remarks about the novelist
that stud the critic's diary (published by Victor Giraud in 1926 under the title of *Mes Poisons*).]

2. [Ed. note: François Villemain (1790–1870) was a professor, critic, and Minister of
Education from 1839 to 1844. Emmanuel-Joseph Sieyès (1748–1836) was one of the founders of
the Jacobin club.]

3. Pierre Nicole (1625–1695) was a Jansenist philosopher and author, notably of *Essais de
morale;* Louis Bourdaloue (1632–1704), a Jesuit priest, was the author of *Sermons,* celebrated
for their clarity of style.

4. Jean de La Bruyère (1645–1696), was the author of one of the classics of French
literature, *Les Caractères* (Moral portraits).

The Genius of Balzac   Hippolyte Taine*

When we speak of a man's genius (*esprit*) we mean the general shaping
of his thought. There is in every one a certain ruling habit which obliges him
to look here or there, which suggests to him a figure of speech, a philosophical reflection, or a jest—so that no matter what he may be working at, he falls
into one of these habits by the very necessity of his nature, his mind and his
taste. Savants call this method; artists call it talent. Let us examine it in
Balzac.

*Reprinted from *Balzac: A Critical Study* (New York and London: Funk and Wagnalls, 1906),
109–20.

He began in the fashion not of artists, but of savants. Instead of painting, he dissected. He did not enter into the souls of his characters violently and at a single bound like Shakespeare or Saint-Simon; he walked round and round them patiently and slowly like an anatomist, lifting a muscle, then a bone, then a nerve, and only reaching the brain and heart after he had traversed the whole cycle of the organs and their functions. He described the city, then the street, then the house. He described the foundations, the front, the structure and the materials of the entrance, the jutting of the plinths, the color of the moss, the rust on the bars, the cracks in the windows. He notes the arrangement of the rooms, the shape of the chimneys, the age of the tapestries, the quality and arrangement of the furniture; then he would expatiate on the clothes. Arrived at his character, he exhibited the structure of his hands, the curve of his spine, the shape of his nose, the size of his bones, the length of his chin, the size of his lips. He counted his gestures, his winks, his warts. He knew his origins, his education, his history; how much he had in land and income, what circle he moves in; what people he saw, what he spends, what he ate, the brands of his wines, who formed his kitchen force,—in brief, the innumerable multitude of circumstances infi- nitely ramified and intersected, which go to make up, influence, and modify the surface and the depths of nature and human life. There was in him an archæologist, an architect, an upholsterer, a tailor, a costumer, an auction- eer, a physiologist, and a notary: all these make their appearance in turn, each one reading his report, the most detailed in the world and the most exact. The artist listened with pains and scrupulous care, and his imagination did not take fire until he had made out of this infinite paper scaffolding a solid structure according to his idea and desire. "I am," said he, "a doctor of the social sciences." A pupil of Geoffroy Saint-Hilaire, he announced[1] his project of writing a natural history of man. Animals have been catalogued, he would furnish the inventory of manners. He has done it; the history of art has never presented an idea so foreign to art, nor a work of art so great; he has almost equaled the immensity of his subject by the immensity of his erudition.

Hence numerous defects and merits; in many passages he bores many readers. I said, a moment ago, that there is a crowd of artisans and bailiffs in his waiting room; we are there with them and it is disagreeable to be kept waiting in an anteroom. The artist keeps us too long; you feel like swearing at him when he keeps you waiting in the cold for an hour among a crowd of his employés. This crew, nevertheless, is nothing if not diverting. Memoirs of carpenters and stories of lawyers, however, end by giving you a headache; the odor of the registry-office, the courtroom and the shop becomes suffocat- ing. One must be an observer by profession, a critic for instance, or still better, a business man, to be at home in this atmosphere. If we were not all plebeians and amateurs of science we would have flung up M. Goriot at the beginning of his fatal apoplexy, and flung Cæsar Birotteau into the fire at the first deficit of his balance sheets; the author would have seen the half of his public vanish if the nineteenth century had not invested cataplasms and bills of protest with a sort of romance.

But the worst of it is that the book often becomes obscure. A description is not a painting, and Balzac often thinks that he has produced a picture, when he has merely given a description. His compilations reveal nothing; they are merely catalogs; the enumeration of the stamens of a flower, never brings before our eyes the image of the flower. It requires the poetical faculty of George Sand or Michelet, or the violent sorcery of Victor Hugo or Dickens, to conjure in our minds the shape of physical objects; such writers transport us beyond ourselves, and emotion places all in a clear light. The minute explanations of Balzac leave us in quiet and in darkness. It is in vain that he describes so minutely; the intersections of the bars of the Hôtel du Guénic, or the nose of the Chevalier de Valois; these crossbars and this nose remain obscure; only a physiologist or an archaeologist might divine something; the common run of readers will pause, mouths open in respectful astonishment, secretly wishing for the aid of some sketch or portrait.

A final misfortune is that the description carried at too great length falsifies the impression. When the imagination perceives an imaginary character it is as if by a flash of lightning; if you linger over a trait or a feature, through a dozen lines, nothing at all is perceived. One no longers knows whether the figure is lovely, grandiose or fine. Its physiognomy has disappeared; there remains a mere bundle of flesh and bones. Is it a woman that you see here, or is it not rather a mass of anatomical shreds?

"The arch of the strongly penciled brows extended over both eyes, the flame of which scintillated momentarily like that of a fixed star; the white of the eye is not of a bluish tinge, nor sown with red veins, nor is it of a pure white; it has the *consistency of horn,* but is of a warm tone; the pupil of the eye is bordered with a circle of orange; it is like *bronze surrounded with gold*—but living gold, animated bronze. This pupil is deep; it is not double as in certain eyes, nor has it that metallic cast which reflects the light, resembling the eyes of tigers or cats. This depth has something of the infinite, just as *eyes reflected in a mirror* have a suggestion of the absolute." The portrait is continued thus through two hundred lines. A friend of mine, a naturalist, asked me one day to come and see a magnificent specimen butterfly that he had just been experimenting with. I found it cut into about thirty pieces, pinned separately to a paper. Those disgusting bits, when put together, formed the magnificient butterfly.

Nevertheless what power there is in all this! What striking qualities and what relief this interminable enumeration gives to the character! How we recognize him in every action and in every detail! How real he becomes! With what precision and energy he becomes imprinted in our memory! How thoroughly he resembles nature, and how perfect the illusion! For such is nature; its details are infinite and infinitely drawn out; the inner man leaves his imprint on his external life, on his house, on his furniture, on his business, his gestures, his language; it is necessary to explain this multitude of effects in order to wholly explain him. And on the other hand, it is necessary to bring together this multitude of causes in order to present him in his completeness. The food which nourishes you, the air which you breathe, the buildings that surround you, the books that you read, the most trivial habits in which you give a glimpse of yourself, the most imperceptible circumstances which you allow to influence you—all contribute to make you the man that you are; an infinite amount of endeavor has been concentrated in the formation of your character, and your character is revealed in an infinite number of endeavors; your soul is a crystal lens which gathers to a focus all the luminous rays darted from the boundless universe, and like a radiator, reflects them back into infinite space.

It is on this account that every man is a being apart, absolutely distinct, capable of being multiplied to an enormous extent, a sort of abyss whose depth is equaled only by his prophetic genius and enormous erudition. I dare to assert that in this respect Balzac has mounted to the level of Shakespeare. His characters live; they enter into familiar conversation; Nucingen, Rastignac, Philippe Bridau, Phellion, Bixiou, and a hundred others are men whom we have seen, whom we cite to give an idea of some real person, whom we meet in the street. As he himself says of original artists, he has created "emulation in civic life."

If he is so strong it is because he is systematic; this is a second trait which completes the savant; in him the philosopher is combined with the observer. Along with the details he sees the laws which connect them. His houses and his physiognomies are the molds in which he fashions the souls of his characters. In these all things are inter-related; there is always some passion or situation which is at the bottom of them, and which prescribes what happens. This is why they leave so powerful an impression; each action and detail concurs to drive it home; tho innumerable, they are brought together for a unique effect. We feel them all in a single sensation; the characters are more expressive than actual living beings. They concentrate what nature has dispersed. This is still more apparent in his plots. His order is admirable; it required an extraordinary power of comprehension to connect all these events, to maneuver this army of characters, to combine these long series of machinations and intrigues. He is like a circus driver who reins in fifty powerful and spirited horses, keeping them to their course, without lessening their speed. Many of his plots are so skilfully contrived that one loses his way in them; it is necessary to be a merchant to understand *Cæsar Birotteau,* and one needs to be a magistrate to follow *Une Ténébreuse Affaire;* the latter is beyond the sounding of ordinary faculties, it is a concert so rich, composed of so many novel instruments and of so varied and intricate ideas, that our ears, accustomed to the simplicity of the classics, can with difficulty grasp the ensemble and conception of the composer.

Moreover, and what is still more notable, he always has some great idea which serves as the center round which his story revolves. He may be wrong in announcing it, but the announcement does not deceive. He not only describes, he thinks. It is not enough to observe life, he understands it. Celibacy, marriage, government, finance, luxury, ambition, all the leading occupations, all the secret depths of passion: such are the foundations of his work; he is the philosopher of humanity.

*   *   *

Note

1. Preface of *The Human Comedy*.

[The Balzac I Knew]   Théophile Gautier*

*   *   *

With his profound instinct for reality, Balzac understood that the modern life he wished to depict was dominated by one great fact—money—and in *La Peau de chagrin* he had the courage to show a lover anxious to know if he had moved the heart of his beloved, but equally anxious about having enough money to pay for the carriage in which he is taking her home. This audacity is perhaps one of the greatest ever perpetrated in literature, and in itself would be enough to immortalize Balzac. There was deep stupefaction, and the purists were enraged over this infraction of the rules of the genre. But all the young men who, going to spend the evening with some pretty lady, ironed their gloves with starch and crossed Paris like dancers on the points of their dress shoes fearing a spot of mud more than a pistol shot, sympathized with Valentin's anguish because they had experienced it; and they were passionately interested in the hat that he cannot afford to replace and which he cares for so meticulously.[1] At moments of greatest poverty, the discovery of a hundred-sou coin left among the papers in his drawer by the modest, commiserating Pauline, had the effect of the most extravagant dramatic crisis, or of the appearance of a fairy in a tale of the Arabian nights. Who has not discovered, on some day of distress, a wonderful coin forgotten in a pair of trousers or a vest; a wonderful coin that saves you from the misfortune that youth fears most: to be embarrassed in the presence of a beloved woman over a cabriolet, a bouquet, a chair rental in a park, a program at the theater, a tip to the usher, or some trifle of that sort?

*   *   *

Balzac's way of proceeding was the following: when he had carried a subject around and lived with it for a long time, he sketched out a kind of scenario in a few pages of rapid, angular, abbreviated, almost hieroglyphic writing, which he sent to the printers, from whom it returned in proofs— that is, in columns set in the middle of large sheets of paper. These proofs,

*Translated and reprinted from *Honoré de Balzac* (Paris: Poulet-Malassis et de Broise, 1859), 63–141.

which gave his embryonic work an impersonal character that the manuscript did not have, he read attentively, and then applied to this sketch the great critical faculty that he possessed, as if it were the work of someone else. He was working on an object; approving or disapproving his work, he kept some things and corrected others; but above all he added. Lines branched out from the beginning, the middle or the end of sentences toward the margins—right, left, upwards, downwards, leading to developments, interpolations, parentheses, epithets, adverbs. After several hours of work, it looked like a display of fireworks drawn by a child. Rockets took off from the original text and exploded everywhere. And then there were plain crosses, re-crossed crosses like those of a coat of arms, stars, suns, Arabic or Roman numerals, Greek or French letters—every imaginable kind of footnote sign mixed in with the lines. Strips of paper attached with sealing wax or pins were added to the insufficient margins, crisscrossed with lines of fine writing so as to save space, and themselves full of black lines, because the new corrections were already corrected themselves. The printed proof almost disappeared in the midst of this cabbalistic scribbling that the typesetters passed around, none of them willing to "do" more than one hour of Balzac.

* * *

Six, seven, and sometimes ten proofs returned slashed and reworked, without satisfying the author's desire for perfection. We have seen, on a library shelf at Les Jardies[2] reserved for his own works, proofs of a single work each bound separately from the first sketch to the definitive book; the comparison of Balzac's thought in its various stages would be extremely interesting, and would contain profitable literary lessons. Near these volumes a sinister-looking book, bound in black morocco, without any gilding or decoration, attracted our glance. "Look at it," Balzac said, "it's an unpublished work that is worth something." Its title was *Comptes Mélancoliques* (*Melancholy Accounts*): it contained the list of debts, the due dates of IOUs, his tradesmen's bills, and all the menacing paperwork that moves through the legal system. This volume, in a kind of mocking contrast, was placed next to the *Contes drolatiques,* "of which it is not the continuation," the author laughingly said.

* * *

Much criticism has been written on Balzac, and he has been spoken of in many ways, but one very characteristic point has not been emphasized: that is the absolute modernity of his genius. Balzac owes nothing to antiquity. For him there are neither Greeks nor Romans; he needs to fight free of them. In his talent will be found no trace of Homer, Vergil, or Horace, not even of *de Viris illustribus;* no one was ever less classical.

Like Gavarni, Balzac has observed his contemporaries; and in art the supreme difficulty is to paint what is before one's eyes. One can live through one's own times without noticing it, and that is what many eminent intellectuals have done.

To be of one's times—nothing seems simpler, yet nothing is more difficult! To wear no colored spectacles, to think with one's own mind, to use current language rather than rehash into resounding strophes the expressions of one's predecessors! Balzac possessed this rare merit. The centuries have their perspective and their depth of field; at a distance the large masses can be seen, the lines are visible, confusing details disappear; with the help of classical recollections and the harmonious names of antiquity, any rhetorician will turn out a tragedy, a poem, or a historical study. But to find oneself elbowed in the crowd, to grasp its appearance, understand its currents, distinguish individuals, sketch the appearance of so many different beings, show their motives and actions: this requires a very special genius, and the author of the *Comédie humaine* possessed that genius to a degree that no one has equalled and probably never will.

This profound understanding of things modern made Balzac, one must admit, rather insensitive to plastic beauty. He looked at the white marble poetry of Greek art, singing the perfection of the human form, with a careless eye. In the Museum of Antiquities he observed the Vénus de Milo with little enthusiasm; but his eye sparkled with pleasure at the Parisian lady who had stopped in front of the immortal statue, draped in a long cashmere sash flowing without a crease from her neck to her heel, wearing her hat with its little Chantilly veil, her narrow Jouvin gloves, and with the polished tip of her rain boot showing under the hem of her flounced dress. He analyzed her coquettish attractions, he savored her knowing graces, and agreed with her that the goddess was very thick-waisted and would certainly not cut a good figure at Madame de Beauséant's, or Madame de Listomère's, or Madame d'Espard's.[3]

* * *

The difficulty that Balzac experienced in the execution of his work derived, without his realizing it, from the *modernity* we are stressing. The French language, purified by the classical writers of the seventeenth century, is appropriate—if one conforms to its rules—only to render general ideas and to paint conventional figures in vague settings. To express a multiplicity of details, of characters, of types, of architectures, of furnishings, Balzac was obliged to forge a special language for himself, composed of all the technologies, all the jargons of science, art, theater, even of students. He welcomed every word that expressed something, and to receive it his sentence opened a parenthesis and obligingly extended itself. This is what has led superficial critics to say that Balzac didn't know how to write. He did have a style, although he didn't believe it, and a very handsome style: the necessary, inevitable, and precise style of his idea!

* * *

This is perhaps the place to define *truth* as Balzac understood it; in this period of realism one must be clear on this point. Truth in art is not at all truth in nature. Any object rendered by art must contain an element of convention: as small as it may be, it is still there, whether it is merely perspective in painting or language in literature. Balzac accentuates, enlarges, prunes, adds, shades, highlights, distances men and things or draws them near according to the effect that he wants to produce. He is certainly *truthful*, but with the additions and subtractions of *art*. He prepares dark backgrounds for his high-lighted figures, he puts white backgrounds behind his dark figures. Like Rembrandt, he adroitly places a point of light on his character's forehead or nose; in descriptions he sometimes obtains amazing and bizarre results by placing a microscope before the reader's eye without any warning. Then details appear with supernatural clarity and exaggerated minuteness—incomprehensible, formidable enlargements; tissues, scales, pores, hairs, moles, fibers, capillaries acquire enormous importance and transform a face that is insignificant to the naked eye into a kind of chimerical grotesque, as amusing as the masques sculpted under the cornice of the Pont-Neuf and eaten away by the passage of time.

*   *   *

Notes

1. [Ed. note: The reference is to Raphaël de Valentin, the hero of *La Peau de chagrin*, who has precisely these worries in the first part of the novel.]

2. [Ed. note: Les Jardies was a home that Balzac had constructed near Versailles. It figures among the more lamentable of his financial fiascoes.]

3. [Ed. note: These ladies are all characters from the *Comédie humaine*.]

Politics and High Scholarship: 1900–1950

Balzac's Prophecies

Paul Bourget*

Tomorrow the magazine *Minerva* will publish an eloquent essay on Balzac by M. Paul Bourget. Our readers will be happy, on the eve of the inauguration of his monument, to be able to read this all too short preview given to *Le Gaulois*:[1]

Among the symptoms permitting us to measure the movement of ideas now taking place in the political mentality of the French elite, none is more meaningful than the present position of Balzac vis-à-vis contemporary thought. For us, the sociological lesson that emerges from the *Comédie humaine* is an integral part of that movement and indeed its crown. This cycle of novels or, to speak more scientifically, of *observations*, culminates in a powerful doctrine scattered throughout, and of which the *Préface générale*, *Le Médecin de campagne*, *Le Curé de village*, *Les Paysans*, *L'Envers de l'histoire contemporaine*, *Les Mémoires de deux jeunes mariées*, and the introduction to *Catherine de Médicis*, contain the most explicit nonfictional expression. It was not so for our elders. I am not speaking of spiteful individuals like Sainte-Beuve, in whom the legitimist Balzac provoked this epigram: "He is a novelist seeking respectability in aristocratic society"; or like Eugène Pelletan, who dared write of this great man: "How can critics be so naive as to fault M. de Balzac's political beliefs and his backpedalling beyond our two revolutions? My heavens, talent, in all its forms, always has its little machinations . . . When Rousseau puts on his fur hat, it is simply to attract the wandering attention of Parisians." We should all read the well-documented chapters that one of our perspicacious critics, M. Edmond Biré, has devoted to *Balzac royaliste*. M. Caro, a philosopher courageous enough to defend the royalist cause, makes the same point: "*I write by the light of two eternal truths: Religion and Monarchy.* Is this M. de Bonald or M. de Maistre making a statement of faith?[2] No, it is the author of *Les Parents pauvres!* And notice that he was relatively sincere with himself. This trait makes the thing all the more peculiar." Two novelists who derive directly from these *Parents pauvres* and who recognized and proclaimed that heritage, felt no less astonishment faced

*Translated and reprinted from *Le Gaulois*, 14 November 1902.

with these declarations of their teacher. Listen to M. Emile Zola: "Balzac was, according to himself, of aristocratic opinions. Nothing is more peculiar than this supporter of absolute power whose talent is essentially democratic, writing the most revolutionary work that can be read . . . His genius went against his convictions . . ." And Flaubert, after reading Balzac's *Correspondence:* "And he was Catholic, legitimist, a property owner! An unbelieveable fellow, although of second quality." Even M. Taine, who in admiration of his psychology did not hesitate to place him on a level with Shakespeare and Saint-Simon, expressed some reservations when he came to judge his politics: "In politics," he said, "Balzac was only a novelist."

I imagine a reader of 1902, someone who has never opened the *Comédie humaine,* beginning to study it after having learned of this agreement among the critics of twenty-five or fifty years ago about the supposed sociological fantasies of the author. This reader chances upon a novel dating from 1837. Imagine his astonishment upon discovering these lines, which prophesy, with tragic exactness, the distress of present-day France: "A proletariat no longer used to feelings, without any god other than jealousy, with no fanaticism other than that produced by the despair of hunger, will advance and put its foot on the country's throat. Foreigners, raised under monarchical law, will find us with no law in our legality, no property owners in our elections, no strength in our free will, no happiness in our equality." Such sentences reveal in the one who wrote them more than sixty years ago such sharpness of vision that our reader continues to page through the novel, and then the series to which it belongs. Pell-mell he realizes that Balzac foresaw everything about our current miseries. He foresaw the helplessness of our legislators: "You will see that as it is presently organized, the Chamber of Deputies will end by governing, and that will be legal anarchy . . ." He foresaw the scandals of our journalism: "Such is the future of our beautiful land, where everything will be periodically called into question, where there will be endless discussions instead of action, where the press, having become sovereign, will be the instrument of the basest ambitions . . ." He foresaw the ignominy of universal suffrage and the frenzy of the class struggle: "If, God forbid, the bourgeois opposition overturned the higher social classes against which it rebels under the flag of political opposition, the triumph would immediately be followed by a sustained battle between that same bourgeoisie and the people, who would see in it a sort of aristocracy—mean-minded it is true, but whose fortunes and privileges would be all the more odious for being nearer to them . . . If that disturbance occurs, it will be because of the voting rights endlessly extended to the masses . . ." He foresaw the dominance of Russia and England in the twentieth century, and its cause: "England owes its existence to the quasi-feudal law that allots family lands and establishments to the eldest born. Russia is based on the feudal rights of autocracy. Thus, these two nations are today following a path of prodigious progress." He also said: "The English navy is seizing whole areas of the globe under the nose of Europe, to satisfy the requirements of English commerce and to dispose of their malcontents . . . In England, everything concerning governmental action is prompt, whereas in France everything is slow; yet they are slow by nature and we are impatient! Among the English, money is bold and busy; among us, it is nervous and suspicious . . ." Announcing at that early date, when the July Monarchy seemed so prosperous, the national disasters we have all witnessed, he wrote: "I don't know to what depths the present system will lead us . . ." And he shows France having become "a country exclusively occupied with material interests, without patriotism or conscience, where authority is without strength, where elections—the fruit of free choice and political liberty—cause only mediocrities to emerge, where brutal force must be used against popular violence, where argument extends to the least thing and stifles all political action, where money dominates all questions; a country where individualism, the horrible product of legacies that destroy the family, will devour everything, even the nation that egoism will one day lay open to invasion. . . When that invasion comes, the people will be crushed. The people have lost their great strength. They have lost their leaders."

Is it probable, is it even possible, that an observer capable of this infallibly penetrating scrutiny might have suddenly lost that exactness of mind when it came to indicating the remedy for the national dangers that he had seen with such clarity? Let us continue to follow the impression produced on our hypothetical reader, and let us suppose that he begins to reason by analogy. He will naturally compare Balzac, who called himself a doctor of social sciences, to a physician. Will our man not reason like this: "How does a doctor inspire confidence in me when I am sick? On the one hand by clearly defining for me the nature of my illness, and on the other hand by precisely describing the coming symptoms and their development." The prognosis is the proof of the diagnosis, and both of them, by their uncertainty or their exactitude, reveal a corresponding authority in the learned man who has made them. And he will conclude that Balzac's social theories acquire a singular authority from sentences like those we have gathered almost at random—and they are innumerable. He will come to such a conclusion especially if he has followed the development of ideas in the nineteenth century and if he has become aware of the astonishing illusion of which France was victim until the war of 1870.[3]

The lamentable attempt that we have been witnessing since then to apply revolutionary theories is just beginning to dawn on thoughtful minds. Before this experience, there was a dogmatically admitted supposition that the principles of 1789 contained within themselves all progress. There was an axiom, engraved on the minds of those very people who, in the name of order, laid claims to power, that Democracy accompanied Science, and that these two currents would carry the peoples of the world toward an inevitable Eden of justice and truth. In a simplification that can be found in all the great collective, millenarian errors, these two currents were considered to be absolutely opposed to the currents of the preceding period. The Past was Monarchy and Faith, and both were condemned in the name of Future and Reason. Capital letters are required here to characterize this almost mystical phenomenon, from which Sainte-Beuve himself did not entirely escape, and of which Taine cured himself by studying the true history of the Revolution in the original documents.

These theories, so manifestly false when we look at them now, were endowed with prestige that derived from several sources. First of all, we recognize in them the continuing impudent charlatanism of the eighteenth century "philosophes." The crowning cleverness of the "philosophes" was to proclaim their intellectual mastery with such energy and, in the case of Voltaire, with such incisive irony, that three generations later people still did not dare think contrary to them. Even today do certain circles, for example in the university, dare do so? The densely massed interests that felt themselves threatened by any attack on the work of the Revolution made common cause with this neo-encyclopedism, and also, it must be said, with that suspicion of competence that the traditionalist party has harbored for so long. A cause that had been served by a Rivarol,[4] a Bonald, a Joseph de Maistre could have—should have—claimed for itself all superior minds. But it didn't do so, and Zola was correct in writing, in the essay from which I have already borrowed a few important sentences: "In spite of his display of respect for monarchical ideas, Balzac has found followers only among the new generation, the lovers of liberty."

This is the explanation of the contrast, in itself so extraordinary and so astonishing to our reader, between our elders' admiration for the genius of the novelist and their disdain for his doctrines. They saw in his work a marvellous understanding of the modern world as the Revolution created it, and it seemed unlikely to them that he would not be fascinated, as they were, by what they believed to be a magnificent social development. They saw him apply to the anatomy of human life all the procedures of the natural sciences, and thus prove that he was indeed adept at the methodology of observation. They therefore thought it logical and necessary for him also to be a proponent of what today's negative thinkers obstinately call Free Thought, as if the rational adherence of the mind to a revealed faith were less independent than its revolt against that faith! They concluded a priori that Balzac was a democrat and a nonbeliever. And suddenly they tripped over a monarchist and Catholic Balzac—let us dare use the word: a clerical Balzac. Disconcerted, they rejected the latter in favor of the former. The reader of 1902 clearly sees the coincidence between the two Balzacs. If he is in any way familiar with modern ideas, he has long ago grasped the irreducible contradiction between Democracy and Science, and the ever-clearer alliance between Science and Religion. He recognizes in the author of the *Comédie humaine* a precursor who drew from the most profoundly analyzed individual psychology a very powerful demonstration of religious truth, and from national psychology a no less powerful demonstration of the truth of monarchy—and all done scientifically, even experimentally, if one may use that word in connection with a chronicle of manners. And why not? If the observer of human life is forbidden to conduct actual experiments, can one not consider the innumerable incidents that are provoked around us by the play of passions to be nature's demonstrations, whose interpretation is equivalent to work in the laboratory?

Notes

1. [Ed. note: The statue in question is by Alexandre Falguière, who was commissioned to create a monument when Rodin's proposal was rejected. Rodin's "Balzac" was not cast during the sculptor's lifetime, and was not actually erected until 1939.]

2. [Ed. note: Louis de Bonald (1754–1840) and Joseph de Maistre (1753–1821) were political theorists of monarchist and Catholic convictions.]

3. [Ed. note: This is a reference to the various neo-monarchist regimes that governed France between 1815 and 1870, none of which recognized the emergence of Prussia as a major threat.]

4. [Ed. note: Antoine de Rivarol (1753–1801) was a writer hostile to the principles of the Revolution.]

Knowledge   Ernst-Robert Curtius*

Wrestling with the secret of life, deciphering mystical hieroglyphs, finding the hidden causes of all phenomena—these are what we have considered to be the aims of Balzac's life. We have seen his entire work as being based on a system of "energetics," through which he interprets reality. An unparalleled understanding of all forms and shades of passion, of love, of the will to power, gives his characters their fascinating force. One tends to see Balzac's greatness in his creativity—but the strength of his work is based not only on his creativity but on the notion of knowledge.

Knowledge is the point at which all paths in Balzac's world come together. He places the life of the mind, the sublimated energy of thought, above the ecstasies of love and the thrill of power. "Life is inside us, not outside; to rise above men in order to command them is the blown-up role of a schoolteacher. Those who are strong enough to reach the heights from which they can survey the universe must not look down!" Confused desire and blind will are subjugated to the primacy of the intellect. All longing for love, every drive for mastery achieves eventual fulfillment and is dialecti-

*Translated and reprinted by permission from *Balzac* (Berne: A. Franke AG, 1951), 162–66. Trans. Eveline L. Kanes.

cally resolved in the thirst for knowledge. To understand "what most profoundly holds the world together" is one of Balzac's basic needs; it gives rise to all the Faustian elements of his being and his work.

The Faustian thirst for knowledge drives the youthful Balzac into that feverish rummaging in the philosophies, religions, political theories, and sciences that he transmitted to his Louis Lambert, his Wilfrid, and his Raphaël.[1]

The Balzacian pursuers of truth wander through all these realms of human research because they are looking for a universal science that encompasses all individual disciplines. The unity of the intellect must correspond to the unity of knowledge. "Science," writes Louis Lambert in 1819, "has today become an integrated whole; it is impossible to deal with politics without becoming involved with ethics, and ethics is connected with all issues in the natural sciences. It seems to me that we are on the eve of a great human struggle: the forces are there, but I cannot see any generals." The philosopher Louis Lambert and the doctor Meyraux meet at a lecture on comparative anatomy in the Museum of Natural History. "Both were drawn there by the same research interest: the unity of zoological structures." One of them is driven by "the presentiments of a genius destined to lay out new paths in the uncharted areas of the intelligence," the other by "the desire to deduce a universal system."

These sentences reflect a period of Balzac's own life. Felix Davin, whom he asked to write an introduction for the *Etudes philosophiques*, wrote: "During the years 1818, 1819, 1820, M. de Balzac, who had fled to an attic near the Arsenal Library, was ceaselessly occupied with comparing, analyzing, and reconciling the studies of man's brain bequeathed us by the philosophers and physicians of the ancient world with studies done during the Middle Ages and in the last two centuries." When Balzac refers in his *Physiologie du mariage* to research by Hill, Baker, Eichhorn, Joblot, Gleichen, Spallanzani, Muller, and Bory de Saint-Vincent, he is recalling his own studies.

Balzac's relationship to science becomes comprehensible only in terms of his thirst for absolute knowledge: that is, for the intellectual penetration of the macro- and microcosmos. "We want to seize Nature's secrets," he writes in 1830, "and in some fashion to participate in eternal omniscience by pushing forward to the sanctum in which the mysteries of creation are hidden." Total reality reveals itself only to total science. And whoever wants to comprehend Being—to grasp it, to mold it—needs that "universality of knowledge that transforms a man into the very expression or embodiment of a century."

In a quite superficial but characteristic way, one discovers the universality of Balzac's scientific interests if one follows his critical writing in the *Feuilleton des Journaux politiques* (1830), in *La Caricature* (1832–33), in *La Chronique de Paris* (1836), and in *La Revue parisienne* (1840). That is where he discusses phenomena of the natural sciences like J. F. Herschell's theory of light; works on politics and economics by Gastaldi and A. H. Heeren; travel books on Spain, England, Morea, and Russia; historical writing of the most varied kind; new regulations for cavalry exercises alongside a commentary on the Epistles of St. Paul; a treatise on criminal law and a French-Algerian dictionary; new chemical discoveries and contemporary belles-lettres; philosophy, military strategy, politics, memoirs—in short, his interest is as all-encompassing as the title of one of the books he reviews: *L'Abeille encyclopédique, ou aperçu raisonné de toutes les connaissance humaines* (The Encyclopedic bee, or rational survey of all human knowledge).

One can, in fact, describe Balzac's thirst for knowledge as encyclopedic in the eighteenth-century sense of the word. For him as for the Enlightenment, nature and society represent the two hemispheres of the cosmos in the closest interaction, so that the analyses of physical and "social" nature complement each other. In a text written in 1795, but not published until 1823, Cabanis had expressed this view, which already presages the scientific theories of Saint-Simon and Comte: "Today we see, we know, we demonstrate that there is nothing isolated in man's scientific treatises; they are intertwined, so to speak, like nations in their trade relations; they promote one another like individuals connected by social ties."[2] But in contrast to the Encyclopedists, and to the naturalism and positivism of the Enlightenment, Balzac sees nature as God's creation: "What a feeling of admiration arises in the soul of the philosopher as he discovers that there is perhaps only one principle in the world, just as there is only a single God; and that our ideas and emotions are subject to the same laws as those that move the sun, make the flowers bloom, and give life to everything."

Balzac's image of the world is very closely related to that of modern natural science. He follows all its patterns. He lets himself be guided by it. However, his final goal is to bring all its discoveries and methods back to knowledge of man and of his place in creation. "The secret of the different intellectual spheres through which man moves can be discovered in the study of the entire animal kingdom. The animal kingdom has thus far been looked at only in terms of its differences, not its similarities."

For Balzac the whole of creation is a divine, uniform organic unity. And that is why nature is never "merely" nature and spirit never "merely" spirit. In contrast to materialistic science, Balzac even conceives of a living spiritual force inherent in inanimate matter. But traditional spiritualist philosophy must appear no less unreal and vain to him: in contrast, he clings to all those perceptions about psychophysical interactions to which the materialistic or hylozoistic natural sciences had drawn attention.

Notes

1. [Ed. note: These are characters from *Louis Lambert*, *Séraphîta* and *La Peau de chagrin*, respectively.]

2. [Ed. note: Georges Cabanis (1757–1808), was a physician and follower of Condillac; he belonged to the group of philosophers known as the "Ideologues." Curtius does not identify the source of this quotation.]

The True Duchesse de Langeais   Marcel Bouteron*

In the reign of Louis XVIII, an exceptional man, a hero—Général de Montriveau—passionately loves an indifferent "grande dame"—the Duchesse de Langeais—who is vain, witty, coquettish, and who, with her carryings-on, makes him undergo the worst emotional suffering: such is the general subject of Balzac's novel entitled *La Duchesse de Langeais*.

If one believes the novelist's repeated confidential revelations, the tale of the tortures inflicted on Montriveau by the cruel duchess is the accurate tale of the tortures inflicted on Honoré de Balzac by the Marquise de Castries in 1832: "I alone," he will later write to a friend named Louise in 1837, "know the horror in *La Duchesse de Langeais*." And this murderous love was so deep in his heart that he declared to his friend: "It took five years of wounds for my tender nature to detach itself from an iron character." The same confessions, the same reiterated lamentations, are found in Balzac's letters to Mme Carraud and Mme Hanska.

The novel, *La Duchesse de Langeais*, and these letters to Louise, to l'Etrangère, to Mme Carraud, were until now our only materials for reconstituting the love adventure of the novelist, with the result that the heroine appeared to us as the most detestable coquette of times past and to come.[1]

Happily for her, new and more reliable documents have emerged: first, fifteen letters from the duchess, collected by the Viscount Lovenjoul after the death of Mme de Balzac;[2] but above all, sixteen letters from Balzac, kept at Vienna in the archives of the Metternich family and coming from the Duchesse de Castries via her son Roger d'Aldenburg. After having tried for over twenty years to see these letters, I was able, a few months ago, to see them, thanks to their current owner, M. Simon Kra.

These thirty-one letters, together with valuable documents from my friend the Count de Miramon-Fitz-James,[3] have allowed us to contrast Balzac's portrait of an unfeeling and coquettish Duchesse de Langeais with a more accurate figure: that of a sentimental and romantic "grande dame" whose loving and tormented heart Balzac, blinded by spite, was unable to understand.

The Marquise de Castries was, at the end of September 1831, on vacation at the manor of Quévillon, near Rouen, where her uncle, the Duc de Fitz-James, lived. Having read *La Peau de chagrin*, which had just ap-

*Translated and reprinted from *La Revue des deux mondes*, 1 July 1928, 164–77.

peared, she could not help communicating her impressions to the author, whom she had never seen. She therefore wrote to him, signing her letter with an imaginary English name and, not knowing the novelist's address, simply wrote to "Monsieur de Balzac, Paris." The letter, after having wandered between the rue Cassini and Saché,[4] finally reached its addressee on October 5.

Balzac answered immediately and at length, defending himself from the accusations of his unknown correspondent by protesting his devotion to the cause of women. Very sensitive to the "touching elegies" of the marquise, he assured her that his solitary soul lived uniquely by thought, avid only for feminine sympathy.

Five months later, the Marquise de Castries, having given up anonymity, summoned Balzac to wait upon her; the novelist accepted with gratitude.

"It is so rare," he answered Mme de Castries on 28 February 1832, "to meet noble hearts and true friendships; I, more than anyone else, am so deprived of sincere support that I accept, at the risk of losing a great deal upon a personal acquaintanceship, your generous offer."[5]

Deprived of sincere support! Balzac cavalierly forgot the protective love of Mme de Berny, the deep affection of his sister Laura, and the tenderly clairvoyant friendship of Mme Carraud. But he is fascinated by this feminine prey, this novelty: a truly great lady, the flower of the French *Almanach de Gotha*.

The Marquise de Castries was then thirty-five years old. Born on 8 December 1796, Claire-Clémence-Henriette-Claudine de Maillé had married, on 29 October 1816, Edmond-Eugène-Philippe-Hercule de La Croix, Marquis de Castries. Her mother, who had died in London in 1809, was a Fitz-James. Her father, the Duc de Maillé, General of the Army, hereditary duke and Peer of France, First Gentleman of the Chamber and Governor of the Castle of Compiègne under Charles X, Knight of the Order of Saint-Esprit, was one of the most authentic representatives of French aristocracy and was descended from that Hilduin de Maillé La Tour-Landry whose name appeared as of the eleventh century in the charters of Touraine.[6] The Duc de Fitz-James, the marquise's uncle, a scion of the royal house of Stuart, held, in 1831, a prominent place in the legitimist party, which had remained faithful to Charles X and the Duchesse de Berry. Parliamentary records have transmitted to us the memory of his oratorical successes as Opposition Deputy, under Louis-Philippe.

The Castries family was no less blue-blooded: Charles-Eugène-Gabriel, grandfather of the marquis, was that famous Marshal de Castries, renowned under Louis XV and Louis XVI, who was Minister of the Navy from 1780 to 1787, then an emigré in the retinue of the Comte de Provence, and who died in exile in 1801. Armand-Charles-Augustin, the marquis's father, had followed Lafayette to America; when he was a Deputy to the Estates-General, he had a famous duel with one of the Lameths, and during the Revolution he commanded a corps subsidized by England.[7] His fidelity was rewarded under the reign of Louis XVIII by a hereditary duchy and appointment as Gentleman of the Chamber and Governor of the Château of Meudon. He died on 19 January 1842, at eighty-five years of age, in his mansion at 22 rue de Varenne, as a retired Lieutenant General, Knight of the Royal Orders, Commander in the Legion of Honor, and even, as a souvenir of his youth, decorated with the American Order of Cincinnatus.

The young Marquis de Castries, the husband of our Marquise and the son of Charles-Eugène-Gabriel, was born in 1787. His mother was the very noble Marie-Louise-Philippine de Bonnières, daughter of the Duc de Guines. He had seen service under the usurper, and as first lieutenant in a company of Gendarmes de la Garde had been taken prisoner in 1813. Louis XVIII named him colonel of the Arriège Mounted Chasseurs, then of the Mounted Chasseurs of the Royal Guard. He died on 1 August 1866, widowed for five years, holding the rank of General.

Such were the connections of the aristocratic correspondent of M. de Balzac, the author beloved of women, unsuccessful Carlist candidate in the legislative elections of 1832. But Henriette de Castries had other claims to Balzac's sympathy than her noble coat of arms and her legitimist connections: she had been in love.

Her marriage, a loveless union of two ducal families, had left her emotionally unsatisfied. She was still waiting for happiness when, in 1822, she fell in love with a young man, hardly twenty years old, as delicate and romantic as she could have wished: Prince Victor de Metternich, Imperial and Royal Chamberlain, Knight of Malta, attaché in the Imperial and Royal legation of Austria in Paris. He was the eldest son of the Chancellor and his first wife, Marie-Eleonore, the daughter of the Prince de Kaunitz. A portrait by the famous Viennese miniaturist Daffinger shows him in all his youthful grace: a rosy face with blond curls, a wide, dark-blue cape lined with scarlet velvet thrown back over one shoulder, revealing a high, black cravat cleverly tied around a collar of fine white linen and showing the edge of a grey, striped vest.

The young Marquise de Castries was then in the first bloom of her beauty: "a noble and courtly figure, a Roman rather than Greek profile, red hair rising from an elevated and very white forehead," so striking in her luster that when she stepped into a salon, at the age of twenty, dressed in a carnation-colored robe that revealed shoulders worthy of a Titian, she literally outshone the chandeliers.[8]

Her adventure with Metternich, consecrated by a de facto separation from the Marquis de Castries, was semipublic; Stendhal, who began *Armance* in 1826, wrote to Mérimée concerning a character in that novel: "Mme d'Aumale is Mme de Castries, whom I made a little wiser."

The dried flowers and the gouaches of an album[9] allow us, at a century's distance, to follow the lovers' progress: scabious flowers, pansies, forget-me-nots, daisies, violets, carnations, and roses, gathered from 1822 to 1829, in France, Switzerland, Italy, at Bois-Roger, in Béziers, in Saint-Germain, in

Rolle, in Geneva, at Lord Byron's villa Diodati, in Terni, in Florence, at the Coliseum *mezza notte*.

On 21 October 1827, a son Roger (named Baron d'Aldenburg by the Austrian Emperor) was born to these romantic lovers. But the days of happiness were ending: Victor was afflicted with tuberculosis and the marquise, following him at a hunt, fell from her horse and broke her spine.

Chateaubriand, whom she visited in Rome in December 1828, was moved at seeing her: "She is still," he wrote on 11 December to Mme Récamier, "one of the little girls whom I held on my lap, like Césarine, Mme de Barante. The poor woman is terribly changed; her eyes filled with tears when I recalled her childhood at Lormois. It seems to me that the traveler had lost that quality of enchantment. What loneliness! and for whom?"

The dream was rudely shattered on 30 November 1829, by Victor's death.

The dazed marquise returned to France and took up residence with her orphaned son in the rue de Grenelle-Saint-Germain, in the Castellane mansion. During the nice weather she stayed at Lormois, near Montlhéry, with her father, the Duc de Maillé. In July she went to the ocean baths at Dieppe, made fashionable by the Duchesse de Berry; in autumn her uncle Fitz-James received her at Quévillon, his property near Rouen. She kept up with literary matters: she read a great deal and was interested in the popular writers.

Balzac was one of the latter. In 1831, when he received the first letter from the Marquise de Castries, he was already the author of the *Dernier Chouan*, of the *Physiologie du mariage*, of the *Scènes de la vie privée*, of *La Peau de chagrin*, and was a contributor to the legitimist newspaper *La Mode*. He was very "fast" and met the marquise's uncle, the Duc de Fitz-James, at the home of the easygoing Olympe Pélissier, who later became Mme Rossini and served as model for the Foedora of *La Peau de chagrin*. Women were infatuated with his work, and his heart was free.

His liaison with the ardent Duchesse d'Abrantès had ended. He was seeking new and less fiery loves, and he was thinking of marriage and a political career: he wanted to settle down. Near him in the shadows there was always the tender, devoted *Dilecta*, the woman who had "formed" him, Laure de Berny. But the love of an aging mistress no longer satisfied him. He wanted to have a young, distinguished, loving, wealthy woman, widowed if possible, whom he dreamt of and whom he could marry. In 1831, his ambitions were not only literary and sentimental, his desire was not only to be a great writer, a profound thinker, and a happy husband; he aspired to political glory and looked to a rich marriage more to provide electoral eligibility than conjugal bliss.

His ideas had changed remarkably since his youth. He was far from the times when, in 1822, his publisher Grégoire-Cyr Hubert wrote to him about his novel *Jean-Louis:* "You must rid your narration and your political reflections of that seditious warmth, which will do *Jean-Louis* great harm in the present times." Balzac is now quite near absolutism, very much as the result of the influence of the Duchesse d'Abrantès. Mme de Berny was unhappy about it, for she was liberal and didn't like the Bourbons; the republican Mme Carraud, the purest of Balzac's friends, was also pained by this sudden metamorphosis. The two women sensed that if Balzac didn't refuse the advances of the Marquise de Castries, he would sink deeper and deeper into his monarchist convictions.

But how could he resist the attentions of the charming woman who, on 16 May 1832, sent him for his name day, Saint Honoré's day, a splendid bouquet of flowers; how resist the flatteries of the great lady who can compliment him so exquisitely for his work on *Le Rénovateur*, the legitimist newspaper subsidized by the Duc de Fitz-James?

So Balzac, very much the dandy at this moment, went every evening to visit his new friend, in his brand-new cabriolet, accompanied by his groom in elaborate livery. Conversation lasted well into the night but didn't suffice for heartfelt torrents and shared secrets. At the same time, they exchanged notes; Honoré sent manuscripts: *La Transaction* (later called *Le Colonel Chabert*), *La Femme de trente ans, Les Orphelins* (later called *La Grenadière*).

Balzac left Paris at the beginning of June 1832 to go work first at Saché, where his friend M. de Margonne lived, then at the powder depot of Angoulême with the Carrauds; but the gracious vision of the Marquise de Castries pursued him everywhere. He wrote to her every week, sent her, at Aix-les-Bains, a copy of the ardent letter from *Louis Lambert* to his beloved angel Pauline, which he had just composed. Finally, after many hesitations, he allowed the Marquise to extract a promise to join her in Savoy, where she was taking the waters. Gathering the little money he had, Balzac left Angoulême on 22 August and arrived at Aix on the 26th, with a paralyzed leg—he had injured it en route, on the step of the stage-coach.

Mme de Castries had reserved for him, at two francs a day, a pretty little room in Roissard's boarding house, from which one could see the whole valley of Aix, and, on the horizon, a series of hills, the high mountain of the Dent-du-chat, and the lovely Lake Bourget. Relentlessly he arose at five-thirty or six in the morning, for he had much work on his hands: the *Contes drolatiques, La Bataille*, articles for the *Revue de Paris,* and others. He sat at his work table in front of the window until five-thirty in the evening, stopping only to take a light lunch: milk and an egg that a restaurant sent him for fifteen sous.

At six in the evening, Balzac went to the marquise, dined with her and spent the evening in her company until eleven, having worked twelve uninterrupted hours.

Mme de Castries was full of attentions: she coddled him, gave him excellent coffee. When his leg got better, she took him out for rides in her carriage, took him to Lake Bourget, to the Carthusian monastery, romantically lingered with him beside a brook and a disused mill. She was charming and although her given name was Henriette, she permitted Balzac to give her a name for the two of them alone: Marie. But she refused the essential: love.

"I came here," groaned the unhappy Honoré, "to seek much and little. Much, because I see a gracious, amiable person; little, because she will never love me . . . She is the most refined type of woman: Mme de Beauséant[10] to the nth degree; but aren't all these pretty mannerisms indulged in at the expense of the soul?"

What disillusion! He, who had expected to discover in Mme de Castries a young and more willing Mme de Berny!

His disappointment was great, but he had suspected it even before running to her, and his letters show him very hesitant about the appropriateness of a trip to Aix: "Shall I go to the lady of Aix?" he wrote in July to Mme de Berny. "Ought I go to Aix?" he anxiously asked Mme Carraud in August. "Why did you send me to Aix?" he wrote her bitterly in September.

The direct and honest Mme Carraud immediately replied:

> Why did I send you to Aix, Honoré? Because only there could you find what you wanted. . . You want a woman of ever-changing forms, with stimulating ways, a truly elegant type, and you hope to find in this satin envelope a large and colorful soul. That isn't possible. . . I let you go to Aix because we don't have a single thought in common, because I despise what you deify, because I will never understand that the person who has earned a glorious reputation wants to sacrifice it to *money*. You are in Aix because you are to be bought for a political party, and a woman is the price of the transaction, because your soul has been falsified, because you reject true glory for petty vanities. When your duchesses are gone, I will still be there, offering you the consolations of true understanding.

But Balzac's heart is firmly caught, and, despite his complaints about the insensitivity of the marquise, he agrees to follow her to Italy. In his heart he still hopes to conquer her. Did she not formally offer, one day, to courageously go away with him to a house in the country? And Mme Carraud herself, did she not recognize in this offer an undeniable mark of love? On 23 September he announced his decision to his mother: the departure from Aix will take place on 10 October and his publisher Mame, for whom Balzac has just written *Le Médecin de campagne* in three days and three nights (or at least that is what he says), will see to the expenses of the trip. The novelist was to travel in the carriage of the Duc de Fitz-James: "I will take this wonderful trip," he wrote to his mother, "with the Duke who will be like a father to me. So everywhere I will meet high society. I'll never be able to find such a chance again." The projected stops were Geneva, Genoa, Naples, and Rome.

At the first stop, Geneva, all the wonderful plans fell apart. Did Balzac, at the last minute and at his mother's insistence, give up an onerous trip, out of proportion to his resources? Did he have an argument with the marquise in Geneva, or during a walk at the Villa Diodati? Perhaps. In any case, we know that at the beginning of October 1832, he left Geneva upset, cursing everything, hating the woman, having wept on the paths of Diodati, "when after having permitted him so many caresses, a woman was able, with a single word, to cut the web that she had seemed to take such pleasure in weaving."

The despairing Balzac took refuge with his old friend, Mme de Berny, at La Bouleaunière, near Nemours; he wept over his lost illusions, but he was not cured, for he still thought of rejoining his indifferent marquise in Naples, in February. And in fact all was not over, for she also wrote to him. Nevertheless, Balzac sought to relieve his pain by expressing it. He painted it into a confession in the *Médecin de campagne*, written under the stress of anger and disappointment, but which he never used:[11]

> That is my whole terrible story. It is the story of a man who for several months enjoyed all of nature, all the effects of the sun in a rich countryside, and who has lost his vision. Yes, monsieur, a few months of delights, and then nothing. Why was I given so many enjoyments? . . . Why did she call me her beloved for a few days, if she intended to take the title away from me, the only title my heart cares about? . . . She confirmed everything with a kiss, a suave and holy promise . . . A kiss can never be erased . . . When did she lie to me? When she intoxicated me with her glances, murmuring a name given and kept for love (Marie), or when she broke the only contract that linked our two hearts, which blended forever two persons in a single life? Somewhere she lied. You will ask me how this frightful catastrophe came about? In the simplest possible way. The previous evening I was everything to her; the next morning I was nothing. On that evening her voice was harmonious and tender, her glance full of enchantment; the next day her voice was hard, her glance cold, her manner abrupt. During the night a woman died, the one I loved. How did it happen? I don't know . . . For several hours, the demon of vengeance tempted me. I wanted to make the whole world hate her, expose her to everyone, tied to the stake of infamy.

Balzac savored vengeance in 1834 when he wrote *La Duchesse de Langeais,* but he had it in hand as of 28 February 1832, when his publisher Gosselin forwarded to him a letter signed "L'Etrangère" ("the stranger") mailed from Odessa. He did not reply, not knowing where to send his response,[12] when on 7 November 1832, a new letter from the mysterious Etrangère arrived. It ended thus: "A word from you in *La Quotidienne* will assure me that you have received my letter and that I can write to you without fear. Sign it: A l'E – H. B." Balzac hesitated not a moment and on 9 December, *La Quotidienne* carried in its classified ads the requested reply. The rest of this story is well known, and culminated seventeen years later, on 15 March 1850, in the marriage of the Etrangère, Eveline de Hanska, née Comtesse Rzewuska, to Honoré de Balzac.

Just in time to replace the cruel marquise, Balzac found another great lady, from one of the best Polish families, whose love was to avenge him generously for the refusal of Mme de Castries.

When the marquise returned from Italy in June 1833, vengeance was well under way. Balzac did not fail to confide to his newly beloved the tortures that the heartless marquise had inflicted on him. We can even believe that he very cleverly used the memory of Mme de Castries to maintain a very advantageous jealousy in the heart of Mme Hanska:

> I have returned to silence and solitude [he wrote to the Etrangère at the end of March 1833]. It took a great disappointment that has fascinated all of Paris to propel me into this extremity. There is some Metternich again in this affair;[13] but this time, it is the son who died in Florence. I have already spoken to you about this cruel experience, and I don't really have the right to tell you about it. Although I am separated from this person out of consideration for her, everything isn't over. I suffer because of her, but I do not judge her. But I believe that if you loved someone, if you had drawn him into the heavens with you every day, you would not leave him alone at the bottom of a frigid pit, after having warmed him at the hearth of your soul. But forget all this: I have spoken to you as I would speak to my conscience. Do not betray a soul that takes refuge in yours.

It was a superfluous discretion, since Balzac, pursuing his vengeance, was going to display in *La Duchesse de Langeais* the atrocities with which he reproached the Marquise de Castries.

Another meeting in Geneva, in December 1833 and January 1834, will permit the novelist to renew *viva voce* his oath of fidelity to the Etrangère; and it is also there, near her, at Pré-l'Evêque, that he will write most of his novel of vengeance: *Ne touchez pas à la hâche* (which became *La Duchesse de Langeais*), in which the characters of Général de Montriveau and of the duchess are none other, finally, than Balzac and the Marquise de Castries.

Notes

1. [Ed. note: In a later version of this article, Bouteron noted that six letters to Mme de Castries also refer to this affair, as well as a letter preserved in the Municpal Library of the city of Nancy.]

2. Lovenjoul Collection, A 313, fol. 28 ff.

3. These unpublished letters and documents are about to be published, together with illustrations (also unpublished) by Lapina, in the sixth issue of *Cahiers balzaciens*. [Ed. note: These documents were indeed published, and are moreover included in recent comprehensive editions of Balzac's correspondence.]

4. [Ed. note: Saché was the small manor house belonging to Balzac's friends M. and Mme de Margonne, where he spent a fair amount of time during this year. The rue Cassini was then his address in Paris.]

5. By a singular coincidence, it was on 28 February 1832 that Balzac received the first letter from Odessa mysteriously signed *"L'Etrangère,"* which was to shape the rest of his life.

6. See L. J. Arrigon, *Les Années romantiques de Balzac* (Balzac's romantic years) (Paris: Perrin, 1927), 144 ff. See also the same author's *La Femme et la flamme: scènes de la vie romantique* (Women and flame: scenes of romantic life) (Paris: Jouve, 1928).

7. [Ed. note: Charles de Lameth (1757–1832) and his brother Alexander (1760–1829) were well-known French politicians.]

8. [Ed. note: This description is taken from Philarète Chasles, *Memoirs* (Paris: Charpentier, 1876–77), I, 303.]

9. This album belongs to the Comte de Miramon-Fitz-James, who has been kind enough to give us access to it.

10. The heroine of *La Femme abandonnée*.

11. Published as *"Le Médecin de campagne: fragments inédits,"* *La Revue*, (1 July 1914). Cited by Arrigon, *Les Années romantiques*, 239–48. [Ed. note: In his revision of this article, Bouteron cites the excellent analysis of this passage in Bernard Guyon, *La Création littéraire chez Balzac* (Balzac's literary creation) (Paris: Colin, 1951), 254–56.]

12. [Ed. note: In the 1954 revision of his article, Bouteron took note of Bernard Guyon's discovery of an ad Balzac inserted in the *Gazette de France* for 2 April 1832: "M. de B. has received the letter sent to him on 28 February; he regrets not being able to reply, and if his wishes are not of a nature to be published here, he hopes that his silence will be understood."]

13. As in Balzac's affair with Mme d'Abrantès, who had taken Metternich as her lover during the Empire.]

The Peasants   George Lukács*

In this novel, the most important of his maturity, Balzac wanted to write the tragedy of the doomed landed aristocracy of France. It was intended to be the keystone of the series in which Balzac described the destruction of French aristocratic culture by the growth of capitalism. The novel is indeed such a keystone, for it goes into the economic causes which brought about the ruin of the nobility.[1] Earlier, Balzac had depicted the death-struggle of the aristocracy as it appeared in the hinterland of Paris or of some remote provincial towns, but in *The Peasants* he takes us to the theatre of war itself, to the economic battlefield on which the struggle between aristocratic landowner and peasant farmer is fought out to the bitter end.

Balzac himself considered this novel to be his most important work. He says of it: ". . . in eight years I laid aside a hundred times and then took to hand again this most important book I want to write. . . ."

Yet, for all his painstaking preparation and careful planning, what Balzac really did in this novel was the exact opposite of what he had set out to do: what he depicted was not the tragedy of the aristocratic estate but of the peasant smallholding. It is precisely this discrepancy between intention and

*Excerpt from *Studies in European Realism* by George Lukács, 21–28. Trans. Edith Bone. © 1964 by Grosset & Dunlap, Inc. Reprinted by permission of Grosset & Dunlap and Merlin Press.

performance, between Balzac the political thinker and Balzac the author of *La Comédie Humaine* that constitutes Balzac's historical greatness.

The ideological roots of *The Peasants* strike back much farther and deeper than the immediate preparatory work Balzac himself mentions as such. He was still in his early youth when he already wrote a pamphlet arguing against the dispersal of the large estates and advocating the maintenance of the right of entail in favour of the eldest son; and long before he completed *The Peasants* (in 1844) he had already put forward in the two Utopian novels *The Country Doctor* and *The Village Priest* his views on the social function of the large estate and the social duties of the great landowner. But having written these two Utopias he crowned the work by showing in *The Peasants* how social realities destroyed all such Utopias, how every Utopian dream evaporated at the touch of economic reality.

What makes Balzac a great man is the inexorable veracity with which he depicted reality even if that reality ran counter to his own personal opinions, hopes and wishes. Had he succeeded in deceiving himself, had he been able to take his own Utopian fantasies for facts, had he presented as reality what was merely his own wishful thinking, he would now be of interest to none and would be as deservedly forgotten as the innumerable legitimist pamphleteers and glorifiers of feudalism who had been his contemporaries.

Of course even as a political thinker Balzac had never been a commonplace, empty-headed legitimist; nor is his Utopia the fruit of any wish to return to the feudalism of the Middle Ages. On the contrary: what Balzac wanted was that French capitalist development should follow the English pattern, especially in the sphere of agriculture. His social ideal was that compromise between aristocratic landowner and bourgeois capitalist which was achieved in England by the "glorious revolution" of 1688 and which was to become the basis of social evolution in England and determine its specific form. When Balzac (in a paper dealing with the tasks facing the royalists after the July revolution and written in 1840, just when he was about to begin *The Peasants*) severely censured the attitude of the French aristocracy, he based his criticism on an idealized conception of the English Tory nobility.

Balzac blamed the French aristocrats for having in the past (in 1789) "contrived petty intrigues against a great revolution," instead of saving the monarchy by wise reforms, and for having in the present, even after the bitter lessons of the revolution, failed to transform themselves into Tories, introduce self-government on the English model and put themselves as leaders at the head of the peasantry. It was to this that he ascribed the ill-will existing between the nobility and the mass of the peasants and believed that the revolution had triumphed in Paris for similar reasons. He says: "In order that men should rise in arms, as the workmen of Paris have done, they must believe that their interests are at stake."

This Utopia, this dream of transplanting English social relationships to France was shared by many others besides Balzac. Guizot, for instance, in a

pamphlet published immediately after the revolution of 1848, followed similar lines of thought and was scathingly critized by Karl Marx. Marx ridiculed
the "great enigma" which had baffled Guizot and "could be solved only by
the superior intelligence of the English," and then proceeded to solve the
"enigma" by pointing out the difference between the bourgeois revolutions
in England and in France. He wrote:

> This class of large landowners was linked with the bourgeoisie . . .
> they were not, as the French feudal landowners had been in 1789, in
> conflict with the vital interests of the bourgeoisie, but in perfect harmony
> with them. Their tenure of land was in fact not feudal holding at all, but
> bourgeois property. On the one hand they supplied the industrial bourgeoi-
> sie with the manpower their manufacturers required; on the other hand
> they were able to develop agriculture in the direction the needs of industry
> and trade demanded. Hence the community of interest between them and
> the bourgeoisie, hence the alliance with the bourgeoisie.

Balzac's English Utopia was based on the illusion that a traditional but
nevertheless progressive leadership could mitigate the evils of capitalism and
the class antagonisms resulting from them. Such leadership could in his
opinion be given by none save throne and altar. The English land-owning
nobility was the most important intermediate link in such a system. Balzac
saw with merciless clarity the class antagonisms engendered by capitalism in
France. He saw that the period of revolutions had by no means come to an
end in July, 1830. His Utopia, his idealization of English conditions, his
romantic conception of the supposed harmony existing between the great
English landowners and their tenants, together with other ideas of a similar
nature, all had their origin in the fact that Balzac despaired of the future of
capitalist society because he saw with pitiless clarity the direction in which
social evolution was moving.

It was this conviction—that a consistent development of capitalism and
the concomitant consistent development of democracy would inevitably lead
to revolutions which must sooner or later destroy *bourgeois* society itself—
that induced him to extol every historical figure who attempted to halt this
revolutionary process and deflect it into "orderly" channels. Thus Balzac's
admiration for Napoleon Bonaparte is quite out of keeping with his English
Utopia and yet, precisely in its contradictory quality, it is a necessary complement of that Utopia in Balzac's historical conception of the world.

In the two Utopian novels that preceded *The Peasants* Balzac intended
above all to demonstrate the economic superiority of the large estate as
compared with the peasant smallholding. He noted quite correctly certain
aspects of the economic advantages of rationalized large-scale husbandry,
such as a systematic policy of investment, large-scale stockbreeding, rational
forest conservation, proper irrigation schemes, etc. What he did not see—
and in the two novels mentioned did not wish to see—was that *mutatis
mutandis* the limits imposed by capitalism applied just as much to large-scale

agriculture as they did to the peasant smallholding. In *The Village Priest* he had to resort to artificial, non-typical conditions in order to prove by an apparently realistic experiment the feasibility and excellence of his Utopia. Balzac was rarely guilty of distorting into non-typicality the essential features of economic reality, and the fact that he had recourse to such distortion more than once in connection with this particular point reveals that it was the crucial point, the point which caused him to despair about the future of bourgeois society and that it was this problem that he regarded as decisive for the survival of "culture."

For in Balzac's eyes the question of large-scale land-ownership was not merely a question of evolution or revolution; it was also the question of culture or barbarism. He feared the destructive effect the revolutionary mass movement might have on culture; in this respect he saw eye to eye with Heine, although the latter held far more radical political views; yet he never failed to stress also the deep-seated barbarism of the capitalist system whenever he depicted conditions in the France of his time.

Caught in the meshes of these contradictions, Balzac was driven to idealize the disappearing culture of the aristocracy. Engels said of him that "his great work was one long elegy deploring the inevitable decline of "good society"!

When in his quality of political thinker he nevertheless sought a way out, he looked for it in the preservation of the large estates as the basis of those aristocratic material resources and that undisturbed leisure which from the Middle Ages to the French revolution had created the aristocratic culture of France. In the long introductory letter written by Emile Blondet, the royalist writer in *The Peasants*, this conception can be very clearly discerned.

As we have seen by now, the theoretical basis of Balzac's Utopia is contradictory enough. But however greatly he may distort reality in these novels by a propagandist, exhortatory, non-typical bias, the great realist and incorruptibly faithful observer breaks through everywhere, rendering even sharper the already existing contradictions. Balzac always maintained that religion—and specifically the Roman Catholic religion—was the only ideological foundation on which society could be saved, and he did so with particular emphasis in the two Utopian novels mentioned in the preceding.

At the same time he admitted, however, that the only economic basis on which society could build was capitalism with all that it involved. "Industry can be based only on competition" says Dr. Benassis, Utopian hero of *The Country Doctor*, and it is from this acceptance of capitalism that he derives his ideological conclusions: "At present we have no other means of supporting society except egoism. The individual has faith only in himself . . . The great man who will save us from the great shipwreck towards which we are being driven will doubtless make use of egoism to rebuild the nation."

But no sooner has he laid this down, than he brings faith and interest into sharp conflict with each other: "But to-day we have no more faith, we now know only interest alone. If everyone thinks only of himself, from where do you want to derive civic virtue, particularly if such virtue can only be achieved by renouncing self?"

This irreconcilable contradiction which Dr. Benassis (who voices Balzac's own Utopian views) blurts out so uncouthly, is manifested in the whole structure of both novels. For who are those who put Balzac's Utopia into practice? It would be quite in order for them to be exceptionally intelligent individuals, for Balzac lived in the era of Utopian socialism and we might concede a wise millionaire to him as willingly as to his older contemporary Fourier. But there is a decisive difference between these two: Fourier's socialist Utopias were conceived in a period when the working-class movement was as yet scarcely born, while Balzac laid down his Utopian way of saving capitalism at a time when the working class was already vigorously surging forward.

But apart from this Balzac was a poet and had to present his millionaires in literary form. The way he chose is most characteristic of the contradictions inherent in the Balzacian Utopia. The heroes of both novels, Dr. Benassis in *The Country Doctor* and Véronique Graslin in *The Village Priest*, are penitents. They have each committed a great crime and thereby ruined their personal life and individual happiness. They both regard their personal life as ended and do their work as a religious penance—on no other basis could the realist Balzac conceive people willing and able to turn his Utopia into reality.

This conception of the principal characters is in itself an unconscious but not the less cruel condemnation of its reality. Only those who give up everything, only those who renounce all thought of individual happiness can serve the common good sincerely and unselfishly in a capitalist society: such is the unspoken but implied lesson of Balzac's Utopian novels. With this mood of renunciation Balzac does not stand alone among the great bourgeois writers of the first half of the nineteenth century. The aged Goethe also regarded renunciation as the great fundamental rule for all noble, high-minded men who wished to serve the community. The subtitle of his last great novel, *Wilhelm Meister's Wanderings,* is "The Renouncers." But Balzac goes even further in the tacit condemnation of his own Utopian conceptions. In *The Village Priest* a young engineer employed by Véronique Graslin tells of his experiences in the days of the July revolution. He says: "Patriotism now survives only under a dirty shirt and that spells the doom of France. The July revolution was the voluntary defeat of those who, through their name, their wealth and their talents, belong to the upper ten thousand. The self-sacrificing masses defeated the rich and educated few who disliked making sacrifices."

Balzac here reveals his own despairing conviction that his Utopias run contrary to the economically determined instincts of the ruling classes and hence cannot become the typical norm governing their behaviour.

That he himself did not really believe in the social feasibility of his dreams, is shown by the whole structure of these novels. Too much attention is focussed on the non-typical heroes and their non-typical behaviour, often obscuring the actual purpose of the novels, which is to depict the blessings of rationalized large-scale agriculture. But even the passages relating to these blessings are sketched in with a superficiality rarely encountered in Balzac's writings; he skates over details and picks out isolated non-typical episodes as a means of throwing light on wide issues.

In other words, what Balzac does in these novels is not to describe a social process, the mutual social impact on each other of large-scale landowners, land-hungry peasants and agricultural labourers, but to give an almost exclusively technical description of the great advantages offered by his economic ideas. But these advantages—again quite unlike Balzac's usual practice—operate in a complete vacuum. He does not show the people at all. We know only by hearsay of the general poverty which had existed before the experiment and then, when the experiment has been carried out, we again only hear that everyone is now better off and contented. In the same way the commercial success of the ventures is taken for granted and shown only as an accomplished fact.

That Balzac thus deviates from his usual methods shows how little inner confidence he felt in these Utopias, although he consistently remained true to them throughout his life in every sphere save in his work as a writer.

It was in *The Peasants* that Balzac, after long preparation, depicted for the first time the actual impact on each other of the social classes of the countryside. Here the rural population is shown realistically in a rich variety of types, now no longer as the abstract and passive object of Utopian experiments but as the acting and suffering hero of the novel.

When Balzac, in the fulness of his creative powers, approached this problem with his own most personal method, he provided in his quality of writer a devastating criticism of the opinions which he in his quality of political thinker stubbornly held to the end of his life. For even in this novel his own point of view is the defence of the large estate. "Les Aigues," the Comte de Montcornet's aristocratic seat, is the focal point of an ancient traditional culture—which in Balzac's eyes is the only possible culture.

The struggle for the preservation of this cultural base occupies the central position in the story. It ends with the utter defeat of the large estate and its carving up into peasant smallholdings. This is a further stage of the revolution which was begun in 1789, and which in Balzac's view was destined to end with the destruction of culture.

This perspective determines the tragic, elegiac, pessimistic keynote of the whole novel. What Balzac intended to write was the tragedy of the aristocratic large estate and with it the tragedy of culture. At the end of the novel he relates with deep melancholy that the old chateau has been demolished, that the park has disappeared, and that only a small pavilion is left of all the former splendour. This small pavilion dominates the landscape, or rather the smallholdings that have taken the place of the landscape. After the demolition of the real castle, the pavilion seems a castle, so miserable are the cottages scattered all round it, built "as peasants are accustomed to build." But the probity of the realist Balzac as a writer finds expression even in this mournful final chord. Although he says with aristocratic hatred that: "the land was like the sample sheet of a tailor," he adds that "the land was taken by the peasants as victors and conquerors. It was by now divided into more than a thousand smallholdings and the population living between Conches and Blangy had tripled."

Note

1. [Ed. note: Although this article appeared in English in 1964, it was actually written and published in Hungarian in 1934. Despite its Marxist orthodoxy, it does not arouse universal admiration among some followers of Lukács who see *The Peasants* as a flawed and uncompleted work.]

Balzacian Mythologies   Armand Hoog*

Proust's Mme de Villeparisis is astonished that her nephews can admire Balzac. She had seen the fellow long ago, at her parents' home, among batches of literary men. She could tell many a funny story about this man, compared to whom Beyle seemed "good company." In a word, she reproached Balzac "with having presumed to portray a society *in which he was not received,* and about which he retailed a thousand improbabilities." A thousand improbabilities! Mme de Villeparisis's complaint goes further than one might think. It is clear that the old lady, around the time of the Dreyfus affair, objects that she cannot find in *La Comédie humaine* a photograph of the times and the drawing rooms that she had known long ago, when she was about eighteen. Naive young men like her nephews can be fooled: they had never met the Villèles, the Montmorencys, the Blacas of those great days, nor had they seen the Paris of the Restoration period. But the marquise has passed judgement on Balzac.

Mme de Villeparisis would be astounded to be told that, like Zola whom she surely detests, she is a partisan of the realist esthetic in literature. She wants literature to "resemble" things. She is in favor of photography, trompe-l'oeil, and imitations. And it is true that Balzac's novels are not documentary; that the Paris of *Ferragus* and of *La Fille aux yeux d'or* is not exactly the Paris of Louis XVIII; that the social mysteries of *La Dernière Incarnation de Vautrin* do not correspond, detail for detail, to the secrets of the aristocracy under Charles X; that *La Peau de chagrin* or *Z. Marcas,*

*Translated and reprinted from *La Gazette des lettres,* 28 May 1949, by permission of Armand Hoog.

finally, allude to obscure forces not officially recognized by the July Monarchy. It is true that Balzac, who wished with all his strength to *create* reality, did not believe that realism was photography. Baudelaire was the only or nearly the only person to understand.

A short time prior to Balzac's period, the greatest creative mind and the greatest imagination in Germany (one is tempted to write its greatest novelist)—I refer to Hegel—proposed this idea: that reality and history cannot appear to us better than they do. Balzac's fearful strength comes precisely from his having taken the contrary position, from his having imprinted on the world a change in appearance that upsets its laws by conferring upon it new necessities and a new structure *truer* than the former. I stroll in a post-Balzacian Paris that would not be what it is without Balzac. Something of the society that Mme de Villeparisis did not recognize has passed into our own; a bit of *Le Lys dans la vallée* into French love; a bit of *Séraphîta* into our women; a bit of Vautrin into our secret curiosities; and a bit of *L'Histoire des treize* into our reveries. We are both Balzac's readers and his characters. The fact is that "reality" never exists as such, as a kind of pale, decomposed phantom. It exists only in our eye, in an iris bathed in our mythologies.

So we must articulate what mythologies Balzac has implanted in modern sensibility, so deeply that they have become inseparable from our vision. I see, first of all, the image of the mysterious city born of the nineteenth century and of that greatest of human revolutions, the industrial revolution. The point at which a confusion of realms takes place, where the realm of stone complicates its architecture so well that it begins to resemble a forest or the bottom of the ocean—this is the spectacle that Balzac was the first to see and which he has transmitted to us. Let no one say, citing Montaigne, Boileau, or Réstif, that it has always been that way. Those writers did not know modern horror with its magic spells of plaster and iron. Their Paris is not ours. Their cities are as far from us as ancient Rome. But because one evening in February, at the beginning of the Restoration, Auguste de Maulincour saw Mme Jules Desmarets walking in the squalid rue Pagevin toward the rue Soly, and because Balzac told about it in *La Fille aux yeux d'or*, we will always be fascinated by "vulcanized" cities.[1] That Pagevin neighborhood, where Ferragus, the chief of the Dévorants lived, disappeared under the pickax of the Second Empire. But the urban enigma, liberated so to speak from its stones, still floats in our streets, in the streets of Europe and America. Baudelaire took it into his dreams. Apollinaire made *L'Emigrant de Landor Road* out of it. That is the mystery I find when I visit Chicago. The planet is Balzacian.

I see the other mythology created by Balzac primarily in the organic evocation of society, in which the French novelist preceded Marx. There are the strange ramifications of the Life Principle in *La Pathologie de la vie sociale*. (In contrast to Marx, economics does not explain everything here.) Whereas a Proudhon stresses the defense of mankind against new incarnations of fate, a Balzac is struck by the reciprocal interweaving of the individual and the social tissue. The famous song of the Ecole Normale is wrong for once: Durkheim is not the Pope here.[2] Myths of collective participation and representation we owe not to a professor, but to our greatest novelistic genius.

The most important Balzacian mythology is well known: it is the mythology of invisible forces that exist *in* and *beyond* reality. And I mean the surreal powers of *Louis Lambert* and *Séraphîta* as well as the secrets of modern vital energy; the horrible and majestic birth of modern energy which gives to the old, classical tragedy its nineteenth-century successor in the *Mémoires de Vidocq* and its twentieth-century successor in crime literature.

The City, Society, the Invisible. . . In France, the role of literature will always move beyond literature. Before our eyes, a novelist engenders a part of the universe. We walk in a world that Balzac has created for us.

Notes

1. [Ed. note: The reference is to Balzac's description, in *La Fille aux yeux d'or*, of Parisian workers "vulcanized" and burnt out by the pace of their lives.]

2. [Ed. note: The reference here is to a song, sung by students at France's most prestigious school, the Ecole Normale Supérieure, referring to the sociologist Emile Durkheim.]

Balzac and the Art of the Novel   Gaëtan Picon*

Everything tends to isolate Balzac's work, to detach it from the genre to which it seems to belong. How can we fail to recognize the universe of poetry itself in the chiaroscuro of gigantic shadows jostling and confronting each other, in the smoke of an infernal forge sliced through by fissures of azure blue, in the frenetic and sublime gesticulations with which the Passion of Man is fulfilled, in the damnation and the coronation of the Will, in the endless, closed world touched by a light that seems to emanate from within? If Balzac makes us think of someone else, it is of Shakespeare. Dickens had barely read Balzac (he had only the *Contes drolatiques* in his library), Flaubert hardly liked him at all, Zola misunderstood him. But Hugo, Baudelaire, Wilde, Browning, and Hofmannsthal understood immediately. And yet this unclassifiable work represents a decisive stage in the genre against which it seems to rebel; this poet transformed the novel, catching it at a precise moment in its evolution and marking it with a sovereign stamp. So that, to penetrate to the heart of Balzac, there is no better way than to seek to grasp

*Translated and reprinted by permission of Madame Gaëtan Picon. From *La Gazette des lettres*, 20 May 1949, 15.

the formation and the nature of his technique, to catch what the novel, as a particular artistic form, became in his hands.

Of course we are tempted to admit the anteriority and independence of characters and situations with respect to the work—to believe that Balzac first dreamed his world and then wrote it. The way in which Balzac speaks of his heroes, as if they were persons living outside the work that imprisons them ("Do you know whom Félix de Vandenesse is marrying?" . . . "Call Bianchon!") contributes to this illusion; so does the fact that the Balzacian novel, as is indicated by the sketchbooks, seems usually to be born of a theme or of the imagining of a situation; so does the fact, moreover, that Balzac makes little progress on the *Comédie humaine* until he has established the general plan and discovered the titles of his books, and the fact that he dated the true birth of his work from the day he intuited its unity. But how can we fail to see that the characters and themes become Balzacian only at the instant the Balzacian world appears—and that the appearance of this world coincides with the emergence of a particular technique?

And surely it is not simply a matter of technique. If Balzac had had nothing to say, the discovery of how to speak would have been pointless. Technique does not clothe a prior vision: by the same token it does not draw it out of nothingness. The moment at which there appears a technique in tune with a ghostly ensemble of imaginings and thoughts is the very moment at which the phantoms materialize; it is in the creative process that thought changes into vision. In any case, the conquest and mastery of a new form was of decisive importance to Balzac. In order for the diffuse but imperious world he carried within himself to become vision and creation, he needed a technique that was neither that of *Adolphe* nor of *Delphine,* no more that of *Melmoth* than of *Ivanhoe*.

Although every novel by Balzac is the telling of a "story," and although the entire work is an unequalled repertory of plots and situations, Balzac finds his full powers only at the moment when the novel becomes for him something other than a story. It is in the instant when the novelistic technique reveals itself capable of communicating a total and internally coherent visionary universe that that universe appears. For Balzac, the usual technique of storytelling is useless, because it detaches the story element from all external materials, sacrifices everything to intelligibility and to the presence of the reported facts. What could he draw from this independence of the story, from this destruction of the world in favor of a privileged event—he who needs to make every detail the captive of a totalizing vision, not to accentuate the reality of the detail but because the totalizing vision is his true and only story? What is taken for Balzacian realism is the thickness of this visionary universe: but there is no Balzacian realism. Realistic description detaches and underscores; it fixes the framework of a tableau; the famous Balzacian "inventories" create an unfathomable thickness in which the eye is quickly lost. Not a single Balzac novel lives in our memory with the precision of *Madame Bovary* or *Anna Karenina*. But we remember the Balzacian universe as we remember no other novelist's universe. The reappearance of characters, the art of correspondences and analogies (of character to physical appearance, of individual to house or clothing, of society to nature, of terrestrial order to a transcendent order), the preparatory technique (which gathers the whole weight of the past behind present actions) joined to the technique of "inventories," contribute to the creation, in all its dimensions, of a closed and coherent universe, which gives so much relief to each scene only by absorbing it into a fascinating unity.

Just as it is the transformation of a story, the Balzacian novel appears as the liberation of fiction—if by fiction one means exterior drama. A drama based on sudden changes in external fortune (on the model of the "roman noir," the fantastical novel, or the historical novel itself) erases the meaning of the event and isolates precisely what Balzac wishes to link. After having waited for fame to come to him from the individual event, Balzac chose to give to each event a greatness that it received no longer from itself, but from its participation in a universe that reveals itself as being as legendary as that of *The Iliad* and as meaningful as that of *The Divine Comedy*.

From that moment on, Balzac's art will become a technique of dramatization. Just as the *processes of thickening* weave each thread into an inextricable web, the *processes of enlargement* give the least event—a word, a gesture, a glance—the dimensions of Myth and Legend. Here we encounter the drama of words (Balzacian pathos does not culminate in scenes but in words), the preparatory mechanisms from which are born tragic feelings of imminence and fate, generalization, emphasis, exaggeration, the epic meaning of enumeration. . . . It is when Balzac gives almost everything to the event and receives almost nothing in return, that we best understand his greatness: in *La Femme abandonnée* better than in *La Femme de trente ans*, in *Le Lys dans la vallée* better than in *La Rabouilleuse*, in *Illusions perdues* better than in *Splendeurs et misères des courtisanes*, in *Honorine* better than in *Ferragus*.

But it is not given to us to "see" this legendary world like a picture: it is carried by a voice. And Balzac is first and foremost a voice—strangely mingled with a vision. The "imperfections" of a style that has so tormented critics are lost in this voice, as rivers are lost in the ocean. Balzac speaks rather than writes, and it is not by chance that he declared that he had wanted to write *Le Lys dans la vallée* in the style of Massillon.[1] This voice, without any doubt, is the voice of eloquence: it is the natural expression of the world it evokes and of its powerful and imperious flux. But it is also something else: it is the unity in which the event and its meaning are joined. Balzac thinks his world and wants it to be understood: it is an archetype, and each appearance refers us back to its meaning. Balzac had to assert his thought without weakening or disturbing his world: his thought, far from being added to his world as a commentary, illuminated it as its immanent meaning. Balzac is accused of digressions and commentaries. But has it been noticed that they have the same tone, the same color as his descriptions, his scenes and his dialogues—that the same stream flows everywhere? The entire work, from one end to the other, in its minutest detail, without interruption or change of perspective, is carried along by that incomparable voice.

And this voice is not that of the spectator involved in an unfolding action, suspended among the uncertainties and hazards of freedom (like Stendhal's voice); nor is it (like Proust's) the voice of memory, which makes the past come alive in its presentness. It seems as if Balzac speaks to us from the depths of a past where everything has happened, where everything has become irreparable, inexorable. And it is because it is carried by the breath of that omniscient voice that knows the last word of the drama as it pronounces the first, that the Balzacian world appears to us to be a total and finished world, one which has exhausted its meaning and its possibilities, which has been everything it had to be—like the world of Predestination and Fatality. And that is also why it appears to us in a legendary remoteness, and why Balzac's work seems less the ever-unfinished history of a living society that exhausts itself attempting to catch up with that history, than in fact a *Divine Comedy*, the epic of a Humanity that has finished living and which, after having given up all its secrets, has merely to await, with its demons and angels, its victims and victors, all petrified in the embrace of battle, the Day of Judgment.

Note

1. [Ed. note: Jean-Baptiste Massillon (1663–1742) was a French churchman and author of celebrated sermons.]

The Modern Period: 1950–Present

Balzac and the Mystery of Literary Creation

Bernard Guyon*

THE THREE STAGES OF THOUGHT

In his analysis of the mystery of literary creation, Balzac . . . attempted not to make the mystery disappear, to resolve it in a pale illumination that would have only destroyed its reality, but to seek its depths, to measure its breadth, to reveal its multiple aspects.[1] In two rather considerable texts, he took pleasure in establishing what he called—long before our modern Doctors of the Sorbonne—the "biography" of the literary work. They are (1) *L'Introduction* to the *Physiologie du mariage* (end of 1829; 32, 3–14) and (2) the opening pages of the *Théorie de la Démarche* (The theory of perambulation) (August 1833; 39, 616–24).

These two texts complement each other, but do not overlap. They permit us to understand certain "constants" in the mechanism of literary creation in Balzac, or rather in the idea he had of this mechanism; but they also show us how dangerous it would be to oversystematize in a domain that is above all one of intellectual realities. It is precisely to avoid such a danger that, contrary to the rule of common sense and prudence that would oblige us to follow a chronological order, we will first analyze the pages of the *Théorie de la démarche*, where Balzac, fully master of his language and sure of his audience, plays the theoretician and gives to his thought a brilliant rather than profound form. In the *Introduction* to the *Physiologie* on the contrary—placed at the head of a work that he does not even dare to sign, written barely two years after the timid and awkward unpublished preface to *Le Gars*—he is less sure of himself but richer, more nuanced, nearer to the living reality that, alone, interests us, and perhaps even more convinced of the importance of the secrets that he is revealing: "If the author is here setting down the biography of his book," he writes, "it is through no movement of conceit. He is relating facts that might serve the history of human thought, and which will undoubtedly account for the work itself" (32, 11).

*Translated and reprinted from *Revue d'histoire littéraire de la France* 50, no. 2 (April–June 1950), 178–91.

La Théorie de la démarche appeared in August 1833 in *L'Europe lit-téraire*, at a moment when through repeated successes the novelist had acquired the right to impose such an austere text on a magazine. He attrib-uted great importance to it. A fragment of that *Pathologie de la vie sociale* about which he had already been thinking in 1830, the *Théorie de la démarche* was to constitute, with the *Physiologie du mariage*, the *Anatomie des corps enseignants*, and the *Monographie de la vertu* (A study of virtue), an ensemble in which the essentials of his moral, social, and political thought would be expressed. Let us then not be led astray by the falsely flippant air that he is obliged to adopt to attract frivolous subscribers, and let us consider the text with a certain respect:

> A thought has three ages. If you express it in the prolific heat of conception, you produce it rapidly in a more or less effective rush, and surely marked by pindaric energy . . .
>
> But if you do not seize the happy initial experience of mental creativ-ity, and leave barren this sublime paroxysm of excited intelligence during which the agonies of birth disappear in cerebral overexcitement, you sud-denly fall into a mire of difficulties: everything sinks; you get tired; the subject softens; your ideas wear you out. The postillion's whip, which you had used to drive your subject like a post-chaise, has fallen into the hands of those fantastic creatures themselves; then it is your ideas that exhaust you, wear you out, whip you with whistling blows about the head, and drive you to revolt. Observe the poet, the painter, or the musician taking a walk, strolling on the boulevards, bargaining for a cane, buying old trunks, smitten by a thousand fugitive passions, taking leave of his idea the way one abandons a mistress who is more loving or more jealous than she ought to be.
>
> And so the final stage of thought arrives. It is implanted, it has taken root in your soul, it has matured there; then, one evening or one morning, when the poet is taking off his neckerchief, when the painter is still yawn-ing, when the musician is about to blow out his lamp thinking of a delicious bit of ornamentation, picturing a woman's delicate foot, or one of those bits of nothing that occupy us as we fall asleep or wake up, they perceive their idea in all the grace of its efflorescence and foliage, the malicious and voluptuous idea, beautiful as a woman, magnificently beautiful, beautiful as a pedigree horse.
>
> And then the painter kicks off his quilt, if he has one, and cries out: "That's it! I'll paint my picture!"
>
> The poet had only an idea, and he now sees a whole work before him.
>
> "Let the world watch out!" . . . he says, throwing his boot across the room.
>
> This is the theory of the behavior of our ideas. (39, 616–17).

Balzac immediately applies this scheme to the very work he is present-ing to his readers at that moment, the *Théorie de la démarche*.

The first moment or "age" is that of conception. It is a moment of inspiration, of creative upsurge, of joy, of ecstasy, born of an event insignificant for others but which, for the artist, is of decisive importance. Here, the event is a worker's losing his balance in the courtyard of the Messageries; a fact which in Balzac's mind is immediately related to a childhood memory, in which he sees his sister laboriously lifting a box that she thought was full and which, being empty, made the gesture ridiculous. So the mind, having juxtaposed "these two dissimilar facts that derived from the same cause," begins to work in a manner that is all the more active for not being willed. A phenomenon occurs in Balzac, similar to what Stendhal, speaking of the birth of love, had called "crystallization." What else can one call a phenomenon described this way:

> Then there surged forth a thousand questions that were addressed to me, in the shadows of my intelligence, by a quite fantastical being, by my *Théorie de la démarche* already born.
>
> Indeed, a thousand tiny, daily phenomena of our nature came to group themselves around my first reflection, and rose en masse in my memory like a cloud of flies that rises, on our approach, from a fruit whose juices they are sucking at the edge of a forest path.
>
> Thus, I recalled at that moment, rapidly, and with a singular power of mental vision:
>
> Cracking of knuckles, stretching of muscles, and somersaults, which I and my friends, puny schoolchildren, permitted ourselves . . .

There follows a brilliant enumeration of these thousand little facts, at the end of which Balzac, out of breath, declares: "My petulant thought reveled in its childhood" (39, 619–20).

This period of creative enthusiasm lasts a certain time that Balzac does not bother to define for us. He merely describes the joy of his discoveries, and the grandiose ambitions that they engender in his soul, with this curious admission: "What tears I shed on the jumble of my knowledge, from which I had extracted only miserable stories, whereas there might have been a human physiology to be found there." (39, 621).

Nevertheless, from discovery to discovery, he is led to the edge of a veritable chasm: "Here, my *Théorie de la démarche* acquired proportions so out of scale with the small space I occupy in the great barn where my illustrious colleagues of the nineteenth century keep their provisions, that I abandoned this great idea, like a frightened man at the edge of an abyss. I entered into the second stage of my thought" (39, 622).

This second age is that of doubt, of fatigue, of fright before the immensity of the work to be done. The author no longer knows where he is headed, he despairs of reaching the end. That—note it well—does not prevent him from working. He couldn't do otherwise. He is caught, spellbound by his idea. It pursues him everywhere. And here is another moving revelation: "So I began an immense effort that would, in the words of my elegant friend Eugène Sue, have worn out an ox less used than I to walking in the furrows, day and night, in all weather, impervious to the whistling wind, to the blows and the offensive forage dispensed by journalism." (39, 622).

An immense effort, but, alas, a vain one: "How many thoughts have I not thrown into that bottomless pit . . . How many nights have I not spent vainly imploring inspiration from the silence . . . A man who did not have my thorax, my neck, my cranium would have lost his mind in the end." (39, 623).

And yet, even if he had not advanced beyond this second stage, even if he had never mastered the temptation of doubt and discouragement, Balzac would have regretted nothing for, like all "poor, predestined scholars," he had known "pure joy." He had sung of it two years previously in one of the most beautiful pages of *La Peau de chagrin*, where, leaving the terrain of the fantastic for that of humble reality, he had been able to find a note of purest lyricism to describe the intimate movements of his mental life:

> I lived in this aerial perch for nearly three years, working night and day without a break, with such pleasure that study seemed to me to be the most magnificent theme of human life, the happiest answer to its puzzle. The calm and silence necessary to the scholar have a certain gentleness, a certain intoxication that resembles love. The use of our powers of thought, the search for ideas, the quiet contemplations of knowledge dispense indescribable, ineffable delights, like everything that participates in our mental life whose phenomena are invisible to the outer senses. Thus we are always forced to explain the mystery of the mind through material comparisons. The pleasure of swimming in a lake of pure water, amidst rocks, trees, and flowers, alone and caressed by a warm breeze, would give to the uninitiated a very faint image of the happiness that I experienced when my soul bathed in the glow of a mysterious light, when I listened to the confused and terrible voices of inspiration, when, from an unknown source, images showered into my throbbing mind. To see an idea dawn in the zone of human abstractions like the sun in the morning, to see it rise like the sun, or better yet, to see it grow like a child, arrive at puberty and become virile, is a joy above all other terrestrial joys; rather, it is a divine pleasure. Study covers everything around us with a kind of magic . . . (27, 100–1)

Balzac does not repeat here the description of the joys experienced by the artist in his passionate search; he is content to recall them in a single word. Then, just about to write *La Recherche de l'absolu* (June–September 1834), having perhaps already conceived this terrible subject of a man devoured by the demon of science, he writes this sentence, which is an advance justification of his hero's madness: "The most wonderful life, the most fulfilled, the least subject to disappointments, is surely that of the sublime madman who seeks to find the unknown of an equation having imaginary roots" (39, 623).

So much work, so much suffering is nevertheless going to find its recompense: here at last is the third stage of thought. The author enters it as

gratuitously, as arbitrarily, as he entered into the first stage. Strangely antici-
pating the revelation experienced by the young Proust through Vinteuil's
"Septet," Balzac's "theory" appears to him as he listens to "Tamburini's duet
in the first act of *Mosè*." *Gratia gratis data*, a theologian would say; or, to
speak a more profane language, and more in keeping with the images that
spontaneously emerge from the novelist's pen: a capricious woman's return
to fidelity. He writes, "My theory appeared to me smart, joyous, lively,
pretty, and came obligingly to lie down at my feet, like a courtesan, upset at
having overdone her coquetry, fearing she has killed love" (39, 623).

And the next day, having rigorously outlined his subject, having final-
ized his method and given up dreaming, he truly sets to work.

In the introduction to the *Physiologie du mariage*, Balzac, as we have
said, insists even more on the mysterious and complex nature of the phenomena that accompany intellectual creativity. Here, still at the beginning, he
discovers a very old but vivid impression that has left a deep mark on his
mind without his having been conscious of it. This vivid impression is the
one he felt when, as a young law student, he read the pages of the Civil Code
devoted to adultery, and principally the words pronounced on this subject by
Napoleon before the Council of State: "These words," he says, "struck the
author of this book; and perhaps without his knowing it, they planted in him
the seeds of the work that he today offers to the public" (32, 4). Then came a
series of reflections on marriage and adultery as they occur in books and in
life, and the discovery that "of all human knowledge, that of marriage was the
least advanced." "However, " Balzac cleverly notes, "that was a young man's
observation; and in a young man, as in so many others, it was lost in the abyss
of his tumultuous thoughts like a rock thrown into a lake." So the idea aborts,
but not definitively, for the work of the subconscious continues to feed it
until the day when it will reappear in clear consciousness, the day of its true
birth: "Nevertheless, the author continued his observations despite himself;
then, there slowly formed in his imagination something like a swarm of more
or less accurate ideas on the nature of conjugal affairs. Works form in the
mind perhaps as mysteriously as truffles grow on the fragrant plains of
Périgord" (32, 4).

So here he is, having entered what the *Théorie de la démarche* called
"the first stage of thought": the stage of inspiration. In the present case, the
latter takes form immediately; but it is still a mediocre form: "minimal
thought in which his ideas were formed"; a "small, conjugal pamphlet."
Nevertheless, around this nebulous, primitive notion, the process of "crystallization" immediately begins. The author, Balzac says, "spent a delicious
week grouping around this innocent epigram a multitude of ideas that he had
acquired without realizing it and that he was astonished to find within himself" (32, 5).

Here, suddenly, a new blockage of inspiration occurred. The stoppage
was provoked by an external interference about which Balzac unfortunately

is chary of information: "This playing about," he tells us, "collapsed at a judgmental remark. Susceptible to others' opinions, the author returned to the insouciance of his lazy habits." That sounds very much like the renunciation of literature provoked in the young Proust by the "magisterial" pronouncements of M. de Norpois on the day the younger man showed him his first essays. And yet, just as M. de Norpois's young friend gives up a writing career, believes he is wasting his time in the society life into which he has plunged, and yields to the "insouciance of his lazy habits," yet is really amassing—without intending to and without clearly knowing it—the materials of *Le Temps retrouvé* (The Past Recaptured). So Balzac continues to nourish, in the mystery of the subconscious, the idea of the *Physiologie*.

Although the description he gives is slightly different from the one we already know, one can say that he then enters into the second stage of thought. He insists less on the difficulties of his subject than on the unconscious nature of the work that is taking place in him, and, this time, to describe it he uses (is this a discovery? a recollection?) the famous Stendhalian metaphor:

> Nevertheless, this delicate principle of science and wit was perfecting itself all alone in the fields of thought: each sentence of the disparaged work took root there, gained strength, remaining like a little branch of a tree, which, left on the sand on a winter's evening, is covered the next day with those white and bizarre crystallizations designed by the capricious frosts of the night. Thus the sketch lived and became the point of departure for a multitude of mental ramifications. It was like a polyp reproducing itself. The impressions of his youth, the observations that an importune power obliged him to make, found support in the smallest of occurrences. Better yet: this mass of ideas acquired harmony, animation, almost a personality, and moved into those fantastical countries where the mind likes to let its peculiar progeny wander. Despite the preoccupations of the world and of mundane life, there was always a voice in the author that made the most mocking revelations to him at the very moment when he watched with greatest pleasure a woman dancing, or smiling, or chatting. Just as Mephistopheles . . . (32, 5)

And there goes Balzac, launched on an ultraromantic comparison in which the devil plays the role of the Muse, so as to make us feel very concretely the spell cast by the Idea over the artist. The obsession is interrupted for a few years because the author has fallen in love and "the devil would have taken on more than he could handle if he had returned to a dwelling occupied by a woman" (32, 7). But one day, the obsession does return, stronger than ever, provoked by one of those chance occurrences that never happen to fools, a story heard one evening in a Parisian drawing room about a terrible affair of adultery that once occurred in one of the most austere families of the city of Gand:

Suddenly, the word *adultery* rang in the author's ears; and then a kind of carillon awoke in his imagination the most lugubrious figures of the cortege, which, not long since, had filed along behind those prestigious syllables. From that evening onward, the fantasmagoric persecutions of a nonexistent work began again; and at no point in his life had the author been assailed by so many fallacious ideas on the subject of the book. But he resisted his mind courageously, although the latter connected the smallest events of life to this unknown work, and, like a customs clerk, stamped everything with his mocking mark (32, 9).

"He resisted his mind courageously." This resistance to the injunctions of inspiration show us that the author has not yet entered the "third stage." How will he enter it? Once more by a fortuitous and seemingly unimportant occurrence: a conversation with two charming and witty women. They were discussing the unhappiness of husbands, the uncertain virtue of wives; he revealed to his interlocutors the "project of a book that was persecuting him"; "they smiled and promised advice." Back in his home, the author said to his demon: "Come on! I am ready. Let us sign the pact! The demon never returned" (32, 11). "It is perhaps of no small interest to anatomists of thought," he adds, "to know that the soul is feminine. Thus, as long as the author forbade himself to think of the book he was to do, the book seemed written everywhere . . . The day he said 'This work that is obsessing me will be written,' the whole thing fled from his mind" (32, 11–12).

There appears to be a certain vagueness in Balzac's description. We thought that he had finally reached the "third stage," the one of realization, of serious and rewarding work. And suddenly here he is plunged into the "mass of difficulties" with which the *Théorie de la démarche* had characterized the "second stage"!

Let us look more closely. The vagueness will seem less evident to us. In fact, in the *Théorie de la démarche*—in the opening outline as well as in the detailed analysis that illustrates it—Balzac, after quickly defining this "third stage" of thought, stops on its threshold. And how well we understand him! For it would be no less than the process of describing the sufferings of the creator during the time of production itself. It would be like describing the pains of childbirth! Nowhere has Balzac given us this description in a complete and systematic way; it would require something quite different from mere *Préfaces*. But he gave us certain elements of it that we must now examine to complete our task.

"WHEN I CAME TO DO IT, EVERYTHING CHANGED!"

In fact, nothing is finished when the painter, kicking off his quilt, shouts, "It's done! I can do my painting!" On the contrary, everything remains to be done. The picture is painted only in his imagination, not on the canvas where eyes other than his own can see it. At this moment, a thousand technical difficulties begin. We will not follow the novelist through the analysis of these difficulties; it would mean a whole book on the novelist's art. It would mean, above all, repeating the excellent work of Maurice Bardèche.[2] We will only elucidate one essential characteristic of Balzac's literary creativity, one of which he himself was aware and whose various causes he analyzed quite exactly. "The poet had only a single idea, and he finds himself confronting a whole work," he wrote in the *Théorie de la démarche* to define the unconscious progress of the Idea during the "second stage." It is by an entirely analogous process that *in the very course of composition* the work will become more and more extensive, thus confronting the author with technical problems that are sometimes insoluble.

It is in the creation of the *Comédie humaine* itself, taken as a whole, that the process appeared most clearly to Balzac. He described it at length in the *Introduction* to the *Etudes philosophiques* dictated to Félix Davin in 1834, at a moment when, without having yet found the high-sounding title of *Comédie humaine* for the ensemble of his work, he already saw it as forming a whole, divided into two vast compartments: the *Etudes de moeurs* and the *Etudes philosophiques*. Moreover, he insisted that this plan did not spring full-blown from his brain—not merely to excuse the defects of the arrangement (lacunae, repetitions, ill-placed parts), nor to publicize himself as claimed by many critics who cite the *Introduction* only to mock it, but, as Marcel Proust saw with the insight of a fellow genius,[3] because it corresponded to a living reality:

> Did the author himself contemplate the size of the canvas that he filled each day? [asks his mouthpiece]. We don't think so. If his plan had emerged complete from his mind like one of those marvelous unities that artists of long ago used to spend an entire life conceiving, but which the all-consuming pace of our century no longer permits us to create, perhaps he would have dropped his pen . . .
>
> The creation of the works of M. de Balzac is a curious phenomenon, worthy of examination—as are the unexpected developments that have enriched them and the vast additions that have extended them. The history of literature surely offers few examples of this progressive elaboration of an idea, which, originally indecisive in appearance and expressed in simple stories, suddenly acquired a breadth that places it at the center of the loftiest philosophy.
>
> Now that the erection of several important sections lets us see the shape of the edifice, now that the innermost sense of the general formulation expressed by the author in his many observations of humanity begins to dawn on us, may we not naturally suppose that one day, comparing the various thoughts engraved in his works, he acted like the weaver who, by chance, steps around from the rear of his tapestry and examines his design in its entirety? At that moment, and because the elements of a superb synthesis were already in him, he began to contemplate the effect of the ensemble. Suddenly, mentally filling the gaps in this enormous fresco,

imagining a group here, a principal figure there, further off a background of echoing colors, he fell in love with these tableaux and returned to work with an overweening *French fury,* because he was still young enough not to have any misgivings. Then, once engaged upon his task, this man with the unbendable will so admired by those who were acquainted with it, and which will one day be as prized as his talent, this man uninterruptedly went forward each day without a thought for the work and the fatigue of the preceding night . . .[4]

The two texts that we have just analyzed have shown us the development of Balzacian creativity subjected to two sets of influences: the first are internal and the most important, and can be summarized as *the progressive realization by the author of the dimensions of his work.* The second are external: the requirements of editors of magazines, newspapers, and publishing houses. And there are others that form a kind of transition between these two. They are internal insofar as it is the author who, by a conscious meditation on his creativity, dictates modifications to himself that he judges to be necessary; external insofar as this esthetic decision is in the end inspired by a desire to succeed, by a desire to please the public. On this point, Balzac made a veritable confession in the *Préface* to *Le Curé de village.* Any reader of this novel cannot fail to be struck by the difference between the first part, an admirable "scene of provincial life," intensely dramatic, linking a deep psychological analysis with a mystery novel, and the second part, full of vast projects, strong thoughts, edifying scenes and lovely landscapes, but at the same time calm, without any action or passion. Now there is no doubt that this second part was, in the author's eyes, the true subject of his book: "By what means did Father Bonnet make a pious, progressive, and excellent population, of the best cast of mind, out of an evil population—one that was backward, unbelieving, devoted to misdeeds and even to crime? There, surely, was the book."[5]

Then why did he precede this novel with another one quite different in spirit? Solely because he was *afraid of boring* a public too frivolous to follow him down such an austere path. Listen to his formal confession:

> Here, as in all the *Scènes de la vie de campagne,* it was less a question of telling a story than of spreading new and useful truths . . . Thus from the author's point of view, far from offering the novelistic interest so avidly sought by readers and which makes them rapidly turn the pages of an octavo volume they will never reread once the explanation is known, this book seemed of such little interest to the public at large that he thought it necessary to enhance it with a realistic, dramatic idea, but one in harmony with the tone of the work—two immense difficulties that the reader will hardly care about (*Le Curé de village,* 637).

Let me conclude by citing a passage from the famous article in the *Revue parisienne* on *La Chartreuse de Parme (The Charterhouse of Parma),* in which Balzac, to explain the impression produced on him by the figures of Mosca and Ranuce-Ernest, appealed to the laws that governed his own creativity. Struck both by the "prickly intentions" that appeared in them (he was convinced that Stendhal had taken Metternich and the Duke of Modena as models) and by their good taste and great propriety, he found the explanation of this double aspect of their natures in an intellectual phenomenon that he knew well, and which we have analyzed at some length: the modification of the work in the course of its execution.

> Without any doubt, this is what happened in the very creation of these two creatures. Carried away by the enthusiasm necessary to anyone who handles clay and putty knife, brush and paint, the pen and the treasures of moral nature, M. Beyle, who started out to portray a small Italian court and its principal diplomat, ended with the type of the *Prince* and the type of the *Prime Minister*. The resemblance that began as the fantasy of a mocking spirit ended when the genie of the arts appeared to the artist (40, 378).

I know that Stendhalians do not like this generous article, in which Balzac, among so many compliments, took the liberty of slipping in, with much goodwill and honest simplicity, a few technical criticisms. Moreover, I think Balzac's hypothesis is chancy for many reasons; we know that Stendhal denied having taken for Mosca and Ranuce-Ernest the models that Balzac thought he had taken. But if I cite this text, it is to show the multiple perspectives which Balzac's views open on the genesis of the literary work. If, instead of judging in the absolute, the critic attempted to take the author's point of view, to see what he wanted to do, to make us feel the obstacles he encountered, the solutions he found to overcome them, what precious light would not be projected on his work? Using documents where they exist, appealing to a sort of divinitory intuition where they are lacking, founded on a solid knowledge of the "métier," it would permit us to cast over this work a glance at once exacting and tender—and, consequently, the most intelligent and the most accurate—that of the creator himself.

Notes

1. [Ed. note: In the preceding sections of this very lengthy article, Guyon has discussed "The Mystery of Genius" and "The Life of Ideas" according to Balzac. Except where otherwise noted, references in the text are to the Conard edition of Balzac's work (*Oeuvres complètes de Honoré de Balzac* [Paris: Conard, 1912–40], 40 vols).]

2. Maurice Bardèche, *Balzac romancier* (Paris: Plon, 1940).

3. M. Proust, *A La Recherche du temps perdu* (Paris: Gallimard, 1954), 3, 160. Proust speaks of "retrospective illumination."

4. [Ed. note: Quoted from the *Introduction* to the *Etudes philosophiques*, Bibliothèque de la Pléiade (Paris: Gallimard, 1979), 10, 1201–2].

5. [Ed. note: Quoted from the 1841 preface to *Le Curé de village*, Bibliothèque de la Pléiade (Paris: Gallimard, 1978), 9, 638.]

Balzac and Visual Imagery   Jean Adhémar*

About fifty years ago, Paul Bourget was one of the very first to point out that Balzac never took time to rest, "to look around him, to study men through daily and familiar contact"; never, according to him, was Balzac able to have recourse to direct observation, for he slept during the day, wrote during the night, and had hardly a few minutes to spend on visits, walks, or love.

And, in fact, if one looks at the way he spent his time, one ascertains that he went to bed at 8:00 p.m., arose at midnight, worked until 8:00 a.m. Then he breakfasted, looked out of the window, bathed, received printers and publishers, and corrected his proofs from 9:00 a.m. to noon. Then, after a light meal, he worked until 5:00 p.m., dined, received friends, and went to bed. On days when he did not work, he slept, exhausted, for eighteen hours, and was unable to do anything for the remaining six.

How, then, did he write? How did he procure those elements of observation indispensable to a novelist so precise in his descriptions, since he almost never left his house?

It appears, and it has not been sufficiently stressed, that these elements came to him from the various newspapers that he received each week as a contributor. Each issue of these publications, *La Caricature, La Silhouette, La Mode, Le Charivari,* contained two or three plates by the best lithographers of the times. Balzac also received numerous albums that were sent to him for review. We know he bought others, for his bills from binders and booksellers were very high each year. Thus, he had at hand an immense repertory of images, similar to what we would have if we were to keep the illustrated magazines that appear weekly.

His interest in the image began in his youth; the engravings that, despite his poverty, he insisted on buying to decorate his modest room in the rue Lesdiguières are a kind of symbol of that interest. Later, in the rue Fortunée, in addition to oils and watercolors, he hung a dozen prints in the stairwell, entry hall, and corridors—some of which he had been carrying about for years. He must have had boxes of engravings or, more precisely, runs of magazines, for he worked at home, rarely at the Bibliothèque Nationale, even though he was a friend of the curator of the Department of Prints, Duchesne aîné, who dined with him to celebrate the success of *Séraphîta* in 1835.

*Translated and reprinted from *Arts*, 26 January 1951, 8, by permission of Mme Jean Adhémar.

When he was a child, he also saw, not far from the rue du Temple, the wallpaper dealers on the Boulevard Bonne-Nouvelle,[1] above all the establishment called *Les Deux Indiens*, to which the curious were drawn by "the fire screens that decorated its exterior," and the shops on the rue Saint-Denis and the rue Saint-Martin with their signs inspired by famous paintings by Vernet, Girodet, and other artists.

For the print, the handiest form of the image, was not the only one that struck him; he was also interested in painting—although in a rather secondary way. This taste perhaps came to him from his father, who had had himself painted at least twice in his life, incredible for a bourgeois of his times. One of these portraits was attributed, according to a believable tradition, to Mlle Godefroid, and might date from about 1822; this would explain the relations of Balzac himself with Baron Gérard, whose student and constant friend Mlle Godefroid was. Introduced into Gérard's circle, and rapidly gaining respect there, Balzac received from him engravings of his most famous paintings, which constituted in 1830 what Balzac called his "Museum." Very early on, moreover, his friend Théodore Dablin (Pylade-Dablin) highly praised the works of the best "modern" painters, Girodet and Guérin.[2]

Here then are the elements that formed his taste. The Napoleonic portraits and subjects of Gérard, the sweet and highly finished works of Guérin are for him the very summits of art; he equates them with the insipid reproductions of Raphaël virgins and Carlo Dolci allegories that grace the displays of the print dealers; he sets them alongside wallpaper, the lithos of Deveria, Lami, and Gavarni, decorative clocks, and shop signs. They constituted nearly his entire "Museum," a singularly mixed bag as one can see, and which, having been formed before 1830, excluded the great romantics for the most part but included a few caricaturists as well as a few of the very first new painters.

Among the caricaturists, Henri Monnier occupied a preeminent place. Balzac met him in 1824, and they remained on intimate terms for a long time. He was the one who revealed to the novelist (his lithographic work being finished by 1830) the comedy of the life of the petits bourgeois and of *Les Employés;* he is also the one who told him the story of Napoleon that will find its place in the famous pages of the *Médecin de campagne*. The lithographer Gavarni, like Monnier, was one of those "fruits" that Balzac could squeeze; Gavarni taught him to dress correctly, persuaded him to buy several dozen pairs of yellow gloves each year, and above all showed him the various aspects of elegant life through his lithographs.

Thus constituted, Balzac's "Museum" was of enormous help to him all through his life, for images, once he had seen them, sank into his consciousness and remained with him for a long time; he had an extraordinary visual memory, like his Louis Lambert, who not only "recalled objects at will, but also saw them within himself, illuminated and colored as they had been at the very moment when he had first seen them." He constantly referred to his

"Museum" for descriptions of persons and places. Montauran, in *Les Chouans*, comes from a lithograph by Girodet; the elegant gentlemen and misers of the *Comédie humaine* are described according to Gavarni, whose series "Les Lorettes" inspired many pages of *Illusions perdues*. Beautiful Esther[3] resembles Raphaël's "Madonna of the Chair," except when, in her amorous delirium with Lucien, she makes us think of a sensuous decorative figure on a mantelclock. Before Joseph Bridau[4] got to it, Sigalon had painted a "Venetian Courtisan," and the "Dido and Aeneas" of Guérin is a constant source of reference, as is Daumier's "Robert Macaire" and Henri Monnier's bourgeois types.

Pierrette, in the novel of that name, is exactly the young mother who dominates the "Roman Reapers" by Léopold Robert; *La Fille aux yeux d'or* takes its inspiration from Delacroix's "Young Woman with a Parakeet," and the "Angel's Fall" that is the liaison between Rubempré and Vautrin corresponds in Balzac's mind to a vignette by Johannot.

In the same way, when he wants to show us a landscape, a site, a city, he always falls back on one of those picturesque views that the "Voyages dans l'ancienne France" by Taylor and Nodier spread around by the hundreds. The engraved landscape sufficed to inflame his imagination; he wanted to go to Naples after having looked at the plates in the "Voyages" by Saint Non; "What a sky: the artist, the engraver, the typographer have rendered it miraculously. There is fire under the cold paper." Indeed, he often preferred the life of the image to that of reality; he asserted that a diorama provided him with an impression of relief that the landscape itself did not give him.

Thus images were of constant service to Balzac. Miss Wingfield Scott has catalogued 1600 allusions to works of art and to artists in the *Comédie humaine*, and she is in fact far from the true number;[5] at every moment, a reader of Balzac, if he knows the lithographs of the period around 1830, recognizes an image about which the novelist is thinking, consciously or not.

A few of these images can be seen on the walls of the Mansart Gallery:[6] for each we have ascertained that it antedates the corresponding description by the novelist; thus we have been able to verify the interesting conclusions of Mlle Mespoulet, who insisted as of 1934 on the connection between prints and the realist novel, and on the precedence of the former over the latter.[7] Linked to the research of Jean Seznec on Flaubert, the Balzac Exhibition takes its place at the center of what M. Julien Cain accurately calls "The Museum of Literature," and that is why it has aroused so much interest among historians of that period who are taking it very seriously; let us hope that an exhibition on another of our great classic writers will permit us to make still more contributions of this kind, which help renew, thanks to the Bibliothèque Nationale and its admirable print collection, the study of literary history.

Notes

1. [Ed. note: Wallpaper was hand-made in the early nineteenth century, and was extremely elaborate and quite expensive. Its manufacture ranked as an art.]

2. [Ed. note: Baron François Gérard (1770–1837) was a celebrated painter of historical subjects; Marie-Eléonore Godefroid (1778–1849) was a popular portraitist; Théodore Dablin (1783–1861) was a well-to-do art collector and friend of the Balzac family; Anne-Louis Girodet de Roucy (1767–1824) was a neoclassical painter, but with connections to the romantic movement.]

3. [Ed. note: Esther Gobseck, mistress of Lucien de Rubempré and protagonist of several other novels.]

4. [Ed. note: Joseph Bridau, a painter, appears in many novels: La Rabouilleuse, Les Employés, La Bourse, Le Père Goriot, Un Début dans la vie, Modeste Mignon, Splendeurs et misères des courtisanes, Ursule Mirouet, La Cousine Bette, Les Petits Bourgeois, and Les Comédiens sans le savoir.]

5. [Ed. note: Mary Wingfield Scott, Art and Artists in Balzac's Comédie humaine (Chicago: University of Chicago Press, 1937).]

6. [Ed. note: The occasion for this article was an exhibition of the visual arts connected with Honoré de Balzac.]

7. [Ed. note: The reference is to Marguérite Mespoulet, Images et romans. Parenté des estampes et du roman réaliste de 1815 à 1865 (Paris: Belles Lettres, 1939).]

The Visionary   Albert Béguin*

Is Balzac an observer *or* a visionary? The question is not a new one. But it is perhaps not necessary to decide it, or to consider it as a set of alternatives. Analyzing the workings of Balzacian observation, M. Jean Pommier left the door open to the study of "vision." I will not attempt to follow here the successive steps and stages of Balzac's visionary activity which, seizing hold of the data of observation, transfigures them and reconstructs them to create not an image similar to reality, but an alternate universe: a universe of poetry that will be the equivalent and not the copy of the real universe. My intention is simpler. I would like to demonstrate, without being able to prove anything, the necessary place of the creative imagination, not in the works of Balzac, but at the origins of that work and in the general context of a spiritual life of which La Comédie humaine is the consequence. That is the same as asking, if you will, why Balzac became a novelist and why it was inevitable that he became precisely the novelist that he was.

In a very curious essay on *Louis Lambert*, published in French in the magazine *Esprit* in December 1949, Henry Miller—yes, the Miller of the *Tropics*, who, more than once, in connection with Joyce, Proust, Van Gogh, produced great criticism and even moralistic criticism—offered views of Balzac that were original to say the least. According to him—I am simplifying—

* Translated and reprinted by permission of Flammarion Editeur from *Balzac. Le Livre du centenaire* (Paris: Flammarion, 1952), 224–30.

Balzac was initiated into occultist metaphysics and called to be a magus, but betrayed his spiritual vocation by agreeing to write a novelistic work, whereas he should have devoted himself to the development of a mystical theory. Faithful to his highest destiny when he composed *Louis Lambert* and *Séraphîta*, he supposedly showed himself much inferior as soon as he used his gifts as a writer to describe the human society of his times, thus renouncing the intellectual effort that he should have pursued. This thesis is cunning in that it permits Miller to make a very perspicacious interpretation of the novels that make up *Le Livre mystique*, but I would consider it to be true only on condition that its terms be strictly reversed. Balzac, a born novelist if there ever was one, risked missing his true vocation when he oriented himself in the difficult direction of the explicitly metaphysical novel, and painfully discovered that vocation during a slow apprenticeship.

He was a born novelist to such a degree that novelistic genius can be measured against his gifts; indeed the whole modern novel has arisen from him. The clearest sign of this congruence between Balzac and the novel is the failure of all his preconceived intentions and deliberate purposes. It has often been noted that the programs expressed in his prefaces or the political, social, religious theses defended in the preachier pages of his work are almost always contradicted by the meaning of the work itself, such as it emerges from events, gestures, and the destinies attributed to the characters. Defender of throne and altar, apologist of a strongly hierarchized society and a strong government, partisan of law and order, Balzac's authorial preferences go to creatures who escape the determinations of birth and class, just as they escape the prescriptions of social morality. Because they are closest to his heart, his best characters are outlaws and conspirators, the hidden masters who reign in the shadows and infringe laws, individuals of great imagination who create their own destiny by freeing themselves from all constraints. Courtesans, so numerous in the *Comédie humaine*, play a prominent role not because observation revealed to Balzac their place in contemporary society, nor because they represent forces of disorder that his traditionalism had to condemn. They are elite creatures because they have an exceptional destiny and because they create their destiny themselves, whether that destiny follows the upward movement of a conquest or the downward curve of a great disaster. For Balzac's choice is not between the conquerors and the conquered—any more than it is between good and evil. It is purely the choice of a novelist between adventuresome lives and paralyzed lives that are impossible to incorporate into the reality of the novel, if it is true that the novel is defined above all by movement. It little matters that this movement rises or falls, climbs the steps of the social hierarchy or falls down towards its lower depths: what counts is that the creature upon whom is conferred the dignity of "fictional character" escape the static existence of those who remain "in their place," and that he cross the various layers of society, overturning barriers in his fall or in his race toward honors.

This dynamism, essential to the *Comédie humaine* and contrary to everything that Balzac claimed to be demonstrating, gives to this reactionary's work a revolutionary meaning that he surely misunderstood himself. But precisely because it lies at the opposite pole from the convictions professed by Balzac in the political arena, one must suppose that this meaning has a profounder source, situated somewhere in those zones of interior life where spiritual beliefs and loyalties lie. The novel itself brings us back therefore to consider those metaphysical or mystical certainties that Henry Miller claims Balzac abandoned in order to fall to the rank of novelist.

Metaphysical preoccupations appeared very early and very vividly in Balzac, if we believe the largely autobiographical portrait of Louis Lambert. They quickly assumed the form of death-anxiety, and more precisely of anxiety vis-à-vis the destructive action of time. We know how much Balzac, like his father before him, was concerned with the problem of longevity. He who one day was to cry out "Death is inevitable, so let us forget it," he who consequently turned toward life, how could he not have been haunted by the desire to "live a long time" and by the search for a method of prolonging terrestrial existence? The practice of philosophy was, for him, first and foremost a meditation on the sources of life energies and on the possibility of retarding their expenditure. It is in this perspective that the problem of mind and matter presents itself to him, particularly as he presents it in those novels whose heroes are men of thought. Having persuaded himself that activities of mind are fed from the same sources of energy as activities of the body, he had to come to a tragic view of things, according to which the mind is the enemy of life, the imprudent consumer of the substance of which longevity is made. When he discovers occultism, he believes he has found in it the doctrine that will permit him to respond to that existential anxiety, and he will draw from it a precious conviction formulated in one of Louis Lambert's "thoughts": a day will come when, by a sort of reverse incarnation, it is "flesh that will be made word." No hope appears more frequently in Balzac's work, and in more diverse forms, than that of the Assumption of material nature, spiritualized by the élan of its own movement. Balzac's entire metaphysics of love is contained in the framework of this Gospel, as one can see not only in *Séraphîta*, where it is the central subject, but more or less everywhere, in the stories of the lovers of the *Comédie humaine* and in the play of metaphors that flower whenever the felicity of love is evoked. Séraphîta is an angel, an immaterial creature engendered by the physical love of two creatures of flesh and blood; but as soon as two beings truly fall in love, the instant of their union sees the parallel birth in heaven of an angel, an androgynous being in which they are mingled forever.

Once launched on this track, Balzac could have pushed his reveries very far, and as Henry Miller would have wanted, he could have constructed a complete mystical system. That was his great temptation when he wrote *Séraphîta*. But had he bothered to do so, we would have had from him either some sort of revelatory treatise or else one of those vague constructions such as Ballanche has left us. But he was Balzac, that is to say a man who, haunted by metaphysical questions but more or less self-taught and little inclined toward systematic reflection, risked wasting his admirable intelligence if he used methods of investigation and expression that were not his. He understood in time that his basic questions could not be answered with a doctrinal solution, but rather in the calm found only in the creation of characters and a novelistic world. Painters, he says in *Le Chef d'œuvre inconnu,* think with their brushes in their hands. In the same way, Balzac could think only in living images and scenes, through the invention of creatures who would all possess something of himself. He had once written a myth, the myth of *Séraphîta,* in which he went as far as possible in the substitution of dreamed reality for quotidian reality. But within that myth itself, the dream had lost its initial, transparent purity: the angel Séraphîta had been drawn back into suffering by the painful, hopeless love of creatures of flesh. Balzac listened to the internal logic of his own creation, allowed himself to be led back to everyday existence, and henceforth renouncing the creation of an arbitrary universe, applied his visionary gifts to understanding and giving life to the world as it is. As it is—but not in the eye of just any observer; rather, in the eye endowed with insight or what he called "second sight," capable of discerning *at the same time* the immediate apsect of things and their secret "meaning": the network of hidden correspondences, of relationships and "correlations" that inspired in him the joyous exclamation that we read at the beginning of *Z. Marcas:* "Our globe is plenitudinous, everything corresponds."

From that moment on, the novelistic world of the *Comédie humaine* is no longer "another" world, like that of the first *Etudes philosophiques;* it is our world, but seen "differently." Not a copy of reality, or of what we ordinarily consider to be reality, but a reality exalted and enlarged in such a way that by its very deformation it *expresses* the reality that an exact copy would not express. We praise the exactness of Balzacian descriptions; I ask that they be examined closely and that in particular one consider, by isolating them from the context in which they seem so "true," the portraits of characters or their actions in dramatic scenes. One can choose a hero of thought or of art—Frenhofer, Balthasar Claes, Lambert, Marcas. Their foreheads flash sparks, power of mind illuminates their features, they are made of fire and burning lava. Let us surprise them in action or at the moments of their most tragic lucidity: they abandon themselves to gestures that one would like to call "Elizabethan," to such an extent do the necessities of powerful expression override respect for moderation. And I am not speaking of scenes like the epilogue of *La Fille aux yeux d'or,* where, to end this novel entirely composed of a play of colors à la Delacroix, Balzac, who needs a handsome red, has poor little Paquita assassinated and dismembered: scattered on the white and gold cushions of the drawing room, the bloody parts of the cadaver and the marks of hands on the walls create an ambiance that would be pure melodrama, if we didn't know that it is pure pictorial harmony.

"All literary characters are geniuses," said Baudelaire. We can easily agree, if we are speaking of Claes, of Lambert, of so many other figures, almost all of them tragic, on whom Balzac inflicted the dangerous burden of thought. They have in common a fear of ever-lurking insanity, as if for Balzac the power of genius, which destroys human equilibrium, constantly risked breaching the frontiers of madness. The explanation is that Balzac placed in them his profound experience, and the fear of lunacy that never stopped fascinating him. He knew very well that Louis Lambert had lost his mind because he overused the faculties of vision that dissociate the mind from its earthly body. In a sense, he knew he was a Lambert who had felt the danger in time and who, giving up the exploration of the unknown, had found his salvation in conversion to the novel.

But there are many characters in the *Comédie humaine* who seem to have no trace of genius, a whole population of social climbers, politicians, lawyers, and moneylenders. Well, even in their case Baudelaire was right: created in the image of their author, they received from him the gifts of genius. For a character to receive an entry visa into the Balzacian novel or his legitimation as a character, there has to be something in him of that power of imagination that created the novelist himself. The monologue of Gobseck the moneylender, on the eve of his death, is very revealing in this respect. He is not in love with the gold that he handles every day because of a taste for material possession, but because the fatal metal gives him a double pleasure: the joy of seeing the bared souls of those who come to implore him, and the joy of determining their fate as he wishes. This double delight, of knowledge and power, is that of the novelist who discovers souls as he gives them life and who reigns over their destiny like an all-powerful divinity. Gobseck, in this respect, is very much like Vautrin, who is the hidden master of destinies he has chosen to orient towards triumph or ruin, veritable creator of the young people whose steps he guides and to whom he is bound by a kind of mysterious paternity.

Albert Thibaudet said one day that the *Comédie humaine* was "the imitation of God the Father." This is the profoundest possible comment. Balzac's vast novel is, in all its parts, a myth of paternity, because Balzac's personal expression is the experience of his own fertility. We know that the death of the child he expected with Mme Hanska was, for a mind already touched by partial amnesia, the final blow that put an end, if not to his work, at least to the joy of production. No stroke of fate could injure him more "centrally" than the ruination of his hopes of paternity. But although he was deprived of bodily paternity, he knew the intoxication of a multiple, spiritual paternity, having given birth to hundreds of creatures who resembled him. And they resemble him precisely because, authors of their own good or bad fortunes, they are first and foremost endowed with imagination and indeed with the rich imagination that generates works, successes, dramas, and lived novels.

But in this universe of the joy of creativity, whose creatures are all animated by genius and energy, we feel the old balzacian anguish rumbling:

the fear of death, the fear that life is running out, the permanent threat of insanity. This anxiety is not a foreign element that might be externally contrasted to the intoxication of creative fertility. It is inherent in the latter, it attaches itself to that creativity as if by internal necessity and implacable logic: first of all because the feeling of a loss of energy through the exercise of superior faculties never gave Balzac any rest; secondly because, like any great mind who has chosen to express himself through art, Balzac is anxious about his very choice. Is it not a forbidden, condemned act, a Promethean gesture? Is not the imitation of God the Father precisely what the Angel of Revolt, the one who is also called "God's Double," has attempted from time to time ever since his Fall? It is not for nothing that the sovereign ruler of the Balzacian kingdom is Vautrin, the great rebel, all of whose qualities imitate Balzac's and resemble Satan's. He has a taste for souls, which is surely the name of charity (the sacerdotal gift among Bernanos's priests), which is also the passion of the true novelist, but which, in Vautrin, is an infernal desire. Those whose salvation he claims to achieve are led to death, and one senses that more than once, Balzac trembled before the somber power of this double of himself. Constructed as a response to his principal anxiety, Balzac's work sent back a reflection of that anxiety, but it is in that way that the work acquires the status of myth.

In the description of Louis Lambert after he succumbs to madness, Balzac accumulates expressionist touches that translate interior truth through the deformation or exaggeration of perceptible probability. One of these details is singularly revealing: we see Lambert standing erect, "rubbing one of his legs against the other with a mechanical motion"; and, says Balzac, "the continual rubbing of the two bones produced a terrible sound." As skeletal as one supposes him to be, he is clothed and we have difficulty imagining that his bones can produce this sound in spite of flesh and cloth. The fact is that Balzac, visionary at that moment as he was in his best moments, *really sees* the dead Lambert, Lambert as skeleton. Why is this so, if not because Balzac sought to translate physically the madness of his friend and double, and because for him madness and death are objects of the same anguish, hence synonymous? We would have to collect and study Balzac's strange images, search for the cause of his linguistic excesses, of his improbabilities. Only the interpretation of his uncontrolled metaphors, conducted according to the methods of a Gaston Bachelard[1], would permit us to reach, at the heart of his work, the guarded secret that is the secret of his vision because it is the secret of his obsessions.

Note

1. [Ed. note: Gaston Bachelard (1884–1962) was a French philosopher and psychoanalytic theorist.]

The Spider's Feast: Some Aspects of
Balzacian Creativity

Pierre-Georges Castex*

Paul Valéry, in his pages on *Adonis*, compares the poet to a mysterious spider, watching for its prey and attentive to the "chance occurrences from among which it chooses its food." Confronting any literary work, whether it be poetry or novel, the role of the critic should be to unravel the threads of which it is woven so as to find the creator at the center of the web. The work is not comprehended in the Latin sense of the term until it is apprehended and, so to speak, relived.

Has Balzac's *Comédie humaine* been grasped with all desirable method and patience? There are, to be sure, several basic studies that shed precious light on the novelist's art and method. But there seem to have been too many excursions into biographical anecdote, conducted with somewhat gratuitous pleasure. Questions have been asked such as: Just how many canes did he have, since it has been shown that he had several? The sumptuous menus that he offered his friends have been reproduced. And so a Balzacian fetishism has developed. Critics have also occasionally yielded to the temptation of easy questions, which leads them eternally to reopen the same inquiries. We have a good ten books on the women in Balzac's life; too many, far too many. On the other hand, there are not enough works devoted to a scrupulous study of one of his novels.

It is in the latter direction that Balzac studies should now be oriented. For basic analyses, we have in the Spoelberch de Lovenjoul collection a documentation that until now has been very incompletely used. Let us beware of losing ourselves in Byzantine quibbling over a comma that has changed place from manuscript to printed text; let us not lose sight of the fact that our object must be the understanding of a work whose breadth is surely its most astonishing characteristic. But the time has not yet come to attempt valid, overall conclusions about Balzacian creativity. It would be better, we think, to choose a few great novels and minutely explore their texts over the coming years. As of now, several researchers are at work.

We would like, for our part, to indicate certain results of research that we have been conducting. Generally we will try to avoid the repetition of well-known facts so as to be able, if possible, to propose a few new views of a subject much less worn out than one would tend to think.

The spider at the center of its web seals the fate of the smallest insects that fall into its grasp. Thus the novelist, "at the imaginary center of his uncreated work," as Valéry writes, neglects none of the humble resources that the exterior world gives him with which to nourish his story and make it live. Let us dispense with the image of the visionary blessed with "mystical

*Translated and reprinted by permission from *Annales de l'Université de Paris* 27 (1957): 517–29.

insight" or of a God drawing his work out of nothing: these dangerous metaphors have been overused. Balzac himself warned us that "novelists never
invent anything." But the novelist's glance is sharper, faster, more penetrating than the ordinary man's; his ability to register things is better exercised.
Like the spider, he lies in wait and nothing escapes him. He is extremely
attentive to the smallest chance happenings, because his appetite is insatiable. Think of the multitude of small concrete facts that must be assembled to
write a work that mirrors life! Here are a few examples, apparently trivial, of
this kind of vigilance.

In *Ferragus*, we see a concierge named Fouquereau, to whom the hero,
Auguste de Maulincour, calls several times in imperious tones: "Fouquereau, answer me . . . Fouquereau, I'm counting on you." Fouquereau is the
confidential servant, always at one's disposal. Now, in writing his manuscript, Balzac surely had in mind the name of the foreman of the Everat
printing house, Foucault: it is to him that Balzac turns for everything concerning copy to be delivered or proofs to be returned. We find indications
such as these coming from his pen: "Foucault, you will receive ten sheets at
two o'clock . . . Foucault, I need this proof tomorrow morning . . ." the
novelist needed a proper name: this one was caught on the fly, and modified
slightly. Meager pittance for a spider! But it's that much gained.

In *La Vieille Fille*, the novelist described a certain Polish princess whom
he first called Sapiéha. But, on a proof, we see a correction: Sapiéha becomes
"Goritza." What happened? He had heard the news of the death of Charles X
at Goritz, in Hungary. And in fact the name Sapiéha was clumsy: on the basis
of Goritz he made Goritza, and his princess became Hungarian!

Other borrowings from reality are clearer and more important. In *La
Vieille Fille* again, we find a curious character whom Balzac calls the Chevalier de Valois. This chevalier is fifty-eight years old, but still vigorous. An
aristocrat and convinced legitimist, he insists on dressing in the old style: he
wears a maroon suit with gold buttons, well-fitting trousers, and shoes with
square gold buckles. Physically, he is notable for a thin body, elegant wrinkles and above all a prodigious nose. He has innocent manias and carries on a
continual dialogue with a medallion picturing the Princess Goritza, his
former mistress. This medallion is on the cover of a snuff box, which he
constantly pulls out of his pocket.

Let us concentrate on these details: they seem to have been taken from
a real-life model, and indeed they were. At the end of the nineteenth century a Breton scholar, Hyacinthe du Pontavice de Heussey, published the
letters of Balzac to General de Pommereul of Fougères. In one of these
letters, we read: "Be so good, General, as to transmit my greetings to my
good-natured antagonist, M. de Valois . . ." What does that word "antagonist" mean? An opponent at the gaming table? Perhaps. In a discussion?
Probably. This Valois, faithful to the traditions of his name, was a legitimist,
whereas the young Balzac professed liberal opinions. In all probability, he

gave the novelist information about episodes of Chouannerie in the region around the city of Fougères.[1]

Now du Pontavice was a descendent of this eccentric gentleman, and family documents enabled him to provide a description: he was "a dry, thin little man, with deep, brilliant eyes, a nose like the beak of a bird of prey, a very thin mouth, and a leathery and cleanly shaven face." He wore "powdered hair, a suit of hazelnut color in the French fashion . . . loose-fitting trousers, variegated stockings, and buckled shoes." His principal mania was to play "with a snuff box ornamented with a miniature, into which he dipped from time to time with a tiny golden spoon."

Etienne Aubrée reveals in his *Balzac à Fougères* that this Valois was indeed a chevalier. He was seventy-three years old when Balzac met him, eighty-one at the moment of *La Vieille Fille,* and was to die in 1845 at the age of ninety. At sixty-four years of age he had taken a second wife, a demoiselle Henriette-Reine de France!

There can be no doubt that the novelist remembered him when portraying his aged but still frisky bachelor. But he takes pleasure in muddying the waters. Let us read the opening to *La Vieille Fille:* "Many people must have met in certain provinces of France a certain number of chevaliers de Valois: there was one in Normandy, another in Bourges, a third flourished in 1816 in the city of Alençon, and the south perhaps possessed one of its own" (VF, 811). Balzac is careful not to specify that he himself knew a chevalier de Valois in Fougères. This spider has his tricks.

That was, perhaps, an especially simple example of the transposition into the novel of a real person. Moreover, Balzac lends his hero adventures that are not those of the model and the inspiration for which perhaps came from elsewhere: he is a user of the process of *contamination.* Let us examine an example of this, not apropos of a character but of a place.

The precision with which Balzac set the decor in which his action unfolds is well known. We can be sure that he began by observing the houses that he describes. In *La Vieille Fille* he even gives us the address of his heroine. Mademoiselle Cormon lives in Alençon, "exactly halfway down the rue du Val-Noble." Various indications given by the novel permit us to locate this building quite precisely, at the corner of that street and the Passage des Filles de Sainte-Claire, which Balzac had to take in 1825 on his way from the château to the rue aux Cieux where the engraver Godard had his studio.

Yet let us read *La Vieille Fille.* After the exterior, the novelist describes the interior of the house. On the mantelpiece of the main drawing room there was "a clock whose decoration, taken from the last scene of *Le Déserteur,* proved the prodigious popularity of Sedaine's work. This clock, in gilded copper, displayed eleven characters, each five inches high . . . The paneling in the woodwork was ornamented with the most recent family portraits, one or two Rigauds and three Latour pastels" (VF, 850).

This raises a question. The authentic house of *La Vieille Fille* has been razed and reconstructed. There is no way to know if Balzac had been able to visit it so as to make an inventory of the furnishings, but it is rather improbable. When he came to Alençon, he was quite young and without the least reputation; moreover he spent only two or three days in the town—insufficient to open the doors of a provincial society. Are we then to suppose that having described the exterior of a house seen in the course of a stroll, the novelist then relied on his imagination to describe the interior? No! This extraordinary clock, these Rigauds, these Latours, he saw them . . . but elsewhere.

We have proof of this in a *Guide to Upper Normandy,* written by Messieurs Dimier and Longnon. These local scholars describe the château of Glisolles in the Department of the Eure, which belonged to the Clermont-Tonnerre family, and which unfortunately was destroyed by fire in 1937: "Inside, to the left one discovers two drawing rooms still filled with their antique furniture. In his novel *La Vieille Fille,* Balzac described them as belonging to the Cormons. On the mantelpiece, the novelist says, there was a clock . . ." Here the authors of the *Guide* see no need for further description since Balzac's seems so accurate to them. A historian, M. Vidalenc, confirms their statements in his thesis on *Le Département de l'Eure sous la Monarchie constitutionnelle* (The department of the Eure under the constitutional monarchy). He, too, allows the novelist to describe the château of Glisolles. We know that this luxurious château attracted numerous visitors: Balzac could have gone there during a trip to Bayeux, where his sister lived. His visit would not have been wasted time.

Another example of contamination involves a famous character, the Baron de Nucingen.[2] The Pléiade edition of the *Comédie humaine* proposes for him an equation that is really too simple: "Nucingen = James de Rothschild." If the novelist limited himself to copying real life, the work of the critic would be awkward, there would be no literary creation. When Balzac declares that he does not draw portraits, we must believe him. Moreover, an objection arises in our minds. Nucingen is a grotesque and odious character. Now Balzac had personal relations with Baron James de Rothschild, who had introduced him to the Duc de Fitz-James and had rendered him service by lending him books. Balzac wouldn't dream of displeasing him, and Rothschild does not seem to have recognized himself in Nucingen.

If one looks closely, one sees that Nucingen's career doesn't resemble Rothschild's at all. Nucingen starts as a bank employee in Strasbourg at the beginning of the century; he is Alsacian; he builds his fortune through a series of liquidations. In 1804 and again in 1815 after Waterloo, he maintains that he cannot satisfy his debts, but he avoids bankruptcy by mollifying his creditors with depreciated stocks and profiting personally; later he consolidates his fortune by speculating in wool. Now Rothschild, who is German by nationality, came to France only in 1811; he never liquidated and he never traded in wool. On the other hand, a different banker, Fould, spent his apprenticeship in Strasbourg at the beginning of the century, liquidated twice, in 1804 and 1811, and was very much involved in cotton prints; he was born in Boulay, on the frontier of Lorraine and Alsatia. Such analogies are probably not coincidences.

There is little doubt, however, that in order to create Nucingen, Balzac began with Rothschild, just as he wrote to Mme Hanska. But he took care to take other models, so as to confuse the issue. If Rothschild had had any suspicions, the novelist could have invoked a wonderful alibi by pointing to Fould. Posterity has simplified the matter: it has ignored Fould and retained Rothschild. But we today must try to see things more clearly.

The study of *La Fille aux yeux d'or* allows an analogous observation with respect to one of the two heroines, the Marquise de San Réal. Reading this text attentively, we were stopped by the following passage describing her: ". . . a young girl named Euphémie, born of a Spanish lady, raised in Havana, brought back to Madrid with a young creole girl; having the ruinous tastes of the colonies but happily married to an old and extremely rich Spanish nobleman, don Hijos, Marquis de San Réal, who, as of the French occupation of Spain, had come to Paris and lived in the rue Saint-Lazare" (FYO, 1058). Except for a few details, we thought we recognized in this description the Comtesse Merlin, whose receptions Balzac attended. The Comtesse Merlin was also of Spanish origin; she lived until the age of twelve in Havana; then she spent some time in Spain; she was married in Madrid— not to a Spanish grandee it is true, but to a French general, who, in 1811, brought her to Paris.

We have just been given supplementary proof that Balzac, in describing his heroine, was thinking of his friend. Mr. Wayne Conner has found a detail that had not caught our eye among the variants of the manuscript.[3] In the early versions, the Fille aux Yeux d'or invites de Marsay to meet her not at the home of the Marquise de San-Réal, but at the home of the Duchess de Santa Cruz. Mr. Conner reminds us that Santa Cruz was one of the names of the Comtesse Merlin, born "Mercedes Santa-Cruz y Montalvo, Contessa de Jaruco." We can now see how things must have happened. Balzac, in the manuscript, wrote the name Santa Cruz. But when he was correcting proofs, he realized that such precision is indiscreet and that the Comtesse Merlin might well be angry. She might tolerate his borrowing a few details from her life story, but would not appreciate his going too far. No one ought to be tempted to *recognize* her in the Marquise de San-Réal, a lesbian who, in a fit of jealousy, finally kills her partner!

Moreover, it is obvious that Balzac did not wish to draw a portrait of the Comtesse Merlin. For this story of love between women, he doubtlessly drew inspiration from a scandal that had just occupied Parisian gossip, especially in writers' circles: the liaison between Marie Dorval and George Sand. Balzac was admirably placed to know all the details, since just when he was writing *La Fille aux yeur d'or* he was putting up Jules Sandeau, George

Sand's ex-lover, to whose revelations he lent a willing ear. So much so that the Marquise de San-Réal is the Comtesse Merlin in certain circumstances of her life, but for one aspect of her behavior, George Sand.

One could multiply examples of this sort. Can one, reading *Le Cabinet des antiques* or *Les Secrets de la Princesse de Cadignan*, guess who was the model for the heroine, the extraordinary Diane de Maufrigneuse, a coquette who plays the ingenue? In his unhappily incomplete edition of the *Comédie humaine*, Albert Prioult points to a curious parallel in this connection: the Duchesse de Maufrigneuse, who was Princess de Cadignan in 1830, was born in 1797 and married in 1814 at seventeen years of age; she is twenty-six when in 1823 she meets the Comte d'Esgrignon, and thirty-six in 1833 when she takes up with d'Arthez; the Marquise, later Duchesse de Castries, was born 8 December 1796 and married in 1816 at the age of twenty; she is twenty-six when she meets Prince Victor de Metternich, and thirty-six when in 1833 she strikes up a relationship with Balzac.

It is also true that the Duchesse de Maufrigneuse greatly resembles the Duchesse de Langeais, of whom Mme de Castries was the prototype. The two heroines of the *Comédie humaine* have the same ethereal and enchanting charm. Both are accomplished actresses, who play the innocent with skillful artlessness. The Duchess de Langeais, to avoid the demands of General de Montriveau, evokes conjugal fidelity, then religious scruples; Montriveau lets himself be deluded and naively says to de Marsay: "The Duchess is an angel of candor." The Duchesse de Maufrigneuse also gives herself angelic airs: "She had hit upon the idea of making herself immaculate"; the word "angel" appears like a leitmotiv ironically describing her all through the novel. These two characters therefore embody the same feminine type. Clearly, Balzac remained haunted by the memory of his emotional relationship with the great lady of the Faubourg Saint-Germain.

But he is careful not to stress the resemblances. Mme de Castries, who remained his friend, could not be allowed to see herself in the character of a dissolute heroine such as the Duchesse de Maufrigneuse: her life, although rather adventuresome, was neither wild nor emancipated. In any case, Balzac is not thinking of her when, near the end of *Le Cabinet des antiques*, the Duchesse de Maufrigneuse reappears disguised as a charming young man: at this point other recollections tempt the author. A variant reveals that this "chevalier" was a "groom" in the prepublication text that appeared in *Le Constitutionnel*. Now it was disguised as a "groom" or a "page" that Caroline Marbouty accompanied Balzac on a trip to Italy in 1836. Like the Duchesse de Maufrigneuse, she carried a riding whip as part of her disguise: the detail is really important. We can also suppose that Balzac is thinking of his escapade with her when elsewhere in the same novel he evokes the sentimental journey of the duchesse and the young Comte d'Esgrignon through the cities of Italy.

But let us beware of establishing the equation "Diane de Maufrigneuse

= the Marquise de Castries + Caroline Marbouty"! The character possesses an autonomous life. We would denature the power and richness of Balzac's creativity if we proposed to reduce it to elementary contaminations. We must allow for an often much more complex alchemy.

The complicated problems confronting a critic in connection with one of the principal characters of the *Comédie humaine* can be clearly demonstrated in the case of Henri de Marsay, who appears in about twenty novels. We recall that until about 1827 Henri de Marsay leads the insouciant life of a dandy and distinguishes himself above all by his amorous conquests; that he then becomes a deputy, a minister, and even prime minister for a short while, and thus appears as one of the most prominent politicians of the July Monarchy.

What strikes us in this character is that he discourages identifications. Mr. Wayne Conner drew up a list of possible prototypes, or at least of individuals of whom Balzac might have been thinking for a given detail, but in vain: this list is so long that it permits absolutely no conclusions. The very name of de Marsay first attracts Mr. Conner's attention: he notes the Comte de Mornay, a dandy, diplomat, and lover of Mademoiselle Mars; the journalist and *viveur* Lautour-Mézeray; the Comte d'Orsay, another famous dandy, and his father Général d'Orsay; another general named Marc-Jean Demarsay, who, under the Restoration, was a liberal deputy. Certain episodes of Henri de Marsay's career bring to his mind Charles de la Battut, the famous Lord L'Arsouille, as well as Lord Seymour, who is sometimes confused with Lord L'Arsouille. But it is clear that Balzac could not have had all these individuals in mind. That he borrowed details here and there is obvious. But the essential element remains his secret.

This essential element lies in the extraordinary portrait of Henri de Marsay that we find in *La Fille aux yeux d'or*. Henri de Marsay, the most seductive and the most formidable of libertines, is a terribly powerful man because he takes nothing seriously: "He believed neither in men nor in women, neither in God nor in the devil." This skepticism guarantees him control over himself, over men, and over things. He is drunk with this power, which is the result of his genius: "I experience an immense pleasure in escaping from the stupid jurisdiction of the masses who never know what they want or what they are made to want, who mistake the means for the ends, who adore and curse, build and destroy! What happiness to impose emotions on them and not submit to theirs, to dominate them and never obey them! If one can be proud of something, should it not be of something acquired by oneself, of which we are at once the cause, the effect, the principle, and the result?" (FYO, 1099).

Whom does this disturbing hero resemble? He resemble another Balzacian character who does not appear in the *Etudes de moeurs*, but rather in the *Etudes philosophiques*, and who moreover belongs to European mythology: Don Juan. Or at least the Don Juan whom, five years before *La Fille aux yeux d'or*, Balzac had incarnated in *L'Elixir de longue vie:* "Master of life's illusions, he launched himself into it when he was young and handsome, disdaining the world but seizing it . . . wherever he went, he devoured everything shamelessly, seeking a possessive love, an oriental love . . . A model of grace and nobility, possessed of a seductive spirit, he went only as far as he wished to be led . . . He made light of everything. His life was a mocking that enveloped men, things, institutions, and ideas" (ELV, 485–87).

Yes, this Don Juan is indeed the sketch of Henri de Marsay, but a sketch still full of the impurities of the myth. It was renewed by Balzac, and from it was born a character who will take his place in the society of the Restoration and of the July Monarchy. But we must go still further back. Balzac carried the idea of this human type in himself. If, before creating Henri de Marsay in 1835, he created Don Juan in 1830, it was because as of his twentieth year, he had himself been haunted by a dream of absolute power. "I will force all men to obey me, all women to love me," he confided at that time to one of his old friends from Vendôme: at that moment he naively counted on the power of magnetism whose secrets he was trying to penetrate. Life disappointed him. He thought for a moment that he would make his way in politics and tried to play the character of Henri de Marsay even before he imagined him. But too many elements were lacking and in particular the physical presence that is the basis of his hero's triumphs. He therefore took a kind of literary revenge on life when he molded a character endowed with the attractions that he so cruelly regretted not possessing himself.

Thus, in the case of Henri de Marsay the search for real prototypes would be, in our opinion, an error. We must begin with Balzac himself. Balzac refashioned an ancient myth to his own need; and we get de Marsay via Don Juan.

A final example will lead us again to Balzac himself, and will certainly be sufficiently probing to permit us to discover another of his secrets: it is the example of Athanase Granson, in *La Vieille Fille*. Naturally we do not intend to rediscover the elementary truth that Balzac, a realistic novelist, is also the most personal of all the romantic writers. Everybody knows that he portrayed himself or that he placed details from his own life in Félix de Vandenesse, in Rastignac, in Rubempré, in Raphaël de Valentin, in Albert Savarus, in David Séchard and in Général de Montriveau. All these characters, to repeat a phrase of Pierre Abraham's are "phantoms in the mirror": Athanase Granson is one of them, as is already known.

We think, nevertheless, that we are in a position to contribute a rather striking detail to the point. Here again, it is a matter of reading the text, of examining it closely, and even of reading between the lines. We then realize that Balzac had certain intentions that escape the hasty or ignorant reader. It is indispensable, in this connection, to examine a certain fragment very closely.

Balzac observes that Athanase, in love with the old maid, should have denied his liberal ideas and embraced the monarchist cause in order to please her. Unfortunately Athanase "was ignorant of the fact that at the age of thirty-six, when a man has judged other men, their social relationships and self-interest, the opinions to which he had at first sacrificed his future must be modified" (VF, 879). Now this is a very strange sentence. Athanase is twenty-three years old: why should he preoccupy himself with knowing how a man of thirty-six should act? But Balzac himself is precisely thirty-six years old when he writes this sentence, and it is of himself that he is thinking. He is conscious of having reached that stage of political maturity and practical wisdom without which one cannot make a place for oneself in a stable society. Thirteen or fourteen years earlier, he took fire, like Athanase, at the word *liberty*, which he now declares to be so "badly defined." Athanase is the young man whom Balzac had been at the age of noble impatience and revolt. But the Balzac of a more mature age is aware of having developed as do "truly superior men" by becoming the champion of egoism and of social conservatism. He therefore introduces into this text, as if for himself, an implicit justificatiion of his own conduct, but so discreetly, in fact, that few readers have noticed it. It is rather curious to see a creator deposit in his work a secret that he will share only with faithful readers patient enough to enter into the intimacy of his conscience and his art.

And so, beginning with insignificant details, entirely foreign to the writer who gathered them from everyday reality in passing and almost haphazardly, we encounter his deepest preoccupations; these are all connected, when examined carefully, to his will to power: for it is indeed in this eternally frustrated and continually exasperated will to power that we believe Balzac's philosophy can be summed up. We have thus witnessed the work of that insatiable and indefatigable spider, ceaselessly creating new architectural patterns, and which, unsatisfied with the prey offered by the spectacle of the world, often nourishes itself on its own bodily substance.

Notes

1. [Ed. note: The "Chouannerie" was a movement of revolt in the western regions of France against the central government of the First Republic. Balzac's letter to the general can be most conveniently consulted in *H. de Balzac: Correspondance*, ed. Roger Pierrot (Paris: Garnier, 1960), 1, 347–49. Unless otherwise specified, references in the text are to the new Pléiade edition of the *Comédie humaine*.]

2. [Ed. note: Baron Frédéric de Nucingen appears in many novels, but most prominently in *Splendeurs et misères des courtisanes* and *La Maison Nucingen*.]

3. [Ed. note: The reference is to Wayne Conner, "La Composition de *La Fille aux yeux d'or*," *Revue d'histoire littéraire de la France* 56 (1956): 535–47.]

[Portraiture and Character in *La Torpille*]

Jean Pommier*

If I. Jarblum is to be believed, "all prejudice against the Jews disappears as soon as a Jewess enters the scene" in Balzac.[1] Now Esther is Jewish through her mother: we do not know her father.[2] Do the manuscript and proofs of *César Birotteau* tell us anything in this connection? Esther is supposed to be the worthy daughter of Maxime de Trailles, who emerged so hale and hearty from orgies "that debauchery seemed to be his very food."[3]

Six years before writing *La Torpille,* the author of *Louis Lambert* had created the figure of Pauline de Villenoix, the granddaughter of a Jew and a Catholic woman: "Her features offered the characteristics of Jewish beauty in its greatest purity, those oval lines . . . that . . . force the imagination to think of the Orient and the unchanging blue of its sky. She had lovely black eyes . . . a biblical innocence suffused her brow."[4] Later, Balzac will compete in the art of female portraiture with Theophile Gautier. We refer to the latter's article "Mademoiselle Falcon" (*Le Figaro,* 5 January 1838);[5] Balzac recalled it to portray Coralie,[6] and, perhaps, before her, Esther. The peculiarities of the Hebraic type [according to Gautier] "are long faces . . . red lips . . . eyes with heavy eyelids circled lightly with blue and with a luminous center[7]; a languid glance full of sunlight in which all the ardor of the orient gleamed . . . Poetry that carries one a thousand leagues away from our own little world." This, Gautier notes, is a type adopted by the painter Lehmann, creator of *La Fille de Jephté pleurant sa virginité sur les montagnes* (Jephtés daughter mourning her virginity on the mountains) shown in 1837. And in fact, under her turban, Mlle Falcon "entirely resembles one of the companions of Jephté's daughter, if not Jephté's daughter herself." It is rather remarkable that Balzac, a few pages after the portrait of Esther, should also allude to "the scene of Jephté on the mountain" (Werdet, 438). And of course we also remember Vigny's poem (1822).[8]

In Balzac, description extends itself so as not to leave unrevealed any quality of appearance, temperament, or race. The art and science of the novelist compete in this esthetic and naturalistic composition of which the author was very proud, if we are to judge by a passage written a few months later:[9] "The public is unaware of the efforts of conception an author undertakes when pursuing truth in all its consequences, and of how many slowly acquired observations one must bury in apparently unimportant expressions that will impress one man in a thousand. There are certain sentences in certain portraits, that of La Torpille for example, that have cost a whole night's work, the reading of several volumes, and that perhaps raise important scientific questions." And here Balzac reproduces a page of his third

*Reprinted and translated by permission from *L'Invention et l'écriture dans 'La Torpille' d'Honoré de Balzac* (*Creativity and Composition in Honoré de Balzac's 'The Eel'*) (Paris and Geneva: Droz, 1957), 62–67.

chapter, the one that raises the "problem of race."[10] We know that Stendhal didn't hesitate to retouch his published prose; there are some kinds of *marginalia* that drive publishers to despair. Balzac also had that mania: in this case, in addition to two variants that are justified in the Extract,[11] he adds an aberrant reading in his corrections. Instead of "several generations hardly reform the instincts . . ." we read in the *Préface:* "generations pass before the reform of the . . ." For an analysis of this transformation, we refer the reader to a previous article.[12] And as for the suppressed expressions (or rather the surprising expressions), the reader will be able to amuse himself by seeing them in their successive contexts, to which we will return.[13]

Despite slate-grey eyes which become blue-black in the light (Werdet, 433), Esther should not be thought to have dark coloring. She had, and as abundantly as the Duchess of Berry,[14] "admirable blond hair." (Werdet, 424). Blond as that of Madame Guidoboni-Visconti, Balzac's mistress, as that of the Madeleine, as that of Venus born of that element whose undulations, whose streaming, whose enveloping caresses are copied by La Torpille.

Why, thereupon, must a contradictory recollection arise? Was Balzac very reluctant to justify one of his characters, Genestas, falling in love with a Polish Jewess? "The little thing was seventeen, white as snow, with velvet eyes, lashes as black as rat tails, and thick, shining hair that invited touching."[15] In a word, Judith was "as beautiful as a Jewess, when she keeps herself clean and *is not blond* . . ."[16] Was this an expression of [Balzac's] bitterness, at that moment, against the Titian blondness of Mme de Castries? No, the officer's ethnic observation is more deep seated, and fifteen years later, Balzac will express the same idea in a different form, apropos of Noémi Magus, "beautiful as are all Jewesses when the Asiatic type reappears purely and nobly in them."[17]

And so the composite of 1838 quickly disintegrates. As of 1839 another figure emerges from Balzac's hands, one who recalls Esther a bit too closely. Coralie "was the kind of girl who can deliberately fascinate men."[18] She "exhibited the sublime type of the Jewish face . . . with a mouth as red as a pomegranate, a chin as fine as the edge of a goblet . . . a languid glance in which the heat of the desert sometimes gleamed. Eyes deeply shadowed by an olive-colored circle . . ." But the singularity—should I say the anomaly?—of the blond hair has disappeared: Coralie's dark brow was "crowned with two ebony bands, on which the light gleamed as on varnish." The Jewess has returned to her physical type. Jewess? But Coralie seems Christian, since she is reconciled with the church before dying.[19] Was this, asks I. Jarblum, "a way of discreetly telling us that Coralie's mother had a Jewish lover?"[20]

As for Esther, she has not changed, it would appear, when Giroudeau, in November 1842 calls her "beautiful as an Englishwoman."[21] What happens next? When Balzac, a few months later, reissues *La Torpille*, he doesn't touch Esther's blond hair, and yet you will not see it again. The novelist has another image in mind; the Duchesse de Berry's rival is so well forgotten that her double, so to speak, has become her opposite. This is the meaning of the episode where Nucingen, who is looking for Esther, refuses the blond English girl with blue eyes. He wants "some black."[22] Esther II, in effect, reproduces the Hebraic type of Coralie. "The blue-black of her fine hair[23] was set off by some camellias." Balzac has used an image from one of Lucien's sonnets: "I love to see . . white camellias / In the black hair of a beautiful young woman."[24]

This metamorphosis did not escape Pierre Abraham, who tried to make it fit his system. "The lamentable little prostitute who excites our pity . . . that tender victim, will be blond. As soon as she falls victim to Rubempré's love and is madly desired . . . by Nucingen, she acquires that blackness of hair, the necessary condition for the élan of Balzac the man to sustain the art of Balzac the writer in the depiction and articulation of male desire."[25] The explanation will hardly do, for in the first place Balzac the man ardently desired and in fact possessed blonds (in La Torpille itself, as we have pointed out, the portrait of the crumpled-up, overwhelmed young woman reveals the lust of the author); and in the second place the "little prostitute" appears at the ball as a "respectable woman." Months before, with her aristocratic hairdo and the perfection of her blond beauty, she had caught the heart of Lucien, from whom she hides her past: it is for her that he engages in that "restless search" at the Opera Ball; when he has lost her, he loses all taste for life. What more could he have done for black hair? (See A. Billy, Vie de Balzac [Paris: Flammarion, 1944], vol. 1, 204–5.)

What instead must be noted is the obsession with an ethnic type that Balzac admired for itself and for its mysterious correspondence (taking this word in its Baudelairian sense) with that other reflection of the Orient, the Bible. This book "had determined the destiny" of Louis Lambert, whose childhood was smitten "with the exotic attractions that abound in these oriental poems,"[26] well before he conceived his youthful, ardent passion for Pauline de Villenoix. In the same way there opens, in the heart of an old Israelite, a spring fed by all sorts of memories; to "that iron-bound coffer called Nucingen" Esther belatedly offers the poetic genius of her race. How could he not have been overwhelmed by the "sublime Jewish face that he said was the pic'chuh of the Pipple?"[27]

Is this persistence of an image not, so to speak, the reverse side of a pause in inventiveness, when the artist goes back over a first sketch? In any case, the result for Lucien is that he goes from one Jewess to another, as if the world of amusement offered no other choices. (Toward 1840, Baudelaire's first mistress was, they say, a Jewess named Sarah). I. Jarblum inquires if there were more Jewesses than Christians among prostitutes.[28] Balzac directs our attention toward women from Normandy, who, according to a "scholarly doctor" constituted a third of the contingent.[29]

Also born of a Scottish mother named Sarah, the prostitute of the Cité who, in Les Mystères de Paris (The Mysteries of Paris) answers to the name of "La Goualeuse" (The Singer), and of "Fleur-de-Marie" (The Virgin), is not without connections to Esther I.[30] She, too, aspires to an honest life, but more disinterestedly than La Torpille. She also receives an education (through her father, who has rediscovered her). Later, she falls in love with, and is loved by, a young nobleman; not wishing—like a latter-day Marion—to marry him because of her past, she becomes a nun.[31] We touch, we graze the alternate pattern. Softer and less electric, Fleur-de-Marie is, at the beginning of the *Mystères*, about the same age as Balzac's heroine. Will not this sixteen-year-old child, with "large, blue eyes," "a fine, straight nose" and "magnificent ash-blond hair,"[32] make Balzac feel that his Torpille has been stolen from him? It would be piquant to attribute Esther's transformation to the distaste of an author for a character only too well used by a popular rival; and even—who knows—to his concern with avoiding the accusation of imitating his imitator.[33]

Notes

1. *Balzac et la femme étrangère* (Balzac and foreign women) (Paris: Boccard, 1930), 71.

2. [Ed. note: The character analyzed in this article is Esther Gobseck, nicknamed "La Torpille" (The Eel), who has a rather checkered life in the various episodes of the *Comédie humaine*. The fragment in question here was first published under the title of "La Torpille"; it later became the opening section of *Splendeurs et misères des courtisanes*. Pommier's footnotes refer to the 1838 Werdet edition of this text, to the set of proofs now in the Lovenjoul Collection at the Institut de France and, for other novels by Balzac, to the first Pléiade edition.]

3. Cited by Dr. F. Lotte, *Dictionnaire biographique*, (Paris: José Corti, 1952), 601.

4. *Louis Lambert,* ed. M. Bouteron and J. Pommier (Paris: José Corti, 1954), 141. We are quoting the manuscript here; "black" later disappeared.

5. Collected in *Portraits contemporains* (Paris: Charpentier, 1874), 396–98.

6. See *Illusions perdues*, 333, Note 1, on these portraits of the most beautiful actresses of Paris, which appeared in *Le Figaro* (1837–38). See also Spoelberch de Lovenjoul, *Histoire des oeuvres de Théophile Gautier* (Paris: Charpentier, 1887), 1, 187–89, for the analogies between the portrait of Mlle Georges and that of Camille Maupin in *Béatrix*. [Ed. note: Coralie was an actress and courtesan, and mistress of Lucien de Rubempré in *Illusions perdues*.]

7. Is it not this "light circle" that Balzac, among other delicate aspects of this part of the face; strains to render?

8. [Ed. note: Alfred de Vigny, "La Fille de Jephté," first poem in the collection *Le Livre Antique*.]

9. *Préface* (February 1839) to *Une Fille d'Eve* (Paris: Souverain, 1839), 28.

10. This Extract runs from "There are only races . . ." to ". . . Esther's Jewish face." (Werdet edition, 1838, 433–35; Pléiade edition, 688–89). See *Précieux autographes d'Honoré de Balzac provenant de son éditeur H. Souverain*, sale of 20 June 1957, catalogue number 174.

11. The first sentence is abridged by supressing its ending (after "fascination"), which returns the text to its state in Proof C (folio 98 recto). In the last sentence, the insertion of "Jewish" before "face" finally reveals the origin of the prototype.

12. In *La Revue des sciences humaines*, April–September 1951, 173–74.

13. [Ed. note: In following the variants of the story through its manuscript states, Pommier records the portrait of Esther Gobseck, which includes references to the "thirty perfections" supposedly sculpted on the walls of Persian harems.]

14. Werdet ed., 431; Balzac is paying court. But here is evidence of yet another candidate:

if Philarète Chasles is to be believed (see C. Pichois, *"Les Vrais "Mémoires" de Philarète Chasles,"* *Revue des sciences humaines,* January–March 1956, 77), the wife of the publisher U. Canel pleased the novelist "by the abundant beauty of her hair, which could cover her entire body." I mention this to lessen our confidence in the designation of models: we have only very few cards in our hand, and we are always turning up the same ones. This is not said to discourage research of this sort, when it is pursued, for example, by Antoine Adam.

15. [Ed. note: Genestas is a Napoleonic soldier who, in *Le Médecin de campagne,* falls in love with, and marries, a Jewish woman in Poland.

16. *Le Médecin de campagne* (Paris: Mame-Delaunay), July 1833, 2, 239.

17. *Le Cousin Pons;* cited by Dr. F. Lotte, *Dictionnaire biographique,* 369.

18. On Esther's "power of fascination," see Werdet edition, 433.

19. *Illusions perdues,* 333, 532.

20. I. Jarblum, *Balzac et la femme étrangère* (Paris: E. de Boccard, 1930), 64–65.

21. *La Rabouilleuse,* Pléiade, 3, 1093.

22. Ruth [Heathcote's] father had been looking for a blond and found a brunette. Here it is the contrary. [Ed. note: The reference is to Ruth Heathcote, heroine of James Fenimore Cooper's novel, *The Wept of Wish-ton-Wish,* which Balzac had read. Pommier is suggesting that Ruth may have been one of the models for Esther Gobseck.]

23. Think also of the "Black hair gleaming like satin" of Josépha Mirah (*La Cousine Bette,* 1846; cited by F. Marceau, *Balzac et son monde* [Paris: Gallimard, 1955], 221).

24. *Splendeurs et misères,* Pléiade, 776, 909; and *Illusions perdues,* 267. One would say that it is a brunette with hell-black hair, to use an 1830 expression, that Charles Huard pictures in the Conard edition. But why are these two illustrations placed *at the beginning* of *Splendeurs et misères?* They violently contradict the blond image that this part of the text imposes on us. The Girl with the Golden Hair [*sic*] also has black hair, having previously been described as ash-blond.

25. *Créatures chez Balzac* (Balzac's creatures), 5th ed. (Paris: Gallimard, 1931), 208–9. [Ed. note: Abraham attempted to establish a system of coordination between physical appearance and character in the *Comédie humaine.*]

26. Bouteron and Pommier, ed., *Louis Lambert,* 10.

27. "Sublime face": the expression is enough for the writer, who will not repeat it. (*Splendeurs et misères*) Pléiade, 718.)

28. *Balzac et la femme étrangère,* 53. There is no other information on our subject in this work, nor in that of Raphaël Valensi, "Les Juifs dans l'oeuvre de Balzac" (*Le Monde juif,* June 1950), nor in F. Marceau, *Balzac et son monde* (Paris: Gallimard, 1955), 372–74.

29. *La Vieille Fille,* Pléiade, 4, 243.

30. [Ed. note: *Les Mystères de Paris* was an epic series written by Balzac's friend and rival, Eugène Sue.]

31. [Ed. note: The reference is to Victor Hugo's play *Marion Delorme,* in which an ex-prostitute conceals her past from her true lover.]

32. *Les Mystères de Paris, Première série,* 26.

33. It is true that the type represented by Esther I seems to have persisted; we see it even after the publication of the *Mystères de Paris, Première série.* But we must not draw too significant a conclusion from a routine and cursive comparison: "as beautiful as an Englishwoman." In all probability, that Englishwoman was not *visualized* as a brunette.

[The Three Dimensions of Balzac's Paris]

Pierre Citron*

The cartography of physical, social, and spiritual Paris cannot satisfy Balzac, however much pleasure he takes in sketching it, because the maps are two-dimensional. One can only look at them from the exterior, never enter into them. Everything is transformed when the third dimension intervenes: spatial sense is one of the dominant qualities of the Balzacian imagination. Real Paris is felt not in light and shadow nor in colors, but in the form of real and figurative masses: "In Paris, what first seizes our attention is mass: the luxury of the shops, the height of the buildings, the dense traffic of the carriages, above all the continual contrasts between extreme luxury and extreme poverty."[1] Such is the first impression Paris makes on Lucien de Rubempré—analagous to impressions made on many others from Rousseau on,[2] but different from the others precisely in this sense of mass. And like Hugo, Balzac has a sense of the subterranean and architectural thickness of Paris: nothing is foreign to him, not the geological strata beneath the quarries of Montmartre[3] with its antediluvian carcasses,[4] nor the Conciergerie buried under the Palace of Justice,[5] nor the caverns under the Seine, nor the Catacombs.[6]

Physical Parisian space, in itself more or less secondary in Balzac's work, is paralleled by another, much more important fictional space—the area of what Balzac calls "social nature" that he opposes to nature itself—that is, to the ensemble of material realities: "Like nature itself, this social reality is involved with insects, with ephemeral flowers, with trifling incidents, but it also throws fire and flame from its eternal crater."[7]

It is sometimes possible to isolate this fictional space. It is to be distinguished from provincial space first of all by its altitude. The familiar expression "to go up to Paris" has real meaning in the Balzacian universe. The preface to *Le Cabinet des antiques* evokes "the three great ascentional movements to Paris, those of Nobility, Wealth, and Talent," and also their ebbing, "the catastrophes that thrust families from the capital back into the provinces."[8] The contrast is described in detail in the preface to *Eugénie Grandet*, in which the atmosphere of Paris "where a *simoun* blows that carries off fortunes and breaks hearts" is contrasted to "the slow action of the provincial *sirocco*, which undoes the greatest courage, loosens fibers, and removes *acuteness* from passions."[9] In the provinces, adds Balzac, "there is neither contrast nor relief." One cannot mark any more clearly what distinguishes Paris from the provinces: Parisian space has an additional dimension. Everything exists in relief, whereas the provinces are flat. In *Le Cabinet des antiques* the opposition is clear between "the limited horizon of the prov-

*Translated and reprinted by permission from *La Poésie de Paris dans la littérature française de Rousseau à Baudelaire* (The poetry of Paris in French literature from Rousseau to Baudelaire) (Paris: Editions de Minuit, 1961), 211–18.

inces and the enormous world of Paris"[10]: *horizon* suggests a line delimiting a flat country, *enormous* implies a mass. These are precisely the hierarchies and varieties that distinguish Paris from the leveling and the platitude of the provinces. Here is that platitude in the domain of ideas: "In the provinces one is not permitted to be original: that would be to have ideas that are not understood by others, and what is wanted there is similarity of mind as well as of custom." And here it is in the feminine hierarchy: "In Paris, there are several types of women: the duchess and the financier's wife, the ambassador's wife and the consul's wife, the minister's wife and the ex-minister's wife, the proper lady of the Right Bank and her counterpart of the Left Bank; but in the provinces, there is only one woman, and that poor woman is the provincial woman."[11] Whence her lack of agility, which distinguishes her from the Parisian woman: she is "used to moving in a sphere without irregularities, without transitions."[12] Once again, we think of du Lorens, who also made of Paris, in contrast to the provinces, a fluid three-dimensional mass in which the Parisian bathed: " One can only swim in profound waters."[13]

This geometry returns frequently in the conceptual Parisian space created by Balzac. Bohemia is defined in *Béatrix* as "one of the districts of the moral topography of Paris"[14] (Balzac says *moral* in the sense of *figured*, but he is really speaking of a social topography), and in *Un Prince de la Bohème*, as a "microcosm."[15] When the Duchesse de Langeais says to Mme de Beauséant: "The world is a mudhole, let us try to stay on the heights,"[16] we have again a spatial image of the incorporeal universe. And it is in a purely social atmospheric space that de Marsay, for the guidance of Savinien de Portenduère, situates the career of Victurnien d'Esgrignon: "Alas, his life was like a rocket. He rose as high as the Duchesse de Maufrigneuse, and he fell back into his native town."[17]

Occasionally this figurative Paris is somehow the "double" of the other; it possesses a sky as well as a subterranean density. Here, in *Le Cousin Pons*, are two schoolfriends, one having become rich, the other poor: "One went through life on the frisky horses of Fortune or on the golden clouds of Success; the other made his underground way through the sewers of Paris, and he bears the marks of it."[18] The comparison is banal. The feeling of that social space can be found in the different categories of society: Suzanne du Val-Noble, who goes to Paris to make herself a career as a woman of easy virtue, remains "in the loftiest regions of amorous intrigue."[19] It even happens that the intellectual and the social are confused in the same space, as we have seen the social and the physical mixed together: "Solid footing is the general law of the different social spheres. Only exceptional natures who are not cowed by the presence of their superiors, those who make their place among their true peers, like to climb the heights . . ."[20] It is a naively monarchist conception of an aristocracy of the soul and the mind mixing with that of blood and power. Another spatial image occurs when Bixiou, the archetypical Parisian, says to Lousteau: "You are lowering yourself down into the *third subcellar* of the social theater."[21] The same expression occurs in *La*

Cousine Bette, when Mme Nourrisson appears to Victorin Hulot as "that horrible mysterious woman, called up from a nest of spies, just as, at the wave of a fairy wand in a ballet, a monster rises from the third subcellar of the Opera."[22] The traditional image of the theater takes on another dimension; Balzac infuses new life into hackneyed clichés when he says of newcomers to Paris: "Everything serves them as ladders to climb onto the stage; but since everything wears out, even the rungs of stepladders, beginners in all professions no longer know what wood to use."[23]

The intellectual substance that fills this figurative space is not identical for everyone—just as the geography of Paris varies with its inhabitants. Balzac and his strongest heroes, who know it intimately, give considerable density to the "contents" of Paris. For Vautrin, it is the density of the crowd: "One must enter this mass of humanity like a cannonball, or else slip in like an infection," he advises Rastignac.[24] But if a Balzacian hero lacks knowledge and willpower, space loses any point to which he can attach himself. It becomes the "most frightful desert, a paved desert, a lively, thinking, living desert where everything is worse than hostile—indifferent," as Raphaël de Valentin says, who, as we see, mixes the material "paved" world with the living world.[25] It becomes "a strange abyss," as Lucien de Rubempré writes to his sister,[26] and as Dumay, the cashier from Le Havre, says;[27] or, again, it is an "emptiness" like the one in which Wenceslas Steinbock struggles when he arrives in Paris.[28]

One might say that these are simple stylistic figures, which do not imply any global poetic vision. But first of all the style, and particularly the images, even when they are banal, often reveal profound, unconscious intuitions that, without being strictly speaking poetic, contain possibilities of poetry. Then these two spaces, physical and imaginary, whose manifestations we have just pointed out, take on a true poetic value as of the moment when they partially melt into each other.

Balzac, like so many romantics, seeks the essence of the poetry of Paris in a unity that alone provides a correspondence between the body and soul of the city. And, having given up comparing Paris to a living creature, and having abandoned the convention of Paris-Woman and the vision of Paris-Monster, he must have two spaces when he adopts an image of the world—a body-space and a soul-space—in order to account for the natural unity beneath the diversity of appearances. But where Balzac separates himself from the other poets of Paris is that in his case this idea was not born suddenly; it was prepared by long internal work. His poetry arises solely from a mass of observations, experiences, analyses, and details; its intuitive emergence is based upon the thickness of reality, on a multitude of facts whose juxtaposition—which is prosaic—justifies a generalization from which poetry is born.

What may have led Balzac to the idea of a global Parisian space is the feeling that he had very early on of a fundamental relationship between his characters and the apartments, houses, and even neighborhoods where they live. These new and admirable analyses originate in sociological rather than

poetic investigations. This, therefore, is not the place to review them, especially since they refer as frequently to the provinces as to Paris. Let us
merely note that as of 1830 Balzac went beyond the simple assertion of the
conformity of man to his milieu to the degree that the milieu has shaped him;
and that the correspondences he perceives seem at moments to have sources
deeper than material reality. Here is the portrait of Mme Crochard in *Une
Double Famille:* "The pale, wrinkled face of the old woman harmonized with
the darkness of the street and the mildew of the house. Seeing her resting in
her chair, one would have said that she belonged in the house the way a snail
belongs in its brown shell . . . her large grey eyes were as quiet as the street,
and the many wrinkles of her face could be compared to the cracks in the
walls."[29] In *Les Dangers de l'inconduite* (The dangers of misbehavior),[30] the
usurer Gobseck is described in a comparison of the same type: "He and his
house resembled each other. You would have called them the oyster and its
rock." But these metaphors disappear quickly. Already, in the famous portrait of Mme Vauquer, in the opening pages of *Le Père Goriot,* Balzac
substitutes for the juxtaposition of analogous elements a demonstration by
causality: there is "harmony" between the person of the mistress of the
boarding house and her dining room, but the fact is that "her whole person
explains the boarding house."[31] And, in the later novels, Balzac will be
content in general with precise descriptions of the houses in which the action
will take place, without linking them by quasi-irrational correspondences to
the people who inhabit them. A notation like the one concerning the black
clothing of clientless lawyers and physicians, with their "faded seams that
remind one of the tin of mansard roofs"[32] is rather exceptional in his work
after 1835. Was he sensitive to the mocking of his critics? Rather, it would
seem that in his Paris, he instinctively reserved poetry for a general illumination rather than to establish the relief of details. Instead of being focused on
one or another site or milieu, the poetry of Paris is that of a global space in
which are located both the physical city and its social and conceptual hierarchies, closely linked yet not intermixed and even often opposed to each
other; it is to this space that the novelist makes continual reference in order
to portray the Paris of desire, emotion, and self-interest.

The number and variety of these correspondences are perhaps at the
origin of Balzac's feeling for Paris: the material milieu in which he lives and
the human milieu of which he is an intimate part and in which his imagination moves, these two three-dimensional spaces have convergences, intersections, and common areas that create a single global space embracing the
physical and conceptual spheres, with Balzac passing from one to the other
like Lewis Carroll's Alice moving from one side of the mirror to the other, or
like characters in modern science fiction who find themselves, by chance or
calculation, in the fourth dimension. Sometimes the birth of this space is
facilitated by the use of certain terms that, like the key images in the formation of the myth of Paris, serve as the articulation between the physical and
conceptual worlds. When Balzac evokes "Parisian immensity" in the 1839

edition of *Illusions perdues*,[33] does he not give it an allegorical nuance? In *La Fille aux yeux d'or*, Paris is "a vast field continually stirred up by a tempest of self-interest beneath which there swirls a crop of men, more frequently cut down by death than anywhere else but who are reborn as densely as they were before . . ."[34]. The ensemble of the image is figurative; but does not the physical extension of Paris also play its role in this "field"?

But most often, there is no need for pivotal images to move from one reality to the other. The connection is direct. It is a coincidence of spaces that takes the general form of the city. Paris is built in a river basin; "an immense city, at the bottom of a precipice," he had already written in *Le Doigt de Dieu* (The finger of God); "a space surrounded by hills in the midst of which Paris squirms like an infant in its cradle," we read in *Ferragus*.[35] The "valley of plaster" of *Le Père Goriot* is also "filled with real suffering and frequently false joys, and so terribly agitated that something extreme is needed to make any kind of lasting impression."[36] It is also the *basin*—we will return to this image—the *arena*,[37] the *roulette wheel*. These are all images in which the notion of a hollow is associated with that of the movement that takes place within it: the physical and the moral.

This coincidence of spaces, rather vague when it is applied to Paris in general, has a more intense poetic value when it is found in specific aspects of Paris: Balzac here is no longer carried along by the words and images of contemporary poets who use the myth of Paris, but by a direct sensation of reality. We find it first of all in the description of Paris-as-monster, which we have already mentioned, but to which we must now return: "Its garrets, a kind of head full of knowledge and genius; its second floors, happy stomachs; its shops, veritable feet."[38] One might see in this only quaintness, just as there is perhaps only a stylistic effect in the definition of Paris as "an astonishing assemblage of movements, machines, and thoughts."[39] But the overlapping of the two spaces, the smooth movement from the one to the other, are clearer in the note published by the *Revue de Paris* as an appendix to *Ferragus*,[40] in which Balzac expresses his hope of having "succeeded in painting Paris in several of its aspects, by having crisscrossed it, going from the Faubourg Saint-Germain to the Marais, from the street to the boudoir, from the mansion to the garret, from the prostitute to the loving married woman, and from the movement of life to the repose of death . . ." The next year, with *La Fille aux yeux d'or*, this mixture of spaces reaches its greatest intensity: here Balzac describes the hell of Paris using Dante as a model. The different levels are represented as "spheres" or "circles"; the social hierarchy is materialized in a kind of stratification. Moving from a description of the Parisian working class to that of the petty bourgeoisie, Balzac, in order to introduce the reader to this "second Parisian sphere," writes, "Go up one story to the mezzanine; or come down from the garret and stop at the fifth floor; in a word, enter the world of those who have possessions."[41] The localization of wealth according to the floors of buildings is less simplistic here than in *Ferragus;* but it immediately dissolves into the vision of social

Paris as a kind of pyramid in which four levels are superposed: at the base are the workers and shopkeepers, then the petty bourgeoisie, then businessmen and artists, and finally the aristocratic world, where one feels that "air and space are purified."[42]

Far from being fixed by its structure, this figurative universe is one of movement.[43] P. G. Castex has noted the dynamism of all the images in the opening pages of *La Fille aux yeux d'or*.[44] In *Ferragus*, Paris is already "that astonishing assemblage of movement, machines, and thoughts."[45] The mechanical aspect of this movement is better seen in *La Fille aux yeux d'or*. In that novel, Balzac takes up a view expressed by both Mercier and Vigny: "All the needed gears were at hand, ready to engage their slots." Does this involuntary alexandrine verse—"*Pas une dent ne manque à mordre sa rainure;*"—betray the influence of Vigny's *Paris* in which the same metaphor can be found?[46] And further on, he speaks of men who allow themselves to be caught "in the gears of that immense machine" of Parisian business affairs.[47]

But this kind of image does not account for the play of chance in the life of the great city; it lacks the warmth and freedom that are inseparable from any human mass, and above all it forms an impenetrable universe. Now Balzac conceives of Paris most frequently from within; everything happens as if his deepest sensation was that of swimming in a conceptual Paris as in a homogeneous milieu where his imagination moves in all directions; a more or less dense milieu, but a fluid one; or more precisely a mass formed by fluids in motion. One could define Balzac's Paris by its essential specificity: an imaginary space made up of several spaces molded on each other and partially overlapping, whose fluid nature is physically sensed by its great creator, as he moves within it.[48]

Notes

1. *Illusions perdues*, 4, 602. [Ed. note: Except where otherwise noted, Citron's citations are to the first Pléiade edition (Paris: Gallimard, 1935–1965). References are to volume and page numbers.]

2. This juxtaposition is perhaps not fortuitous. Rousseau is the prototype of the provincial genius who comes to Paris. Raphaël de Valentin, in *La Peau de chagrin*, decides on his hotel because he happens to be in a street where Rousseau had lived (9, 90). The name of the Genevan philosopher recurs several times in *Illusions perdues:* Mme de Bargeton pictures to Lucien the "poor sublime Jean-Jacques" attracted by the capital city (4, 587). Further on, Balzac writes: "Losing his illusions about Mme de Bargeton, as Mme de Bargeton lost hers about him, the poor young man, whose destiny resembled that of J. J. Rousseau, imitated him on this point: he was fascinated by Mme d'Espard" (4, 619). The bookdealer Doguereau flatters Lucien in his attic: "This, my good sir, is the way Jean-Jacques lived, and you resemble him in more than one way" (4, 643). D'Arthez "often ate, like Rousseau, bread and cherries, but without Theresa" (4, 648). And, when Lucien thinks of suicide, Balzac evokes the suicide of Rousseau (4, 1013).

3. *La Peau de chagrin*, 9, 29.

4. *Splendeurs et misères*, 5, 928.

5. Ibid., 927.

6. *Melmoth réconcilié*, see p. 230; also see p. 227.

7. *La Fille aux yeux d'or*, 5, 255–56. In the same way, Molineux is "a grotesque small investor, who exists only in Paris, just as a certain lichen grows only in Iceland." He belongs to "a compound nature, to an animo-vegetal domain that a latter-day Mercier could put together with cryptograms that grow, flower, and die on, in or beneath the chalky walls of various strange and unwholesome houses." *César Birotteau*, 5, 391).

8. *Le Cabinet des antiques*, ed. Castex, 245–46.

9. *Eugénie Grandet*, 11, 200.

10. *Le Cabinet des antiques*, 4, 375.

11. *La Muse du département*, 4, 70.

12. Ibid, 4, 74. The same idea can be found, expressed in a less imagistic way, in the preface of April 1839 to *Un Grand Homme de province à Paris:* "Provincial talent is opposed by provincial life, whose monotony makes any imaginative man aspire to the dangers of Parisian life." (*Illusions perdues*, ed. A. Adam, 763).

13. [Ed. note: The reference is to the *Satires* of Jacques du Lorens, first published in 1624.]

14. 2, 586.

15. 6, 823.

16. *Le Père Goriot*, 2, 911.

17. *Ursule Mirouet*, 3, 357.

18. 6, 664.

19. *La Vieille Fille*, 4, 243.

20. *Le Cousin Pons*, 6, 670.

21. *La Muse du département*, 4, 165.

22. 6, 463.

23. *Le Cousin Pons*, 6, 665.

24. *Le Père Goriot*, 2, 936.

25. *La Peau de chagrin*, 9, 87.

26. *Illusions perdues*, 4, 629. Lucien is described as being "attracted by the bottomless pits of Paris" (735). Balzac insisted on this idea: in the preface to *Un Grand Homme de province à Paris*, he wrote much the same thing about the attraction the capital exerts over Lucien: "The depths have their attraction" (*Illusions perdues*, ed. A. Adam, 763). And thinking again of the way writers are swallowed up by Paris, he cries out in a February 1849 letter to Laurent-Jan: "What a bottomless pit is present-day Paris . . ." (*Corréspondance*, ed. Ducourneau, 490).

27. *Modest Mignon*, 1, 480.

28. *La Cousine Bette*, 6, 191.

29. 1, 927.

30. This work became *Gobseck;* the cited text is 2, 625.

31. 2, 852.

32. *Le Cousin Pons*, 6, 664.

33. A variant given on p. 805 of the edition by A. Adam. Balzac then made a correction: "The desert of Paris" (4, 651).

34. 5, 255.

35. 5, 119.

36. 2, 847.

37. *Ferragus*, 5, 233.

38. Ibid., 5, 18.

39. Ibid., 5, 19.

40. Reproduced by P. G. Castex as an appendix to his edition of *L'Histoire des Treize*.

41. 5, 260.

42. 5, 265.

43. 6, 664.

44. Introduction to *La Fille aux yeux d'or*, Garnier edition of *L'Histoire des Treize*, 367.

45. 5, 19.

46. 5, T. 1, 271.

47. 5, 262 and 264. We also note, in the introduction to the *Etudes de moeurs au XIXe siècle* signed by Davin, this sentence about Paris: "Here true feelings are the exception and are broken by the play of self-interest, crushed in the gears of this mechanical world."

48. On the forms that consistency of the universe takes in the imagination, see G. Bachelard, *L'Eau et les rêves* (Water and Dreams) (Paris: Jose Corti, 1942), 1–2.

[Balzac's Esthetics]   Pierre Laubriet*

If we reflect again, after having tried to examine and analyze the movement of Balzac's thought the way he himself observed the movement of Parisians, on the definition he proposed of esthetics—that is, of a system of general laws that facilitate the production of Beauty—it is impossible for us to deny the existence of a Balzacian esthetics, clearly apprehended and consciously elaborated by the novelist. "All great poets naturally and inevitably become critics," Baudelaire will say, ". . . a crisis inevitably occurs in which they wish to reflect upon their art, uncover the obscure laws by virtue of which they have produced, and draw from that study a series of precepts whose divine purpose is infallibility in poetic production."[1] Balzac experienced that need, conducted that study, and attempted to work out an infallible method of novelistic creation.

Balzac sought to determine the nature of literary Truth, which he distinguished from the truth of daily experience, and which he discovered was governed by laws one could not violate. Literary truth must be subjected to requirements of verisimilitude and unity that nature is unaware of: if the facts of reality impose themselves by their very existence, the artistic fact imposes itself only through the aforementioned conditions. Moreover, it must reveal what is only latent in the truth of nature. It is at once richer and more systematized. Moving beyond art, or rather attaching art to the world of which it wishes to be the image, Balzac rises to the heights of metaphysics. He possessed a personal world view, whose essential elements appeared very early in his mind, and which he only gradually completed and clarified—a system that derived both from an absolute materialism (since it

*Translated and reprinted by permission from *L'Intelligence de l'art chez Balzac* (The understanding of art in Balzac's works) (Paris: Didier, 1961), 515–20.

bases a world both material and spiritual on the secret, complicated play of physical and chemical forces) and from a certain spiritualism (since it seems to consider that such forces emanate from a divine center—forces that gradually acquire substance). Whatever be the label that the system merits, it is surely the expression of an inextinguishable desire for a total explanation of the universe and of a pressing need for unity. Now art appeared to Balzac to be the way to explain, by re-creation, the unity of the world. Thus he wished to endow his esthetics with universal value. The laws that he discovered are surely valid for all forms of literary art, and indeed for all forms of the arts. According to them he judges, generally quite accurately, the productions of writers, painters, sculptors, and musicians. He also tries to observe their fundamental requirements in his own creativity. Or rather, one might say that he bends his creativity to their imperatives; he makes the novel into a genre capable of responding to them completely.

Esthetically based on a monistic philosophy, the novel must reflect the unity of the world and consequently express the world in its totality. The reality that it reproduces is not limited to mere phenomena, but includes everything that escapes the senses and logical intelligence. That reality offers three stages, which the novel in its turn must present, addressing itself to effects, causes, and principles. It paints the whole story of life, it takes apart its mechanism, it explains its functioning and its laws. It can be seen as richer than life itself, of which we generally know only the surface manifestations, whether concerning individuals or events. The Balzacian novel, perpetually mixing the three levels of reality, exposing "the secrets of the game," gives the illusion of plenitude. It thus enters paths that lead it away from any objective realism: it is as symbolist as it is realist, its reality being entirely figurative. The individual is a type, the event is a symbol, the novel is a myth. Art is consequently choice and concentration, the idealization and spiritualization of nature—veritable laws, precisely like verisimilitude and unity, of an esthetics that aims at universality.

Just as he reflected upon the most general and necessary bases of art, Balzac also considered its purposes. He discovered the two traditional ones: pleasure and instruction, but he seems to insist on the latter. He systematically rejected gratuitous art: the task of art is to teach men to know themselves and the world in its surface and buried realities. However, he does not wish to transform the novelist into a schoolmaster, nor impose on the mind any vision of the world or any system of thought whose existence is affirmed a priori. Nor is art aimed at certain ends. Balzac did not fail to present in his novels a political, social, religious, philosophical, and esthetic system: that is of course true, but he claims to draw his system from facts and not impose it artificially. He seeks to base it upon truth by deducing it from principles that he tries to establish as universally valid; above all, even if one does not forgive him his illusion, he has the honesty of not forcing reality into his system. If he warns us that it would be preferable to establish a world according to his principles, he nevertheless paints the world as it is. He reproduces life in its ugliness as well as in its beauty; by itself the portrait is enough to make us take sides. Esthetics is not intentionally moralistic, but is intrinsically so: by taking the totality of life as its object, it obliges itself to seek sense in life and to judge it.

Balzac chose the novel as the instrument of this esthetic because it alone could satisfy all the latter's requirements. Profiting from the lessons of his predecessors and his contemporaries, but moving beyond them, Balzac creates a new literary genre by building a theory of narrative form broad enough to include within itself all other genres: it is at once epic, short story, drama, history, poem, and essay.[2] It will even include other areas of intellectual activity. Forced by its ambitions to be universal, the novel appeals to science: it draws from science facts and explanatory hypotheses. It becomes an area of experimentation; it tends to borrow from science the rigor of its reasoning and the infallibility of its conclusions. Balzac perceives close correspondences between esthetics and science; he seeks to be a scholar as much as an artist, or rather he envisages the artist as being a particular kind of scholar. However, far from subordinating the novel to science, it is science that he places at the service of the novel; science is an auxiliary of esthetics, the accuracy of whose laws it confirms. Establishing, moreover, close ties among the arts, relying on identity of material and similarity of technique except for the transpositions necessitated by each art, to satisfy his need to make of literary art a total art, Balzac endeavors to enrich it by appealing to productions, techniques, sensations, and emotions created by the other arts. There is thus no domain of human activity that escapes literary art. It is archetypical art, and has become so thanks to the purposes of Balzacian esthetics, which aims to be an esthetics of totality.

Such a position obliged Balzac to reject all schools, adherence to a school seeming to him to be a limitation, especially since schools interest themselves only in a single aspect of the world.[3] Thus he is opposed to them all: the sentence he wrote to his sister concerning his resistance to death is applicable here: "I belong to the opposition that is called Life."[4] Now life is neither romantic, nor classic, nor realist, nor naturalist, nor symbolist; it is everything at once. At the beginning of his article on *La Chartreuse de Parme* (*The Charterhouse of Parma*), after having defined the two great currents of literary art, which he calls the literature of ideas and the literature of images, Balzac declares that there exists a third kind of literature: literary eclecticism. "Certain 'complete' individuals," he writes, "certain 'two-headed' intelligences, encompass everything, desire lyricism and action, the drama and the ode, and believe that perfection requires a total view of things. This school, which would be *Literary Eclecticism*, requires the representation of the world as it is: the images and the ideas, the idea in the image or the image in the idea, movement and revery."[5] And after having assigned to various writers their place in the first two schools, he declares: "As for me, I place myself under the banner of Literary Eclecticism," giving as his reason that "the introduction of the dramatic element, of the image, of the tableau, of description, of dialogue, seems to [him] indispensable in modern literature."[6]

Balzac had a clear sense of his own originality, because he was about the only one to belong to this school: he includes Walter Scott in it, but we know how he criticized him and how superior to Scott he felt, because he, Balzac, knew how to portray the passions[7] and how to make his work into a totality.[8] He defined himself with precision: just as his novels aim to be the representation of all aspects of the world, so his esthetic theory aims at being the synthesis of the diverse elements of all existing theories, in principle as well as application—but a synthesis created with discernment, eliminating all that is incompatible with the great generative principles of Beauty (verisimilitude, unity, universality, the spiritualization of nature), and adopting everything that confirms them. Balzac allows us to witness the work of an artist who wishes to employ every means of reaching perfection. He had always intended this; need we recall the remark of Vandenesse in *Le Lys dans la vallée*, which seems so much like an intimate confession: "I was therefore exacting without realizing it, like those who, without being able to practice an art, immediately imagine its ideal."[9] The proud dreams of his literary beginnings are without doubt the signs of an ideal already present in his mind and which he will work for ten years to attain: his esthetic is the instrument that he succeeds in forging so as to accomplish this ascension. He thus fulfilled the wish of Louis Lambert, who required in a work of art "novelty of thought as much as of form."[10] The originality of his esthetics entailed the originality of his work.

This is not to say that Balzac worked in absolute intellectual isolation. Open to all currents of ideas, curious about all the manifestations of the human spirit, avid to possess the most varied knowledge, he never stopped reading, looking, and listening. Not that he was a cultural dilettante, or a scholar in his study; his ambition was to crack open the enigma of man and of the world. Thus, dissatisfied with traditional explanations, he addressed himself especially to the two branches of knowledge that in his day seemed most likely to bring new solutions: the psychic sciences (still all encumbered with metaphysics), and natural history (mixed with archaeology, anthropology, and sociology). The study of these sciences led him to discover methods of investigation and explanation that he will transpose into the domain of literary art, as well as original novelistic material. The psychic sciences introduced and confirmed in him the idea that reality is multifaceted, and contributed to endowing his work with its symbolism as well as with the enriching principle of correspondences. The natural sciences accustomed him to the rigor of observation, experiment, and reasoning. They led him into the temptation of seeking absolute formulas for art. In a word, he learned through them the dream of an esthetics of perfection, containing and dominating the various values of the two great means of knowledge: deduction and intuition.

However we consider Balzac's esthetic thought, we always find our-selves facing an attempt at synthesis. Certain of his contemporaries were already struck by this. George Sand has perhaps best expressed it in *Autour de la table* (Around the dinner table), where, after having defined his novels as "a mirror in which fantasy has taken hold of reality," she catches the marvel of Balzacian art in this happy formulation: "Balzac, who sought the absolute for so long in a certain type of discovery, almost found in his own work the solution to a problem unknown before him: complete reality in a complete fiction."[11] Balzac, on the threshold of his life as an artist, appears to us thirsting for unity: as early as the *Notes philosophiques*,[12] and even before if we are to believe *Louis Lambert*, he was obsessed by the desire to resolve the antinomy of the world. In every domain, his effort is the same: to bring everything down to a unique principle that would permit a total and easy apprehension of things; be it in psychology, in politics, in science, or in art, this need appears everywhere. It is too persistent and too pressing not to correspond to more than a simple intellectual need. It expresses, we believe, the effort of a divided being to reach equilibrium, internal unity.

How many contrasts does Balzac not represent! Possessing a sensual temperament, he dreams of asceticism and practices it; gifted with an acute sense of reality and taking pleasure in living and enjoying it, he also loves abandoning himself to the caprices of revery and building a fantastical world; a penetrating observer with an accurate and precise view of the world, he is not satisfied with this gift and wants to complete it with a quasi-magical faculty of divination, a desire that manifests itself yet again in the dissatisfaction that a view of a merely external world leaves in him; aspiring to a philosophy that would have the rigor of science, and in love with close reasoning, he is continually tempted to escape it via an imagina-tion that craves the seduction of hypothesis; happy when he is manipulating ideas and disporting himself in abstractions, he cannot escape the need to represent things and to manipulate ideas by incarnating them in the con-crete. Thus Balzac is always caught in the dilemma that he posed early in life, and which is profoundly his: senses, sensibility, observation, imagina-tion, incarnation of the abstract—everything that is attached to matter is on one side. Asceticism, dream, a taste for logic and ideas, a feeling that true reality is disincarnated—everything that belongs to the spirit is on the other side.

Balzac's entire life was devoted to the resolution of this duality in his character. Art was its expression and esthetics was its method. Thanks to its diversity, he was able to satisfy all his gifts, develop all his faculties; thanks to its unity, he found his own unity. He united the man and the thinker in the synthesis of the artist. To the man in search of the absolute, as well as to the writer "full of the book that doesn't exist, that has never been written, and that he would like to be able to create,"[13] that unity brought him the means of attaining the one and creating the other. Esthetics was for Balzac an artistic methodology; even more, it was the instrument he created to resolve the problem of his existence. It was the art of living.

Notes

1. Charles Baudelaire, *Art romantique* (Paris: Conard, 1925), 219. [Ed. note: Except where otherwise noted, all references are to the Conard edition of Balzac's work (Paris: Conard, 1912–40), 40 vols.]

2. Cf., *Lettres à l'Etrangère* (Paris: Calmann-Lévy, 1906–50), 4 vols., 1, 34: "Having undertaken . . . to represent the ensemble of literature in the ensemble of my works . . ."

3. Does he not complain to Nodier that their contemporaries want to enclose each writer in a speciality? (*Letter to Nodier*, 49, 558). Champfleury contends that already in 1825 he refused to pledge allegiance to a school: "He was not a member of the Cénacle [Nodier's group], and accused himself of eclecticism" ("Balzac, Father of Future Criticism," *Le Messager de l'Assemblée*, 14 June 1851). In 1827, V. Morillon also refused to join a school: cf. *Avertissement du Gars*. [Ed. note: *Le Gars* is an early title for what eventually became *Le Dernier Chouan*. Victor Morillon was its proposed pseudonymous author.]

4. *Lettres à sa famille* (Paris: Albin Michel, 1950), 379.

5. *Etudes sur Beyle*, 40, 371.

6. Ibid., 373. He thus confirmed the affirmation of Cyprien Desmarais who, at the end of his work, *De la littérature française au XIXe siècle* (On French literature in the nineteenth century) observed that the revolution of 1830 had given free reign to the last romantic follies, declaring that "letters and arts are therefore now free enough to advance without any obstacles in the path of their rejuvenation, and to brilliantly ally classic purity to romantic daring." (*De la littérature française au XIXe siècle*, 2d ed., 1837).

7. Cf. Avant Propos to *La Comédie humaine*, 1, xxxiii–xxxiv.

8. Ibid., xxix.

9. *Le Lys dans la vallée*, 26, 24.

10. *Louis Lambert*, 31, 108.

11. G. Sand, *Autour de la table* (Paris: Dentu, 1862), 200.

12. [Ed. note: These notes were a youthful composition in which Balzac set out some rather juvenile philosophical theories.]

13. *Lettres à L'Etrangère*, 1, 481.

Creative Reading: Balzacian Imagination at Work
Geneviève Delattre*

Imagination, in Balzac, plays a capital role in the discovery of the imaginary world of books and in the observation of reality, since it is the source of the intuitive vision that permits him to seize truth on the basis of just a sample. One could say, then, without being too paradoxical, that Balzac invents reality

*Translated and reprinted from *Cahiers de l'Association internationale des études françaises*, 15 (1963), 395–406, by permission of Madame Geneviève Delattre.

as much as he observes it, and conversely that he observes the imaginary as much as he invents it. Invention and observation are, in his case, inseparable from each other. The two worlds from which the raw material of the *Comédie humaine* is extracted, the real and the imaginary, are too frequently mingled together for us to dare decide which, for Balzac, possesses the purest reality. M. Jean Pommier, in his work on *L'Invention et l'écriture dans La Torpille* (Inventiveness and writing in *The Eel*), remarked in this connection that the experience of life is not the only nor perhaps even the principal source from which the novelist draws, but that he recalls other literary works that may have impressed him.[1] And, in fact, few works swarm with as many literary recollections as the *Comédie humaine*. When we were attempting to collect in a coherent way Balzac's literary opinions, we were struck by the extent of his reading and the astonishing participation of certain works in the construction of the Balzacian universe. We would like to devote a few remarks here to this connection between reading and literary creativity.

It is perhaps useful to recall first of all that from childhood on Balzac was and remained a voracious reader. The twelve-year-old boy who, in *Louis Lambert*, manages to get a lazy tutor so as to be able to read at his leisure instead of studying mathematics, the same young boy shut up in the closet under the stairs where punishment turns into enjoyment thanks to the librarian who supplies him with all sorts of books, the child who appears stupid to his teachers because his head is already filled with the imaginary world discovered in books—these are all Balzac. There is no volume in the haphazard library of his parents that he has not devoured. And once in Paris, the young Balzac frequents the public libraries. *Facino Cane* shows us the apprentice writer of the rue Lesdiguières leaving his lodgings only to go to the Bibliothèque de Monsieur. When the crushing literary work begins, Balzac will have less leisure for reading; but how often do we see him, in his correspondence, lay down the pen only to take up a book. In Balzac, reading and rereading are activites that seem as essential as literary creativity. When illness strikes him down, or when his overworked mind refuses temporarily to continue its daily routine of invention, we see Balzac deal with his impatience by plunging into reading. When he travels, books often occupy more of his time than tourism. Forced to spend four days in Ajaccio, Balzac quickly tires of contemplating the ocean or looking for Napoleonic relics, and he ends up in the municipal library, where, for lack of anything better, he reads two novels by Richardson that he hadn't known: *Pamela* and *Grandison,* and he rereads the fourteen volumes of *Clarissa Harlowe*.

If we try to explain this taste for reading, we will be led to observe that it is spontaneous. Balzac spent his whole childhood in boarding schools, without his parents participating in the slightest degree in his education. In the Collège de Vendôme, according to all evidence, he stood apart from his comrades. Perhaps only the librarian, a certain Lefèvre, encouraged young Balzac's passion, by placing at his disposal the thousands of books in his charge. It is clear that in his reading the child sought above all an escape from the dismal life of the boarding school and the emptiness of his heart. To love books in childhood is to love escapism and to live imaginatively a thousand lives different from one's own. A child seeks nothing else in reading, since he does not engage in critical reflection. He is therefore a reader in the purest sense of the word, without preconceptions—allowing himself, at the slightest invitation, to be carried off into an imaginary world. He therefore probably represents the ideal reader that every writer dreams of. As Gaëtan Picon observes in his *L'Ecrivain et son ombre* (The writer and his shadow), "the work of art can be compared to the sun, assuredly wishing to be seen, but with a bedazzlement that prevents us from looking at it. Experienced, contemplated, to be sure; but not criticized, commented upon, or judged."[2]

Now this child, struck with wonder on contact with the imaginary world, survives in the adult Balzac, and we discover traces of this fascinated childhood reading when Balzac comes face to face with *La Chartreuse de Parme* (The Charterhouse of Parma). "I am such a childlike reader, so enchanted, so amenable," he writes to Stendhal, "that it is impossible for me to give my opinion after reading; I am the most benign of critics, and I pay no attention to minor blemishes."[3] In such a reader, the imagination dominates and gives to the individual the power of living lives other than his own. But as long as reading remains a total commitment, as in the case of the childish reader (whether actually child or adult), the imagination remains docile, a prisoner of the writer's will, and thus dangerously captive.

Yet in Balzac the desire the create manifested itself from infancy, parallel to the taste for escape into the imaginary world offered by books. The young narrator of *Louis Lambert* neglects his studies not only to read but to compose poems. His comrades had nicknamed him "The Poet." Why should he want to write? That is a question that is surely difficult to answer. Writers have the feeling of simply obeying a force that is in them. But one can hardly imagine a literary work, of whatever form, being born in a sort of spontaneous conception, without its author having the least knowledge of other works. Put differently, it is first through reading that the desire or the need to create must arise. There is hence at the basis of all attempts at literary creation a certain emulation, a "why not me?" thrown down like a challenge to others, but especially to oneself. Now, as M. de Sacy has remarked,[4] the spirit of emulation appears precisely as one of the wellsprings of Balzac's character. The famous formulation "What Napoleon could not finish with the sword, I will accomplish with the pen" is one of its clearest manifestations. On the literary plane, this trait plays a very large role, not only in pushing the emerging writer to measure himself against his elders, but also as a stimulant to work throughout his life. It is this spirit of emulation that, when he reads work that he likes, pushes him to rival it, and to adopt certain of its data in order to develop them differently. Reading for Balzac is thus very often linked to creativity. His imagination immediately adopts the scenes and characters of the work he has read; they are integrated into the imaginary world he inhabits, and they become the subject of observation just as do the flesh-and-blood beings that surround him.

When the initial phase is missing—that is, the phase of spontaneous enthusiasm resulting from the pleasure of the imagination as it receives new nourishment—we see Balzac transformed into a pure and simple critic, coolly judging and reasoning about the merits or faults of a work. The novelist in him then reacts only as a technician, as a professional who can find the fault in the construction at a glance and quickly show what the author should have done. The typical critical article by Balzac is in fact one that is made up of a section that is truly critical, followed immediately by the reconstituting section, the one that begins: "Thus, in a novel with the same characters, the same motivations, the same scenes, one could make an interesting work. But to do so, one should not . . ."[5] Then follow the changes to be made in the work. The presence of the creator can be clearly felt in the critic, since the imagination cannot help intervening to make the technician see the possible sketch of a better work. Nevertheless, the work remains foreign to Balzac; it brings no new element to the imaginary world that his mind inhabits.

If it seems obvious that enthusiastic empathy is necessary to unleash the participation of a work he has read in his creativity, it is also true that there is nothing automatic in this area, and that a work read and enthusiastically admired does not necessarily enter into the *Comédie humaine*. We will cite only the *Chartreuse de Parme* as an example, a novel that Balzac immediately recognized as a masterpiece, a feeling that several successive readings confirmed and that his critical reflection analyzed with all the authority of an accomplished technician. Now it does not appear that the world of the *Chartreuse* ever mixed with that of the *Comédie humaine*, except perhaps to reinforce Balzac's interest in Italy. It could hardly have been otherwise. When Balzac reads, in *Le Constitutionnel* of 17 March 1839, the description of the battle of Waterloo, he discovers with stupefaction that someone else had triumphed over the difficulty—which he had found insurmountable—of describing a battle.[6] That other person was Stendhal, for whom Balzac always felt the greatest respect. "Fascinated, chagrined, enchanted, despairing" (these are his own words), he hastens to read the entire work and accepts with joy the copy that Stendhal offers him. His enthusiasm is well known. Balzac find himself for the first time absolutely won over by a contemporary work at once very like and very different from his own: so like that he understands all its difficulties and can appreciate Stendhal's art; so different that he continually asserts that the work could never have been his own. "*La Chartreuse* is a great and wonderful book," he writes to Stendhal, "and I tell you so without flattery, without envy, because I would be incapable of writing it, and one can sincerely praise that which is not one's own kind of work. I am making a fresco and you have made Italian statues."[7] The comparison is enlightening: Stendhal's novel offers itself to Balzac as a solid block in which each detail is carefully articulated into the ensemble, and from which, consequently, no element could be removed because it is intrinsically linked to the rest. Balzac's pleasure comes above all, it seems to us, from a delicious disorientation, all the more unexpected for taking place on familiar territory. Balzac's imagination does not find the least crack in which to get a controlling hold and is obliged to submit to Stendhal's. Balzac, confronting *La Chartreuse*, has truly become the childlike and charmed reader he described to Stendhal.

However strong the impression left on Balzac's mind by a work or a character, however strong and natural the movement that tends to absorb into the *Comédie humaine* everything that interests him and that he loves, the Balzacian imagination—as highly original as it may be—sometimes meets a resistance it cannot overcome. This is the case with Molière, his most beloved writer, the most admired, the most intimately known. To some degree the *Comédie humaine* surely owes Molière its existence as a picture of society. On the other hand, the economy required by the stage appears to leave the imagination a great deal to dream about: to write a prior or subsequent play, to invent possible happenings, to transplant the hero into a different period and readapt the problem at issue, all these possibilities seem to have fascinated Balzac. They all end in defeat, as is shown by Tartuffe's Balzacian destiny.

Balzac first thought of a female Tartuffe, whom he transposed into a bourgeois drama called *L'Ecole des ménages* (The school for families), in which Molière was completely lost from view. Then he imagined a sequel to *Tartuffe* in which one would see Orgon yearning for Tartuffe because his family bores him. The play, of which only the first act was written, and not by Balzac, carries the mark of neither Molière nor Balzac. He then imagined a prologue to *Tartuffe* in which we would witness the entrapment of Orgon. A more contemporary political and social hypocrisy would be substituted for religious hypocrisy. Tartuffe would be Democratic-Philanthropic. The work would be called *Un Grand Artiste*. "There is a great and beautiful work to be created," Balzac wrote. "Will I succeed? That is the question."[8] He succeeded only in part. In the event, his character began to take on his own life, distancing himself form Tartuffe, becoming one of the great Balzacian characters: the poet Canalis, of *Modeste Mignon*. The idea of a democratic-philanthropic Tartuffe was then transferred to another novel, *Les Petits Bourgeois*, written at the same time. Théodose de la Peyrade, a Balzacian Tartuffe too heavily coated with Molière's clay, never found his final form, since the novel remained unfinished.

Thus Balzac's creative imagination, although stimulated by the reading of Molière and oriented toward certain possibilities of development, finds its liberty limited by overly precise material. The Molière characters that haunt Balzac's imagination are too alive, and too precisely characterized, to enter a world that is not theirs. The necessary condensation of the stage in fact offers openings that the imagination cannot fill except by remaining perfectly faithful to the original material of the author. The Balzacian mark inflicts distortions on the pure lines of Molière's characters that disfigure them without revitalizing them.

We find Balzac confronting the same difficulties when, after having read and reread *Adolphe*, of which he had a high opinion, he undertakes to rewrite Benjamin Constant's novel from the heroine's point of view. What could have given him this idea? Perhaps an article by Gustave Planche, which appeared in the *Revue des deux mondes* in 1834 and is included in the Charpentier edition [of *Adolphe*] in 1839. Now 1839 is the year in which *Béatrix* was composed, in which for the first time the possibility of a counterpart to *Adolphe* appears. It is also very possible that George Sand, who suggested the idea of *Béatrix*, strongly contributed to the refining of Balzac's ideas about a feminine Adolphe during long conversations at Nohant in 1839. As a matter of fact, it is not Balzac who writes the counterpart to *Adolphe*, but Camille Maupin, better placed than he to understand the sufferings of Ellénore.[9] Let us note that she has Claude Vignon beside her, for whom Balzac took his inspiration from Gustave Planche.

The theme of *Adolphe*, scarcely sketched out in *Béatrix*, will not be forgotten. It continues to inhabit Balzac and we rediscover it, now quite painful, when he writes *La Muse du département*. This novel, written at a moment of great physical exhaustion and financial need, is a kind of hasty patching together of various bits and pieces. The second part, concerning the arrival of Mme de la Baudraye in Paris, is the only one created in 1843. And that is precisely the part placed under the sign of *Adolphe*, since the titles of its chapters are: "The Double Chain," and "Commentaries on the novel *Adolphe* by Benjamin Constant." These titles were later eliminated, but this second part of the novel remains an obvious attempt to reshape Constant's novel by treating it from another angle, the one that had struck Balzac: the point of view of a woman who sees a younger and weaker lover escape her little by little, and who, even without yielding to the recriminations of El-lénore, cannot keep him. Let us note that the theme was not new, since it is that of *La Femme abandonnée*, which dates from 1832, and that Balzac did not need either *Adolphe* or commentaries on it to know the anguish that he could have observed in Mme de Berny.[10]

The novelistic situation attracts Balzac because it coincides with a particular sensibility at the deepest level of his being. But Constant's novel, concise, lucid, as polished as a beach stone, cannot be taken apart by the Balzacian imagination. The idea of writing a "female" book (the word is Lousteau's) ends in failure because Balzac does not realize that he is wrong to claim that Constant has not portrayed women's suffering. Those sufferings are there, really there, since they are what cause Adolphe's moral torment. Balzac therefore finds himself struggling with characters and a situation that resist the reworking he wishes to impose upon them. The changed point of view that he believes possible leads him, in his novel, only to reverse the roles, by making Dinah Piedefer play the double role of Ellénore and of

Adolphe.[11] She is both the abandoned and the abandoner. But here the magic of Balzacian invention deceives us, for when Adolphe and Ellénore enter the Balzacian world, they lose all the nobility that is one of the essential traits of their characters. Stripped, then abandoned without any of the sumptuous compensations of which Balzac is capable, they remain sad puppets, and their tragedy becomes a tragicomedy—the tragicomedy of the provincial woman condemned to being ridiculous whatever she does, and the tragicomedy of the cynical, flighty artist incapable of deep sentiment.

Did Balzac realize he had failed? Probably not, for as he is guiding these two unfortunate characters through their mournful adventure, he writes to Mme Hanska: "I hope that in the ending of *La Muse,* people will see the subject of *Adolphe* treated with realism."[12] Everything happens as if Balzac had stumbled against a work so solid and already so perfect in its realism that his imagination had, while he was under way, abandoned the game, allowing the effort toward realism to deteriorate into a simple debasement of the characters. The counterpart to *Adolphe* dreamed of by Balzac changes into parody.

Circumstances are sometimes more favorable to this phenomenon of osmosis between the works read by Balzac and the *Comédie humaine*. If the reprise of the theme of *Adolphe* leads to a half-defeat, that of the theme of *Volupté* (Sensuality) marks a success. Why? Sainte-Beuve's novel does not appear to Balzac with the splendor of *La Chartreuse de Parme* nor the solidity of Constant's novel. The sunspots are much more in evidence, and Balzac, reviewing the work for Mme Hanska a month after its publication, writes: "A book has appeared, a very good one for certain people, often badly written, weak, cowardly, diffuse, which everybody has condemned, but which I had the courage to read and in which there are some very good things."[13] And, a bit further on, he adds this revealing phrase; "There are some beautiful sentences in this book, some beautiful pages, yet nothing. It is the nothing that I like, the nothing that permits me to get into it." It is certain that the situation studied by Sainte-Beuve, like that of *Adolphe*, evoked personal memories in Balzac, and that it was not difficult for him to enter into the character of Amaury.

Nevertheless, this intimate relationship between fictitious characters and their reader was facilitated by the weak and diffuse quality of the work. If the characters had been painted with more vigor, if Sainte-Beuve had specified all the character traits instead of indulging in vagueness, Balzac's imagination would have found less of a foothold. On the contrary, what Balzac calls the emptiness, that is to say the blanks left by Sainte-Beuve in his design, permit the creative imagination to follow its own path. If one is to believe Werdet, Balzac kept *Volupté* open on his desk for months. *Le Lys dans la vallée* was already in gestation, conceived by the desire to do better than Sainte-Beuve of course, but made possible above all by a transfer of identity between Balzac and Amaury and vice versa. Once the character had entered into Balzac's imagination, the novelist could take his destiny in hand and model it as he wished. Félix Vandenesse will know, like Amaury, the tor-menting delights of forbidden love, but Balzac will grant him what, in his view, Amaury lacked—the liberty and the imprudence that accompany pas-sion in France. For her part, Mme de Couaen will become more feminine in the character of Mme de Mortsauf, and the false modesties and discretions described by Sainte-Beuve will be replaced by contained but burning pas-sions whose final, deathbed explosion shows how far we are from Mme de Couaen.

In perceiving in Sainte-Beuve's characters a certain puritanical debility that he judges foreign to the French temperament, Balzac's intelligence finds the angle from which he will be able to refashion them. In fact, it is with the Balzacian seal rather than the French seal that he will mark them, infusing into their veins a good strong dose of his own blood. The transfusion from one work to the other is completely successful because Balzac's imagina-tion can play freely with the elements of Sainte-Beuve's material, and be-cause the latter correspond to an essential experience in Balzac's life yet are flexible enough to lend themselves to a very different inspiration. What must be noted above all is the speed with which Balzac's creative spirit seizes new materials discovered in the course of his reading. The essentials of the *Lys* are already found in the letter to Mme Hanska that we have quoted.

We will not be so naive as to wish to establish rules for success in the assimilation into the *Comédie humaine* of works beloved by Balzac. They enter into it in many ways, often very indirectly. However, where we can retrace what happens between the moment when the imagination is alerted by initial enthusiasm and the moment when creative genius puts its mark on the amalgam formed by the most diverse elements, we observe that certain works are more accessible to Balzacian reconstruction than others, because they have a looser texture and constitute a hollow mold into which the Balzacian imagination can flow. We have instanced here only some particu-larly striking examples. The fantastic impregnation of the *Comédie humaine* by literary memories comes in great degree from a detail, gleaned here or there, separated from the work in which it appears and easily assimilated into a different situation; or from a scene, barely suggested by a writer, but noted by Balzac who immediately sees possibilities of development.

Finally and above all, it seems that very early on, the world that Balzac carried within himself organized itself around certain zones, certain circles we might say, for his cosmography was formed through the reading of Swe-denborg and Dante. These are perhaps the two authors who enabled Balzac to organize the essential masses of his universe; the works and above all the characters who excite his imagination are almost always those who can take their place in the angelic world where Séraphîta soars or the demonic world where Vautrin reigns. There is much more order in Balzac's imaginary world than is generally believed. His observation of the real individuals he encoun-ters in his daily life and of the fictive beings he meets in books functions in exactly the same way; the intuitive observation that is evoked in *Facino Cane* is equally valid for the imaginary world. Given a detail, Balzac reconstructs. Similarly, if too many details are perceived, if the reality imposes itself on the imagination in an overly exact reproduction, literary creativity fails.

Notes

1. Paris: Minard, 1957, 31.

2. Paris: Gallimard, 1953, 12.

3. To M. Frédéric Stendhal, 20 March 1839, *L'Oeuvre de Balzac*, Club français du livre, vol. 16, 268. [Ed. note: Prof. Delattre errs slightly here: there is a letter *from* Stendhal to Balzac dated 29 March 1839; Balzac's reply (from which the quotation is taken) is undated. The signature "Frédérick," with its half-French half-English orthography, was undoubtedly a joke between them. Stendhal's real name was Marie-Henri Beyle.]

4. *Les Deux Univers de Balzac*. 1. *L'Occulte*, in *Balzac* (Paris: Hachette, 1959), 230.

5. "Le Feuilleton des Journaux politiques," a critique of *Samuel Bernard et Jacques Borgarelli, Oeuvres diverses,* (Paris: Conard, 1938), vol. 38, 392.

6. [Ed. note: An extract from Stendhal's novel was published prior to its appearance in book form.]

7. To M. Frédéric Stendhal, 5 (?) April 1839, *L'Oeuvre de Balzac* (Paris: Club français du livre, 1949–53), vol. 16, 269. [Ed. note: See note 4 regarding Stendhal's name.]

8. *Lettres à L'Etrangère* (Paris: Calmann-Lévy 1906–50), vol. 2, 258.

9. [Ed. note: Camille Maupin, the pseudonym of Félicité des Touches, is a writer and composer, a major figure in the *Comédie humaine* and a player in a half-dozen of its episodes. Claude Vignon is a writer and critic who also appears in numerous novels. Balzac's "Adolphe" is therefore an element within the novel, referred to but not actually existing.]

10. [Ed. note: Mme de Berny, much older than the novelist, was Balzac's earliest serious love and possibly the only real one. It is she whom he named "La Dilecta."]

11. [Ed. note: Dinah Piedefer (later Comtesse de La Baudraye) is a major figure in the *Comédie humaine*, appearing in *La Muse du département, Béatrix,* and *La Cousine Bette*.]

12. *Lettres à l'Etrangère*, vol. 2, 126.

13. *Lettres à l'Etrangère*, vol. 1, 186.

Balzac   Harry Levin*

*   *   *

Balzac's collected works, taken in their most grandiose terms, are a titanic attempt to impose a cosmos on the chaos of contemporary life. Every volume may be ticked off, in more intimate terms, as a debt acquitted. In paying off his obligations to society, which itself had been plunged into a state of moral bankruptcy, he was likewise contributing toward its redemption. The threads of vindication, expiation, and rehabilitation are deeply

*From *The Gates of Horn: A Study of Five French Realists* by Harry Levin, 156–59, 164–66. © 1963 by Harry Levin. Reprinted by permission of Oxford University Press, Inc.

woven into the specific patterns and the collective fabric of the *Comédie humaine*. Most of its characters have something to live down. The revolutionary executioner, Henri Sanson, for whom Balzac had ghost-written in the suggestively titled *Mémories d'un paria*, attends a mass for the soul of Louis XVI in *Un Episode sous la Terreur*. In *L'Envers de l'histoire contemporaine* an anti-royalist judge, notorious for his sweeping iteration of the death sentence, is pardoned by his enemies and enabled to vindicate himself by publishing a monumental work on law and order. More familiar with the corruptions of towns than with the countryside, Balzac exhibits his idyllic and utopian strain in two companion studies, *Le Médecin de campagne* and *Le Curé de village*. A protagonist in each case, Doctor Benassis or Madame Graslin, expiates a private sin by setting up a model community, a kind of human reclamation project. Doctor Benassis, the mayor of his village, the father of his people, the Napoleon of his valley, whose biography somewhat parallels Balzac's, dies in the crucial year of 1829. Madame Graslin, like the protagonist of *Crime and Punishment*, ends by submitting to a public confession; but works transcend faith in Balzac's ethical system: "the gospel in action." The Marquis d'Espard, in *L'Interdiction*, acquits a long-standing debt of honor by writing and printing an illustrated history of China; such a book had been among the ill-fated publications of Balzac's actual press.

The liquidation of this establishment did not dampen his commercial zest. Whenever he went on a journey, he came back talking of railway shares and canal concessions, timber rights and mining prospects. He could scarcely pass by a manure pile without undertaking to convert it into a gold mine. His friends vie with one another in their anecdotes of get-rich-quick schemes and glibly munificent speculations, improvised and elaborated with the same admixture of the fantastic and the matter-of-fact that animates his books. Evidently, he drew no distinctions between his literary and his financial interests. He engaged habitually in lawsuits against editors and publishers, and he founded several short-lived periodicals of his own. In his novels he advertised the products of the tradesmen he patronized; he speculated on tickets for his plays; he thought of incorporating his readers into a sort of lottery, a tontine, by combining premiums with subscriptions. Like Defoe, the English novelist whom he most surprisingly resembles, he was a man of innumerable projects. None of them, with the all-important exception of the *Comédie humaine*, ever quite materialized. Taine, as usual, saw the point and overstated it, when he characterized Balzac as "a man of affairs in debt." Balzac was nothing if not a man of letters: literature was his unique stratagem for settling his affairs. His talents and ambitions as organizer, projector, promoter, were finally expressed in his writing. As a writer, he was a consummate business man. Theoretically, he could calculate better than James de Rothschild; we have Balzac's word that his publisher, Souverain, said so. We have also the word of Werdet, one of his previous publishers, that Balzac was not a practical businessman. And, to apply the only canon by which such matters can be tested, we have a significant fact: after Balzac's "Dilecta," his motherly first love, Madame de Berny, had helped to extricate him from the failure of his type-foundry, her son took it over and made a success of it.

Balzac's unsuccessful experiments as a man of affairs confirmed his vocation as a man of letters. Yet it is hard to think of a great writer whose juvenilia are less promising than Balzac's *Oeuvres de jeunesse*. Although their callow sensationalism persists throughout the work of his maturity, they do little to foreshadow his solid accomplishments. "His first operations in mercantile literature," as he candidly termed them, show all of his faults and virtually none of his merits. They bring no new resources to the impoverished conventions of Mrs. Radcliffe and Monk Lewis, or the *bas romantisme* of Pigault-Lebrun and Ducray-Duminil. Indeed it is only the occasional note of parody that detaches them from the gruesome monotony of their models. Only when *Argow le Pirate* supplies the sequel to *Le Vicaire des Ardennes*, and the sinister pirate reappears in the even more sinister guise of a banker, do we catch a first faint glimmering of the Balzacian vision. But Balzac did not discover his subject, nor adjust himself to his métier, until he had been caught in the toils of finance. While Balzac & Cie was being liquidated, he was rusticated to the wilds of Brittany, where he lived "the life of a Mohican." There, a generation before, during the royalist insurrection of the Vendée, the loyal peasants of the Chouannerie had waged partisan warfare against the Revolution. "They were savages who served God and the King by fighting like Mohicans." *The Last of the Mohicans* had lately been translated, and Balzac had begun to regard James Fenimore Cooper as the only novelist worthy of comparison with Scott. One was the historian of nature, the other of humanity, Balzac would write in a later appreciation. Meanwhile, returning to fiction, he felt that he brought to the imitation of both "a passion and spirit which are present in neither." The lost cause he celebrated was that of neither the vanishing redskin nor the Jacobite pretender. It was nothing less than the alter and the throne. It was the old order, to which—brooding over his troubles, and ascribing them to the new disorder—he gradually came to profess allegiance. . . .

. . . It was as if Balzac, like one of his characters, had struck some infernal bargain which empowered him to conjure up a society, on condition that he lived and worked in solitude. His biography is an agenda, a calendar of works and days, a tabulation of profits and losses. His interior life has gone into "the perpetual creation that emerges from my inkwell." There is poignance in the fact that the voluptuous setting for the lurid climax of *La Fille aux yeux d'or* was modelled on the boudoir adjoining his own Carthusian study, or that the interrupted love story of *La Grenadière* was located in a home he had wished to buy. "I have written my desires, my dreams," he confessed to his Countess. We are not surprised that so many of his characters are monomaniacs when we trace their peculiar obsessions back to their creator's all-embracing megalomania. It is surprising that there has been so little investigation of Balzac's imaginative processes, for few writers

have written so unguardedly. His misunderstood geniuses, his unappre-
ciated artists, his persecuted scientists act out the compulsion that bound
him to his desk through the nights. His letters refer to his *grand oeuvre* in
the awe-inspiring manner that the Queen's astrologers, of *Le Secret des
Ruggieri,* assume when they discuss the philosophers' stone. *La Recherche
de l'absolu* intensifies this note by contrasting the comfortable bourgeois
solidity of its Flemish background with the sublimated alchemical quintes-
sence for which Balthazar Claës experiments in vain. The indifferent reception of Balzac's preposterous drama *Les Ressources de Quinola* must have
seemed a confirmation of its thesis—the obsessive Balzacian thesis of the
inventor's sufferings. A contemporary of Galileo's, who has had the temerity
and ingenuity to invent the steamship, is forced to scuttle it by the Inquisi-
tion. "Hell," he concludes, "is paved with good inventions."

Balzac must have touched, in moments of self-questioning, the thin line
that separates inspiration from paranoia. To his composer in *Gambara,* and
to his tenor in *Massimilla Doni,* their own music sounds divine; to the others
it is insane cacophony. The isolated idealists of his *Etudes philosophiques*
stand apart from the social realities of his *Etudes de moeurs*. Reality is the
never quite attainable absolute toward which his laborious researches tend.
It is his own fixed idea that he exposes in *Le Chef-d'oeuvre inconnu,* permitting life itself, in the youthful person of Poussin's mistress, to elude the
endeavors of art, personified by the half-mad Frenhofer. Is that painter an
incomparable genius or a self-hypnotized charlatan? His encrusted canvas
seems to be dismissed by Balzac as a meaningless daub, and yet the reader is
left wondering—until he too seems touched by a gleam of madness—
whether a more percipient taste would not discern some brilliant innovation.
Cézanne identified himself with Frenhofer, while Picasso has published a
dazzling series of illustrations. And Balzac's ambiguities have survived to
perplex other writers. For Hawthorne, in "The Artist of the Beautiful," the
masterpiece of a lifetime takes the shape of a delicate mechanical toy, which
a careless gesture of the merest child can crush. For Henry James, in "The
Madonna of the Future," there are further refinements to "that terrible little
tale of Balzac's." The hesitant perfectionist, who contemplates his blank
easel, while his model waxes buxom and middle-aged, bears a closer resemblance to James than to Balzac. Balzac, after all, has more in common with
the ingenious interloper, who takes possession of the impatient madonna and
thrives upon prolific caricature. His is the last word: "Cats and monkeys,
monkeys and cats—all human life is there."

The allegory should explain why James, probably the least Balzacian of
novelists, bore wistful homage again and again to "the first and foremost
member of his craft." For Balzac specialized in those bustling combinations of
material circumstance, so characteristic of the American scene, which had
eluded both Hawthorne and James, and to which they both preferred the
quest for ivy-covered romance. Moreover, Balzac's works were translated and
circulated in America on a scale which befitted the mass-production of his

brothers Cointet and the supersalesmanship of his Gaudissart. Five-foot sets of dusty editions in any second-hand bookshop will bear witness to this national vogue, as well as to a subsequent ebbing of interest. The ephemeral nature of the Balzacian wave that swept our shores may be blamed, at least in large part, upon bungled and garbled translations. In larger part, it was bound to call forth a school of native Balzacians, who would set their sights closer to home. Borrowing *The Wild Ass's Skin* from the Carnegie Library, Dreiser learned to visualize himself through Valentin and Pittsburgh through Paris. Others in other countries, similarly, readjusted the novelistic focus as they extended its panoramic range. To have represented the bourgeoisie so thoroughly was to retain certain defects of their qualities; and Balzac remains, far more obviously than Goethe or such other household gods, an inspired philistine. By way of compensation, he could claim with his Mercadet: "They will never put a stop to speculation. I have understood my epoch." It is often ambiguous, as we try to follow the curve of Balzac's speculations, whether he belongs with the Mercadets or the Galileos, with the jobbers or the discoverers. But to run up a perennial deficit into one of the most amazing success stories in the history of literature is to be paid in kind.

[Balzac's Theory of Thought]   Maurice Bardèche*

At the risk of repeating ourselves, let us sum up what seems essential to an understanding of Balzac's work. The novelist takes his point of departure in a physiological definition of Man. Every man possesses a certain fund of energy, and his life is the way in which he expends that energy. Thought, which emanates from man in the form of ideas, willpower, desires, sentiments, and passions, is analogous to an invisible fluid, to electricity for example, or radio waves. Man is at once the conserver and broadcaster of this vital energy to which Balzac gives the generic name of "Thought." In varying circumstances, he can be either a conserver or an emitter. The *Etudes philosophiques* are intended to develop this theory and to show its consequences in actual fact. The conserving individual limits himself to accumulating vital energy without projecting it onto anything. He is an energy miser. He ends up with a kind of contemplative life, without expenditure but also without color. He approximates a purely vegetative existence. At the other extreme, the man led by a violent and imperious passion constantly projects a prodigious quantity of energy. He spends it because he feels, but he also irradiates. His energy is creative, transformed into thought, willpower, or influence. Those who are exceptional in this respect have the power of miracle workers. This power can be expressed in a palpable way, as

*Translated and reprinted by permission from *Une Lecture de Balzac* (Paris: Les Sept Couleurs, 1964), 380–90.

in the case of cures obtained by the laying on of hands or simple presence; or impalpably yet almost as powerfully, as in the case of the orator and the leader of men, or the man of action, the initiator, the headstrong individual. The price of this expenditure of energy is the wearing away of life. Finally, this energy can also be economized, spent at the correct moment, and then turned off: this is the principle of life that Balzac attributes to Napoleon and that is imitated by his young ambitious heroes. Strictly speaking, this ballistic concept is what one can call Balzac's *energetics*. In extreme cases, what we perceive as miracles are perhaps only the unknown or misunderstood applications of this energy. Balzac accounted in this way for the history of the early Church, which he felt furnished important testimony about human beings.

Although these extreme cases explain certain of Balzac's characters, they are only rarely brought onstage. In fact, for Balzac, the phenomenon of "Thought" consists of ideas, desires, sentiments, and passions, and crystallizes or, put another way, condenses in each man, unbeknownst to him, in certain characteristic ways. Then man does not lead his life, he does not freely direct his *thought;* he submits to his life because tyrannical "Thought" takes hold of him. This is what might be called no longer Balzac's *energetics*, but his *theory of passions*. Most men thus construct for themselves an intellectual or emotional landscape, which ends by acting within them like a powerful force of which they are not the masters. The storms that occur at the heart of this accumulation of cerebral electricity can create mortal crisis, through the fulfillment or sudden collapse of the dream that every individual carries within himself. But this force that each of us allows to accumulate internally can also slowly kill us through our furious efforts, our exasperated desires, our bitterness, our despair; in other words, either through the violent struggle that man must accept in order to realize what is dearest to him, or through the chagrin of not being able to do so. Balzac's *monomaniacs*, his violent characters, his human wrecks, his passionate creatures, are not only *cases* he has happened to meet; they are above all *cases* that are explained by his system. His observation is profound because his physiology is accurate. He follows the chimeras that haunt every human brain. This is the secret of his great characters. He is an admirable geographer of the phenomena of the imagination, or rather he is one of the few writers who have seen the extent of the imagination's hold on human beings, on women as well as men, for the power of chimeras occupies an equally large place in the psychology of his feminine characters. In this way, his *Etudes de moeurs* are in reality deduced from his *Etudes philosophiques*.

The *theory of energetics* and the *theory of passions* have no moral content. They are the theories of a physiologist or of an engineer. Balzac constantly reiterates that he is a *doctor of social sciences*. The physician does not *reform* his patient. He merely indicates the sources of the illness and, if he can, the remedy. In this physiological explanation, Balzac limits himself to ascertaining that man is essentially different from animals in that the latter cannot harm themselves—the animal is a blind force, it receives and expends, it is a consuming machine—whereas man secretes a substance that can influence his own life. He has the privilege of transforming his vital force into specifically human energy waves that act on other men, or of permitting his imagination to create within himself a kind of cerebral tumor that accumulates all his capacities. Whence the dictum of Rousseau, which Balzac repeats so often that it might be the emblem of his entire work: *the man who thinks is a depraved animal*.

Civilization aggravates these tendencies through *social desires*, temptations, examples, solicitations of all sorts; in a word, through reasons for thinking, which make of civilization a kind of reflector and multiplier of the passions and desires that are embedded in us. In great cities in particular, this reverberation of pleasure, vanity, and luxury is a permanent stimulator of both energy and passions. On the other hand, the frantic race for success and wealth, the tension of willpower, the exhaustion caused by hope or speculation, the maneuvers of all sorts, the mad surfeit, the abuse of pleasures and stimulants—all these cause a rapid exhaustion of life forces that is characteristic of great cities. Finally, comparisons, envy, the proximity of social climbers and the powerful, the spectacle of extreme wealth and extreme poverty cheek to jowl, bring about a profound skepticism, a corrosive and demoralizing thought that is like a poison inevitably accompanying a certain frenetic state of civilization. Journalism, advertising, and books all feed and sharpen this mass of hopes and ideas, and nourish bitter judgments. Finally, there arises from these cities a kind of deleterious cloud of collective thought, an overload of electricity that strains all minds, creating an illness menacing not only the lives of men but the lives of cities, thus realizing another of Rousseau's warnings that also becomes one of Balzac's axioms: *Thought is the most powerful agent of destruction in the modern world*.

This axiom is ambiguous. It identifies, first of all, a certain antihygienic state of life within civilization. But at the same time it goes beyond the properly physiological phenomena that characterize the life of cities. "Thought" itself, transformed so to speak into a material substance for cities and men, becomes a new element of dissolution—no longer of the individual but now of the social organism. The entry of mass populations into political life at the end of the eighteenth century suddenly liberated an enormous amount of "Thought" that until then had lain dormant. Millions of receptors, which had functioned with only normal energy and in a limited locale, received a supplementary supply—an additional excitation that had little effect on some but a drastic one on others, and that also provided the means of using energy over a much-broadened field. Whole sectors of the social apparatus were overcharged. The problems of the modern world emerged at that time because of the appearance of thousands of individual expressions of willpower, creating a force that henceforth had to be reckoned with, and had to be directed, contained, or utilized.

When he encountered this idea, which is, quite simply, an extension of his *system*, Balzac transformed his physiology of man into a physiology of society. One can thus see that the nineteenth century also became a *character:* perhaps the most important character of the *Comédie humaine*. And like the others, it suffers from hypertrophy of thought; it is poisoned by the deleterious fumes rising from Parisian life, the thirst for gold, the rage to succeed, the negation of everything, the cynicism, the uproar of pleasures and ideas: the brain of the century is also "an opera." But this transposition is not without its obscurities. Man was sometimes suddenly *struck down,* sometimes *worn out* by the charge of thought he allowed to accumulate within himself. But the social organism? Neither of these expressions applies to it. "Thought," in reality, is presented as an agent of destruction that *dissolves* social life, that reduces its resistance to a minimum. On this point, then, Balzac does not pursue his idea to its logical end. He does not describe "Thought" as an electrical *overcharge* in the nation that could lead to a concentration of the national will in certain cases, or, on the contrary, discharge itself in abrupt revolutionary storms. Here Balzac abandons his metaphor: he limits himself to ascertaining more simply that this saturation of thought gave rise to an illness in modern society, *individualism,* which is similar to illnesses that attack vineyards or cattle.[1]

Balzac's *system* therefore ends with a politics that is not as complete or coherent as one might wish. Once again it is the physician of the social organism who is speaking. His diagnosis is *individualism*. For Balzac this is not a journalistic idea or an excuse for tirades. It is a diagnosis that is in profound harmony with his understanding of man, and he is convinced of its truth. He exaggerates it, perhaps, but does so in good faith. His description of the century is deliberately overdone and pessimistic: it is *pathetic* and corresponds very well to the instinctively melodramatic inspiration that underpins all his inventiveness. "He is a man of letters," said Proust, "who wishes to create a strong image of the world." Let us note that the remedy proposed by Balzac is short and chimerical. His panacea, *Monarchy and Religion,* only suppresses the problem: you blow at individualism, and it is supposed to disappear. But can one avert this electrical overload with a wave of a fairy's wand, or even reduce it slowly as if it were some monstrous tumor?

But this pessimistic, perhaps even deformative analysis immediately places Balzac at the heart of the modern world. The social illness he describes has only worsened, and the vision of society that Balzac presents is still perfectly adapted to our times. It even enabled him to foresee the struggles that occur when new thoughts oppose and take the place of thoughts and feelings of a former time; and these dramas are not the least moving ones in his work nor the least meaningful for us. But above all, his condemnation of the modern world taught him that the *iron law* of the century plays a dramatic role in all individual lives. It is the wall against which passions and dreams are shattered. His analysis brings onstage a pitiless partner with whom everyone must reckon. And this pathetic view of the modern world renders the greatest service to the novelist, for it is from this confrontation that the drama emerges. Each of the sad or terrible lives that he describes to us is, in the end, the eternal story of the unequal duel that a tragically solitary individual wages against the egoism and indifference of other men in order to preserve the dream that inhabits him and that is dearer to him than his very existence.

This pathetic vision of the modern world is not found inscribed in all parts of Balzac's work with equal intensity. There are gradations in the gravity of the illness, or at least works in which the colors he uses are less somber.

The study of private lives is thus the occasion for showing in another way how the individual is modeled by "Thought." For not only do man's desires, passions, habits, and dreams lead him on to *his own death,* but the direction habitually taken by his imagination also contributes to the imposition, the *prefabrication,* of his own life: that direction gives him his appearance, his manners, his standard of life, his way of being—in a word, everything that constitutes the characteristic traits of his personality. The exploration of private lives and the determination of different social varieties do not, for Balzac, belong exclusively to the descriptive register: the social specimens that he gathers and describes are the product of certain *causes.* "The natural history of society" that he wished to write is complete and intelligible only if one accompanies each *social product* with the enumeration of the causes that made it what it is.

* * *

It is as a "natural history of society" that Balzac insisted on presenting his work to the public in the famous preface written in 1842 for the first edition of the *Comédie humaine.* He wanted to explain, he specifies, the appearance of different *social species.*

One may wonder why Balzac wanted to cast such strong light on this biological conception of the role of thought in the general introduction to his work of 1842, whereas the presentations he had inspired and perhaps dictated to his friend Félix Davin in 1835 give a much better account of the premises of his explanation of the human condition. The reason lies perhaps in chronology. In 1835, Balzac was taking stock of his system, and he presented his work as in fact it had developed: a theory of man accompanied by its applications. Moreover, at that date he needed to push his *Etudes philosophiques,* and emphasis had to be placed on those aspects that would encourage its sales. In 1842, social nomenclature is in fashion, Cuvier is riding high, and the description of "social species" has become an excellent advertising theme. So Balzac presents his work as a natural history of man that he can base upon a prestigious, unitary doctrine of creation, and he thus links himself to an important scientific movement of which his own description of society appears as a magnificent flowering: the destructive effect of thought is nothing more in this perspective than the antenna that guides the great naturalist in his exploration of modern society, an instrument of scientific research as well as the result of his overall conception of the evolution of species. In reality, nothing has changed: the *Etudes philosophiques* are merely the point of departure for an explanation of contemporary life; conversely the description of contemporary life is not reliable if it is not based on a notion of the nature of man.

* * *

Balzac's work is therefore profoundly *unified* even in its details, and we would feel it more strongly if he had had the time to write those *Etudes analytiques* he had announced and whose object was manifestly to coordinate all the lines of force of his work into a conclusion. The analyses on which a whole generation of Balzac scholars has collaborated permit us to get an idea of this profound unity of the *Comédie humaine*. But at the same time, analysis would not be complete if we did not call attention to a few uncertainties of Balzac's thought in this unified construction.

When Balzac speaks of "Thought," as we have seen, he simultaneously gives this word several different meanings. Sometimes it refers to the capital of life-energy that man accumulates or projects in various ways. Sometimes it refers to the desires, passions, and dreams that produce fixed ideas determining and occasionally dominating a whole life. Sometimes it refers to collective ideas—frenzy, seduction, cynicism, individualism—that constitute a dangerous atmosphere menacing the whole social organism. Sometimes, finally, it refers to the habits, the way of life, the *routines* that are acquired by a certain personality and that make it what it is. The way in which "Thought" functions is no less diverse. In the first sense, it ends up as a hygienics of life; in the second, it explains individual destinies; in the third it controls the future of the city; in the fourth it gives shape to individual lives. It is always "Thought" that produces these results—that is, our imagination, our social relations, what Pascal called the multiple aspects of *our amusements:* in a word, our "fantasies." But these mechanisms are sometimes very diverse (in particular, the one that determines private lives almost always emerging from imposed, but only partially accepted "conditions of class"); so it is regrettable that Balzac did not give firmer expression to the theory and that he did not show as did Pascal how, in the end, protean "Thought," even when it seems disengaged, is only the ensemble of diverse modes of condensation of an eternally destructive power emanating from the "depraved animal" when it ceases to live in harmony with nature. This was Balzac's true moral lesson: one feels it, one guesses at it; but nowhere does one find its definitive formulation, marking his work with a distinctive seal.

Note

1. [Ed. note: It is this implied antidemocratic interpretation of the *Comédie humaine* that set Bardèche against many more liberal commentators.]

La Comédie humaine: A Historical Document?

Louis Chevalier*

* * *

In our times, as a matter of fact, an ambitious confrontation is taking place between the *Comédie humaine* and the history of the first half of the nineteenth century. It is created by literary critics and historians who attack the problem more or less the same way, in the same terms, with the same documents and often copying each other as if they belonged to the same discipline—more historical than literary. One can consider that the recent development of social history is partly responsible for these attempts. The historian, with the minimal experience of a few modest quantitative works, thinks he can seize Balzac in a bear hug, and the literary man who has watched the historian believes he can grasp a whole half-century of history. What are these exercises worth? Let us distinguish the identification of characters from the *Comédie humaine* considered in and of themselves from the identification of the groups to which these characters belong and which they incarnate. The distinction is not as artificial as one might believe. The identification of the individuals, so frequent in this kind of research, belongs to literary critics rather than to historians and is marked by an old tradition of literary criticism: I will speak of it only briefly because the field is not mine. The identification of groups, or rather the best judgment of what Balzac says about them, belongs to both literary critics and historians: I will underscore this because it mostly boils down to an importunate or imprudent use of incomplete historical documentation that in no way authorizes such conclusions.

THE IDENTIFICATION OF INDIVIDUALS

I will pass quickly over this first question. The identification of characters belongs to literary history. Balzac himself encouraged his readers to engage in this game. In her important dissertation on the genesis of *Illusions perdues*—the only one of these recent works that it is indispensable to cite—Suzanne Bérard gives examples and proofs in this connection: "Balzac revealed the 'true name' of Mme Firmiani . . .; he formally acknowledged having described Gustave Planche under the name of Claude Vignon, George Sand 'with her own consent' under that of Camille Maupin, etc." That much is clear. However, such unchallengeable identifications are rare. Even when a character is born from a historical person, he quickly begins to differ from the original. He separates from the original, keeps only certain traits (often of minor importance), in order to assume a physiognomy whose complexity discourages any attempt at identification.

This is the case of most of the characters of the *Comédie humaine*. One understands why literary criticism is addicted to the search for what it calls—

*Translated and reprinted by permission from *La Revue historique* 232 (1964): 27–48.

quite unfortunately—"prototypes." This game of "who is whom?" cannot fail to surprise historians. Who is Nucingen, someone asks? Isn't he James de Rothschild? Like Rothschild, he is Jewish and speaks a jargonesque German. One might insidiously add that, like Rothschild, he is a banker and very rich. But let us be serious: the speculations of the two are not at all of the same order. And moreover, Nucingen's father had converted, and that is awkward. Let us look further. Could "the prototype" rather be the founder of the Fould dynasty? Perhaps in some respects, but absolutely not in others. And our literary man, unless it be our historian, consults some manual on the history of the Restoration and of the July Monarchy for other great lords of high finance. Would it not be Ouvrard whose existence is so conveniently recalled by a recent book? Maybe yes, maybe no. And thus, as required by the needs of progress, other possibilities appear in dissertation after dissertation; other discoveries proclaim the meritorious labor of our writers. And Nucingen is still there: a banker of the Chaussée d'Antin who probably resembles numerous other bankers of this financial neighborhood, even if merely by the fact of being a banker—but who above all gives evidence of a prodigious personality. And it is the merit and grandeur of this personality that we ask specialists of literary history to explain to us, rather than wasting their time pillaging history books and gleaning—often at second hand—detailed resemblances of no interest whatever.

THE AUTHENTIFICATION OF GROUPS

If the game of "who is whom?" is justified by a necessity of literature, and if it occasionally helps in the interpretation of a character—I must after all be careful about criticisms and incursions into a domain that is not my own—the same is not true of that other game now spreading, the game of "what is what?" By this I mean the recent efforts of literary historians and of historians as such to set themselves up as judges of the truth of Balzac's descriptions of his times. Here the failure is total. Not concerning the political or economic facts, which are easy to grasp and better explored by historians in works among which Bertrand Gille's occupy pride of place,[1] but concerning social classes considered politically and economically, as well as demographically, socially, and morally: in a word, in what concerns the essential core of the *Comédie humaine*.

This failure characterizes work in literature at least as much as work in history, but on each side it has different causes, implicit in the two disciplines.

To verify the authenticity of Balzac's descriptions, literary scholars use two methods. Transposing into this historical undertaking the habits of literary criticism, they devote themselves to the search for sources. To discover what Balzac knows of things and people, they ask what he might have learned of them: not from the banal, untraceable personal experience common to everybody, but from books that one might reasonably suppose him to have read. A strange procedure, which consists, in a word, of supposing in our novelist a total initial ignorance of the social group he was going to describe—aristocrats, bourgeois, or peasants; which allows him only a book-ish method of informing himself; about whom one would have to say: "He has eyes and he sees not, he has ears and he hears not"; and which in the end condemns him to having read the catalogue of the Bibliothèque Nationale. Suzanne Bérard herself, whose dissertation moves so far from the trodden paths, believes she must, in a chapter called "The Influence of the Teach-ers," search out the books from which Balzac must have drawn inspiration to describe provincials in Paris: and she cites Molière, of whom she says "we are certain that Balzac had read him," as well as La Fontaine and Mme de Sévigné. So we are reassured, and she adds: "And why would he not have read Charles Sorel's *Francion*?"[2]

Historians would be wrong to laugh at this procedure, which can seem strange and useless to them. One must consider it to be a rite of initiation among literary scholars. The tribe of historians—or rather the tribes, for there are several—have their rites as well, which literary scholars must find curious. Unless the document cited has truly had an influence—which is rare—the method is without interest. Balzac was educated in the same way as the Parisians of his times. And let us add that bibliographies of literary scholarship (which all copy each other), display—from the sole point of view of bibliography—strange gaps that condemn the whole undertaking. In the bibliography of a book that aspires to treat "economic and social realities in the *Comédie humaine*," one finds all the well-known and unimportant minor works of picturesque literature, but neither Tocqueville nor Rémusat.[3]

In most cases, moreover, the enumeration of supposed sources is bor-rowed from works of history—a procedure that condemns literary criticism far less than history itself. The main explanation of this awkwardness of research in literary history is in fact the paucity of sociohistorical studies in these areas. Specialists in literature would have no problem in disclosing the authenticity, excesses, and errors of Balzac's descriptions if they could com-pare them to historical models. The latter are still quite rare. And they cannot help being quantitative. Literary minds are repelled by figures: they are quite different in this respect from Balzac himself, whose interest in statistics has never been sufficiently noted. When they refer to a study, they choose studies in social, qualitative, intuitive, philosophical, or merely liter-ary history that I need not cite here: even more commonly, their preferences go to those who are content to borrow from Balzac the essence of their analyses. To verify the authenticity of the *Comédie humaine*, they appeal to works of history whose documentation is basically a compilation of the *Comédie humaine*. If I seem to be exaggerating, one need only consult, in recent books that deal with the relationships between Balzac and his times, the bibliography of historical works. "But you are in them," I will be told. Alas, I am there, but badly interpreted, cited helter-skelter, or simply re-copied and not cited.

To limit ourselves to Paris, the consequence of all this is that the description of the city and its people, done by "Balzacian" historians or by "histori-cal" Balzacians, is encumbered by traditional and legendary themes that we will be forgiven for not enumerating and criticizing here. A few examples, however, will serve to warn those who would insist on work of this sort. From the greater attention Balzac pays the bourgeoisie rather than the working classes, it is usually concluded that the latter are absent from the *Comédie humaine,* as well as from Parisian society, except for a few quaint craftsmen, some criminals, or groups gradually moving into the middle class. Through an identical simplification, the careers of Remonencq[4] and his com-patriots lead critics to lend unwarranted importance to Auvergnats in the *Comédie humaine* and in the regeneration of lower and middle social classes. Balzac, however, in studies of less interesting cases and in observations so valuable and numerous that one could use them for statistical analysis, brings to the problem of immigration to Paris during the first half of the nineteenth century most of its ethnic ingredients: the many and diverse regions of origin, the distribution by trade, class, and often by neighborhood, and finally the influence of regions of origin on the behavior of individuals. As for social mobility, one can consider that until very recently, its study has been skewed by the vision of great middle class careers that have obscured many other careers equally present in Balzac's work but oriented in different ways: obscure, dispersed, merely sketched, or hastily indicated in passing, and yet corresponding more closely to what the most ordinary knowledge of the society of the times permits us to intuit and to what modern research is beginning to confirm.

* * *

From the social lesson that Balzac gives us, let us sketch out, in brief and varied remarks, the principal themes whose study would call for greater developments. On this subject there is a book to be written. Here is what its outline might be.

If we consider that the study of societies of all periods must result in a continuous, homogeneous, and precise description of those societies, in their unity and diversity, their present characteristics and the surviving elements of their past, and above all the relationships that must exist between their highest forms and what Maurice Halbwachs has called "the biological sub-structure of all social life";[5] if such is our definition and ambition, we may consider that the *Comédie humaine* gathers together all the needed givens. Before asking if it reproduces exactly the society of its times, or if it is in conformity with history—a secondary preoccupation—we must observe that it brings to history and to sociology their program and their model. Whether it refers to the past or the present, this is what social description is, failing which it is only a minor exercise whose interest does not go beyond the trivial inquiry that is its pretext and whose contribution will never rival that of the most mediocre newspaper article or novel. Let us enumerate the themes of Balzac's lesson.

It is first of all attention to the foundations and biological aspects of the evolution of societies: the affirmation of the primacy of biology (Preface of 1842); the physical characteristics of the individuals and the groups in which they are assembled; the aging of individuals and milieux thanks to the reappearance of characters; the demographic (that is, physical) aspects of social mobility thanks to genealogies and the reconstitution of families; the problem of generations, evident for example in the description of ambitious young men of all classes and temperaments united by the links and determinism of their age.

The rest is built on this "geological layer of primary terrain" of which Halbwachs speaks. And in the same way, the *lesson* of the rest is drawn from it. First of all, it is a method of defining and studying social classes, present in the ensemble of the work, but most particularly with respect to Paris in the opening pages of *La Fille aux yeux d'or*. These pages furnish the historian with all the givens of the complex problem of social classes that he would vainly seek elsewhere: their enumeration, their hierarchy, their limits, their edges, their contacts, and finally the method of evoking and describing them.

But the interest on these pages goes considerably beyond the study of the first half of the nineteenth century. Their lesson applies to the study of societies in all ages, be it historical or sociological. It teaches us that there is no definition of social classes as such, nor any method to study them that is equally applicable to all classes in all periods; that definitions and methods vary in different periods; and that one would be mistaken to use for the study of a given class at a given moment of the nineteenth or twentieth century these definitions and methods developed for a different class and for a different period. It also teaches us that these definitions and methods are not born of meditation, or from conceptual or philosophical effort; that they result even less from the implantation in a French and Parisian milieu of mechanical classifications and automatic procedures developed in other places for the study of less complex societies and mentalities; and that there is more sociological intelligence in a chapter of Balzac than in a compilation of American research; finally, that those definitions and methods arise spontaneously from familiarity with people and places.

If the characteristic property of historians is to recognize the quality of this lesson in social history and description, the role of literary specialists is to provide the reasons for it. Not by borrowing history from the historians, as do certain recent works that serve as the occasion or rather the pretext for this outline, but by analyzing the way in which Balzac wrote, as Suzanne Bérard does in her dissertation on *La Genèse d'un roman de Balzac: Illusions perdues* (The genesis of a Balzac novel: Lost Illusions); it is the only one of these recent theses that interests history, because instead of getting mixed up in history, it remains literature.

The first problem, to the solution of which Suzanne Bérard makes many contributions, is to understand why, how, and to what degree Balzac experiences and registers the society of his times. Without doubt one sometimes discovers "that this universe," as she puts it, "has only an exterior appearance of solidity, that it is perfectly devoid of authenticity . . . Ages and birthdates of characters are the object of entertaining blunders . . . Balzac, who knows his own weakness and who is singularly suspicious of himself, erases chronologies as much as possible as he corrects. Yet he needs them when he writes, because indications of this sort, as erroneous as they may be, help him create the illusion of reality for himself." For himself and for historians who experience the same need to cling to dates and periods and who, in this detail, recognize in him one of their own.

The second problem is to understand how, starting with this gift of observation that is both conscious and unconscious, devouring and passive, he describes and recreates to the point of giving the impression of imitating nature and of delivering to us not a novel but a document.

Certain givens of this second problem are perhaps more evident to historians than to literary scholars. Historians have spontaneous confidence in Balzac because many descriptions of the *Comédie humaine* can easily be mistaken for those archival documents to which they are accustomed—in both form and content.

Like archival documents, they are often precise and incomplete; they have meticulous respect for detail and disregard for contradictions, rapid composition, imperfection of form, negligence, maladroitness, vulgarity, unevenness. Paul Valéry finds a pebble polished by the ocean and admires the fact that it imitates a work of art. With Balzac, it is the work of art that imitates nature. Whence the temptation of the historian to rediscover in this work, as in the humblest of documents on which he works, the trace of what has been rather than the result of what has been invented.

The illusion is all the stronger in that this work imitates the form of the document as well as its substance. How can we fail to compare Balzac's testimony with Zola's? Sociological history—at least that of the masses—would never be tempted to grant to Zola the total, blind confidence it has in Balzac. Balzac registers; Zola documents himself, and in a necessarily incomplete and partial manner. Balzac reconstitutes, Zola fabricates, and it can be felt. There is always the temptation to charge the errors of the former to truthfulness, and the truth of the latter—as well as his own many errors—to imagination.

* * *

Why does Balzac observe so exactly or rather in such a profoundly historical manner, and why on the other hand does he reconstitute so perfectly? The solution to these two problems—which only specialists in literature can bring us—is itself the essence of the general problem of the authenticity of the *Comédie humaine*. Insofar as the second is concerned, the study of the genesis of *Illusions perdues* explains why Balzac "creates illusion so strongly that, for those who are sensitive to it, it is not easy to forget"—which is the case of historians. Insofar as the first problem is concerned, the problem of observation, literary scholars will forgive the historian for asking them to go further in their analyses. The texts in which Balzac boasts of possessing that exceptional quality that astonished even himself, are well known. In 1828 it is the Introduction to *Le Gars:* "He grew like a plant, abandoning himself to perpetual contemplation . . . living, so to speak, only by the strength of those interior senses that he claims constitute a double being within man, but exhausted by this profound intuition of things"; and again: "This soul was, in Leibnitz's magnificent phrase, a concentric mirror of the universe." In 1836 it is the opening pages of *Facino Cane,* that moreover have the merit of evoking the people of the working-class districts: "In me, observation had already become intuitive, it penetrated my soul without neglecting the body; or rather, it seized exterior details so well that it went straightaway beyond them; it gave me the ability to live the life of the individual toward whom it was directed." Not only does Balzac claim he possesses this intuition, but, as we can guess from these lines, he bases it on a theory and even a metaphysics that literary research, pursued through the totality of the work, could reconstitute. Or rather, why does not this research apply itself to the practice, even to the physics, of the matter: that is, to the analysis of this gift, not through what Balzac says about it, but by what the genesis of his novels reveals and by what our knowledge of the author can discover?

If it is the role of history to demonstrate to literature the authenticity of the *Comédie humaine,* it is the place of literature to reveal to sociological history and description, through the analysis of Balzacian intuition, the secret and the condition of its own creation.

Notes

1. [Ed. note: Bertrand Gille is the author of numerous distinguished historical studies, the most important of which in this context is *Sources statistiques de l'histoire de France* (Geneva: Droz, 1980).]

2. [Ed. note: The reference is to Charles Sorel's *La Vraie Histoire comique de Francion* (The true comic story of Francion), published in 1623.]

3. [Ed. note: The reference is undoubtedly to Jean-Hervé Donnard, *Balzac: Les réalités économiques et sociales dans La Comédie humaine* (Balzac: economic and social realities in the Human Comedy) (Paris: Armand Colin, 1961).]

4. [Ed. note: Rémonencq is a dealer in junk and bric-a-brac who, in *Le Cousin Pons,* rises through a career of fraud and murder from being a peasant of the Auvergne to being the proprietor of a magnificent antiques shop in the exclusive Boulevard de la Madeleine.]

5. [Ed. note: During the 1930s, Maurice Halbwachs published a number of volumes on what he called "social morphology." Chevalier perhaps has in mind a volume bearing that phrase as title, published in Paris in 1938.]

The Author's Point of View   Per Nykrog*

It is at lofty heights where irreconcilable extremes rejoin and melt into each other, where all contradictions are reconciled, that we must finally seek the implicit vantage point from which Balzac conceives the ensemble of his *Comédie humaine* and the intuition or thought that it was to express. At such heights, the contemplation of the world, reduced to causes, means, and principles becomes at once a love affair, a prayer, almost an ecstasy. It is difficult to follow the thinker through these regions, but it seems certain that he did move through them, and it is also certain that his experience provides the key to his intimate and deep religiosity as well as to his intellectual adventure and his vocation.

Was Balzac a mystic, or at least at a certain moment did he have an illumination comparable to that of the mystics? We know that he had probably been initiated, doubtlessly into a group of Martinists, and that this experience had left a strong impression on him. His youthful preoccupations prepared him for it, and the *Livre Mystique* and the *Traité de la Prière* are evidence of it.[1] One can debate the authenticity of such a mystical experience: it seems that it was first and foremost intellectual, marked by strong emotion. But that emotion could have been confused with the intoxication of the writer discovering and deifying his own powers, as he says in *Louis Lambert*. Certainly no one can discover in himself the vocation of devoting an entire life to a work of the dimensions and characteristics of the *Comédie humaine* without immediately experiencing a tumultuous state of euphoric enthusiasm; but, conversely, one may wonder in what mental state a man must find himself in order to discover such a vocation.

This state of intellectual and emotional intuition is directly reflected in the writings that date from the first half of the 1830s—the *Livre mystique* above all, but also texts like the visionary experience of Raphaël de Valentin in the antiquarian's shop: "he exited from real life, rose step by step toward an ideal world, arrived in the enchanted palaces of Ecstasy, where the universe appeared to him in fragments and in fiery flashes, just as the future passed in flames before the eyes of Saint John on Pathmos" (PCh, 9, 24).

Now what is most interesting from a modern point of view is the fact that the texts of 1830 and 1831 offer three similar figures who all experience such a mental state, although they are presented quite differently: old Belvidéro in *L'Elixir de longue vie*, Gobseck in the story that bears his name, and the antiquarian himself in *La Peau de chagrin*. The characters of the *Livre mystique* are presented, practically speaking, only from the inside, from a sympathetic "sphere" within which they are seen as believable (except for Becker in connection with Séraphîta and the brief appearance of Louis Lambert in the background of the *Curé de Tours*).[2] One could also note the

*Translated and reprinted by permission from *La Pensée de Balzac* (Copenhagen: Munksgaard 1965), 387–394. © Per Nykrog, 1965.

important reservations made by the narrator in *Louis Lambert* and the contradictory opinions that Wilfrid and Minna form in *Séraphîta*. The three others, in contrast, are exclusively seen from the outside, from within a "sphere" from which they can be judged; more importantly, we can follow them for a period of their lives. This last characteristic appears again as an important aspect of the presentation of Louis Lambert.

Old Belvidéro grumbles on his deathbed, "I am God" (10, 306); Gobseck, presenting himself as a pure contemplator, similarly declares: "All human passions, exaggerated by the play of social ambition, come to parade before me; and I live in absolute calm. But then, I replace your scientific curiosity—a kind of battle that man always loses—with an understanding of all the springs that move Humanity. In a word, I possess the world without fatigue, and the world hasn't the least hold on me" (2, 630). Further on he remarks: "My vision is like God's" (2, 636). And the antiquarian, in his mysterious solitude, gives himself up to orgies of Thought, "to the sublime ability of conjuring up the universe within oneself, to the immense pleasure of movement unbounded by restrictions of time or space, to the pleasure of embracing everything, of seeing everything, of leaning over the edge of the world to examine other spheres, to listen to God!" (9, 41).

Facing these three figures, presented without the sympathy that surrounds those of the *Livre mystique,* the reader cannot fail to see megalomania and insanity; and their subsequent stories, even though they do not differ essentially from that of Louis Lambert, confirm this judgement. All three, in effect, are brutally reduced to less extraordinary dimensions. Belvidéro disappears totally: his son, by crushing his eye, crushes his memory and his very being (a son who, for his part, almost becomes a saint of the Catholic Church!);[3] Gobseck ends in a state of decay and absurdity when his robust health can no longer direct his thought and commercial activity; the antiquarian, who constitutes the clearest case, falls victim to a vulgar passion and abandons all knowledge and wisdom in order to run after a dancing girl. Conversely, the delirious idealism of Emilio Memmi disappears when his eroticism is satisfied, and so on.[4] In these cases, as always in Balzac, the whole structure of thought changes or collapses when the physical, moral, or social status of the thinker is altered.

Obviously, one can see in this schema manifestations of the well-known idea that it is impossible for Man, that fragile creature, to go beyond his condition bound in Time and Space. These stories would then be merely the implementation of a romantic commonplace. But basing oneself on several of the major themes of Balzacian thought, one can also read them as the mythic developments of a dialectic between interior and exterior universes, a dialectic attached to the complex of illusion, but illusion as Balzac understands it—double edged, at once error and value: "The most beautiful things in life are its illusions. The most respectable are our most futile beliefs" (Phy. 10, 638).

The mechanism of this dialectic is the same as the one that lies at the basis of the Balzacian theory of knowledge and communication, and it can also be found as an essential element in the complex of concepts with which he surrounds existential problems. In analyzing his theory of knowledge, I underscored his critique of a primitive behaviorism: it does not suffice to study behavior. One must subjectively embrace the thought, the feelings, and the motivating forces of the person one is studying. But the terms can also be reversed: one does not completely describe a thought by adopting it. One must, as a corollary, think the thinker who thinks that thought. Now in this operation, the thought changes; having been a value it becomes a symptom. When thinking a thought—whether one has formed it oneself or adopted it from someone else—one accepts it as a value, and above all one implicitly accepts the point of view of the thinker who thinks it as a point of view that if not absolute, is at least valid and not problematical. But as soon as one also thinks the thinker, a distancing takes place; the charm is broken, the absolute point of view reveals itself as relative and personal, subject to error and susceptible to being exchanged for a different one just as valid. A value remains pure only to the extent that it remains an "unknown masterpiece"; that is, to the extent that it has not been contemplated from the point of view of another sphere than the one in which the believer has placed himself.

It is at this juncture that Balzac's ideas on knowledge, on the problem of faith, and on existential and moral problems come together. For it is only on the social level, to the degree that one has contact with others, that problems of morality and faith become pressing. The mystic, the scholar such as Cuvier, and the novelist "see" the world in its totality, and have no moral problem as long as they abandon themselves to their intuition; for in their supreme effort, they have only one point of view at their disposal. Their "faith" even seems linked to their solitude, which (provisionally) excludes from their universe any other point of view, just as it does in the peasant innocent of thought, in the lover, in the adolescent—and in the perfume merchant.[5] It is in the confrontation between the "spheres," on the social level where individuals meet, that the thinker becomes aware of the multiplicity of possible solutions; it is there that one must choose between the different moralities offered by a "linnean" system of Virtue (Phy, 11, 162). Doubt, anguish, and ambiguity are linked to the condition of social man living in "spheres" of contradictory moralities, all relatively valid. For God and for the novelist, who are not involved in the game, there is no definitive morality: any choice is acceptable to them; they need merely deduce its consequences. The anguish of the moral drama lies on the level of individual existence, where the choice is all-important because of its immediate consequences.

In the case that we are considering, the three figures of Belvidéro, Gobseck, and the antiquarian show—in accord with the contradictions between perceptions from different points of view observed in *Louis Lambert* and elsewhere—that Balzac not only lives his illumination and his sense of intellectual power, but also that he reflects on himself and on his thought by looking at himself from the outside via an ironic reversal that takes as a mirror the very idea of the thinker living with his thought. In this mirror, the observer who feels himself to be near absolute truth sees himself as a madman carried away by an idea that is in fact very relative and linked to his personal existence—in a word, an illusion.

The presence of such a dialectical strategy, consciously expressed in the work from the very beginning of its creation, profoundly modifies the character that must be attributed to the initial experience. The point of departure thus includes not only illumination and faith, but also, in an alternative movement often referred to in the preceding pages, their counterpart: relativistic analysis and its resulting doubt. More precisely, the total mystical experience includes not only a mystical illumination but also its negation. Everything in fact seems to indicate that the novelist wanted to succeed in the logically complex operation of making his doubt part of his faith in order to raise the latter to a higher plane. That is why he seems to have wanted to see himself as a character in the great comedy he is describing; why he observes himself ironically, spinning on the same diabolical merry-go-round as the antiquarian, Raphaël, and all the others; why he consciously seeks to launch the "superior" reader into the same whirlwind, comparable to the famous paradox of Epimenides the Cretan, who said that Cretans were not worthy of belief.

(But only the "superior" reader; knowing the social and moral dangers of this whirlwind that risks creating great misfortunes in the short run, the novelist does everything not to trouble the naive faith of the innocent reader, whom at every turn he sends back to the comfort of conformist Christianity and respect for established values).

This merry-go-round leads the fictional character from conviction to disenchantment, from analysis to faith. In Balzac's life it gives rise to two (or three) different lifestyles; in the work, to two or three different narrative techniques. The coexistence, in the same life and the same work, of such different and contradictory manners, in close symbiosis, makes them both appear confusing and paradoxical.

It is useful to recall in this connection a small, meaningful, although frivolous detail. At a certain moment, Balzac, who loved to ennoble his name (*de* Balzac), also took a heraldic coat of arms. He gave this usurped coat of arms a motto: *Jour et Nuit,* and he flanked it with two outer ornaments: "dexter a veiled woman symbolizing the night, as supporter; sinister a bold rooster symbolizing the day, as supporter."[6] Whatever one may think of the aristocratic pretensions of the plebeian novelist, the choice of the motto and the symbolism of the ornaments are revealing.

In the novelist's life, one easily recognizes the equivalent of the veiled woman symbolizing Night, and even more easily that of the bold rooster symbolizing Day. The anecdotal biography of Balzac abounds in information relative to the latter, to his relaxed bohemian existence, to his life as a vulgar and overdressed man about town and a shameless speculator. But the same biography says very little about the unknown, nocturnal existence of the (false) white monk meditating and creating in solitude.[7] We know approximately the number of cups of coffee he swallowed, and we know his approximate schedule, but for the rest we know nothing other than the results: the novelistic work. And yet this is the essential part of his life. And finally we can guess at a third lifestyle, grave and composite, which appears in his relations with certain intimate old friends, the Survilles, the Carrauds, and others, and when he is fighting for his work.

The reader who seeks to know Balzac through the study of his behavior in his "social" existence must meditate a long time on the bold rooster that decorates the right side of the coat of arms: it is indeed the caricature of a style of existence considered essentially inauthentic and caricature-like by the very man who practiced it. It serves to deny and abolish the high but fallacious truths of the Night, above all perhaps with respect to the Self of the thinker. For the bold rooster and the veiled woman mutually abolish and destroy each other: the Night is "light," the interior, moral life, transcendent certainties; but this "light" disappears in the light of Day. Conversely the analytic and pragmatic light of Day is merely nothingness and obscurity in the "light" of the Night. And so on.

The same is true of the work. In it, one discovers at the extreme two contradictory and irreconcilable narrative modes, each corresponding to one of the extreme series we have already confronted. There is "analytic" writing, used for practical, social, and pragmatic problems. It is the writing of the bold rooster. It is journalistic in manner; it displays an intentional though superficial cynicism; it insists on verbal facility and vulgar brilliance. It has surges of emotional generosity, but solely in connection with terrestrial and everyday problems, traditionally considered not very lofty. This is the mode that dominates in the *Physiologie du mariage* and related texts, and it was to mark the whole series of the *Etudes analytiques*, including the *Monographie de la vertu*, very relativistic and corrosive, but nonetheless destined from the very start to be the final word of the *Comédie humaine*.

Then there is the fervent, emotional, and unctuous writing, characteristic of the *Etudes philosophiques* and in particular of the *Livre mystique*. It is the ecstatic writing of the visions of the Night, flying toward the highest transcendental truths, far from any earthly preoccupation. Finally there is a mixed writing, constructed out of simple observations and descriptions, but giving way, in proportions that vary from text to text, either to worldly or political cynicism, or—above all—to a more or less fervent, more or less elegiac emotion. This mixed style, which rather quickly comes to dominate, corresponds to the "cumulation" of the scholar and the madman, of Jean-Jacques and of the Bureau of Longitudes, which are mentioned in the *Théorie de la démarche*; it is destined to link the two complementary "asymptotes" in a synthesis, without masking their essentially different natures.

If one wishes to grasp the novelist's point of view in Balzac's work, it is not enough to take into account "Day Thought," "Night Thought," and the dialectic between the two. One must also introduce the dimension of an evolution in time.

The description given above of the two Thoughts and their dialectic refers, strictly speaking, only to the first phase of his creative years, to the so-called period of ascendancy. During that time Balzac, like Rastignac, proposes to pursue his attack in "two parallel trenches," fully confident of his historic mission as well as his century's; he is still under the spell of his great intuition in its first bloom, but as yet only partly conceptualized. This confidence and faith, simple at night, superior and paradoxical in its totality, is not a naive or elementary optimism: the massive power of social resistance appears as great in the early works as in the late ones. It is at this period that Balzac imagines the creative work of Benassis, who believes and doubts at the same time—"Between the one who always hopes and the one who hopes no longer, I don't know which is the most cowardly" (MC, 8, 502). And one can illustrate that state of mind with the hallucinatory vision of Raphaël in the antiquarian's shop: it shows Man engaged in discovering the meaning of the entire Universe, in making all things come alive.

After about 1835 the tone changes slightly. Already in 1834 (the year he was created) Rastignac had to abandon the idea of advancing on two fronts simultaneously, and it is at that moment as well that the two extreme narrative modes disappear from Balzac's work. The initial intuition is conceptualized, hence exteriorized, with the *Livre mystique*, and this leads to the disappearance of both the "mystographic" and the "analytic" modes at the same time. The last fantastic item in Balzac's work, Melmoth's gift (1835), ends as a worthless certificate on the stock exchange (MR, 9, 305ff.).[8] There remains only the domain over which Day Thought and Night Thought had been in agreement: the functioning of psychic and social mechanism. Creative work is henceforth oriented toward the technical solution newly discovered with *Le Père Goriot*; entirely conceived in the composite mode, it attends to existential and social problems at the level of individual lives, abandoning transcendental conceptions and analytic irony as blurred perspectives that shade off toward both ends of the spectrum. But the novelist has not lost faith, nor the conviction of his pedagogical mission; he has merely narrowed his range, without denying its extreme limits.

As of about 1839 a new attitude gradually takes over, an attitude of discouragement. The *Avant Propos* of 1842 still faithfully repeats earlier ideas, but if one compares them to the works written at that time, one can wonder if they have not merely survived in the form of congealed concepts and convictions. It is not simply for lack of time that Balzac at that moment would have been incapable of rewriting *Séraphîta* or *Le Médecin de campagne*. Everything that Day Thought had in common with Night Thought nevertheless remains alive, and that is a great deal; nearly everything studied in the six parts of this book remains intact.

It is not faith that Balzac has lost at the end of his life, it is hope. He is no longer seeking to indicate a path; he gathers evidence in broadly conceived novels now more frequently left incomplete in a relatively advanced state: *Les Paysans, Les Petits Bourgeois, Le Député d'Arcis*. Another significant fact: the lives of certain characters created in the past are taken up again and given prolongations that turn into mockery. Vautrin the great rebel, Rastignac the ferocious egoist, and other unlikely characters join the mainstream and become pillars of society. It is only in this phase of his life that Balzac adopts, as a title for the whole ensemble, the bitter title of *La Comédie humaine*.

In the last completed great work, *Le Cousin Pons*, the fate of the picture collection counterbalances the revelation experienced by Raphaël in the midst of the accumulated objects in *La Peau de chagrin:* in Pons's hidden museum, the collection was alive; during his death agony, it becomes an object, and at his death it falls into the hands of a world for which its inner value is a closed book. The death of Sylvain Pons and of his paintings marks the disappearance of hope; it is the agony of Night Thought. But it is not its negation: Pons was a reality, and his paintings may well come to life again.

Notes

1. [Ed. note: In the preceding chapters of his book, Nykrog examines six notions that he considers to be fundamental structures of Balzac's thought and consequently of the *Comédie humaine:* Ambition, Thought, Creativity, Spheres (i.e., mutually exclusive modes of being), Life Drama (i.e., characteristic phases of life), Heaven and Hell (i.e., extreme choices in life). All textual references are to the first Pléiade edition, edited by Marcel Bouteron. *Le Livre mystique* was a reissue of *Louis Lambert* together with a few other texts; the arrangement was not retained. The *Traité de la prière* was one of Balzac's many aborted projects.]

2. [Ed. note: In the novel *Séraphîta*, the pastor Becker sees the angel Séraphîta as a female rather than as a superior being.]

3. [Ed. note: Belvidéro asks his son to anoint him with a magic elixir as soon as he has died. But the son, who wishes to keep the elixir for himself, experiments on his father's eye, and finding that the elixir does indeed revivify, crushes the eye and allows his father to remain dead.]

4. [Ed. note: Emilio Memmi is a character in the novel *Massimilla Doni*.]

5. [Ed note: The reference is to César Birotteau, the hero (or rather the antihero) of *L'Histoire de la grandeur et de la décadence de César Birotteau*.]

6. Fernand Lotte, *Armorial de la Comédie humaine* (Paris: Garnier, 1963), 2; reproduced in André Billy, *Vie de Balzac* (Paris: Flammarion, 1944), 1, 70.

7. [Ed. note: The allusion is to Balzac's habit of dressing in a white carthusian monk's robe when he launched himself on an extended period of composition.]

8. [Ed. Note: The reference is to *Melmoth réconcilié*, Balzac's addition to Charles Maturin's fable, *Melmoth the Wanderer*.]

A Balzacian Overture

Pierre Barbéris*

From the young, ardent hack of the 1820s, needy and unknown, to Mme Hanska's husband, the "great mind that Europe has lost," whom Victor Hugo observed on his deathbed; or even from the thirty-four-year-old Balzac, a fantastical Parisian storyteller and the author of only a few *Scènes de la vie privée*, to the Balzac of *Les Parents pauvres*, via the Balzac of the Vautrin cycle: the trajectory is impressive, immense, surely unique in France. During those thirty-odd years, certain major works of our nineteenth century— and of world literature—were conceived and produced. Wordsmith, visionary, journalist, man of letters, caricatured together with Dumas, running after Eugène Sue's popularity, awaited by the critical genius of Baudelaire, destined for Rodin's sculpture—Balzac, if one limits oneself to appearances and diagrams, moves from the universe of Dante to the world of the boulevard and Sacha Guitry. His income, his publishing statistics, his loves, his mad expenditures, his trips, his audacity, his vanity, his collections, his big belly, his hammerblows into the decor of the century, his efforts to be accepted by the right wing, his continued fidelity to the left wing, his rejection of bucolic, messianic, romantic or social styles—everything makes him difficult to classify. He is absolutely unable, in any case, to occupy a place in the literary, idealist, and luminous progress that the romantic nineteenth century wanted to make its own, above all without a *new* revolution, toward an "Open Blue Sky" finally and democratically guaranteed to everyone.[1] Balzac never was exemplary, either in his life or in his work, and even less *classical* (see "Balzac" in elementary school manuals). There is, in the whole Balzacian enterprise, something thick, something not noble, something not "moral," something impossible to mobilize or recapture for any kind of finality or lesson. One seeks in vain in the story of Balzac the equivalent of the tricolor flag of 1830 or of 1848, the rock of Jersey, "the shepherd's house," or an expulsion from the Collège de France.[2]

The fact is that if Balzac's life and destiny are great and sad, they are a private story with all its consequences, as we should have realized right away (as did Hugo), or that we should have understood and sought out. Balzac did not end in glory and honor, in spectacle or celebrity, or even as an author happily and professionally condemned. For him there was no assured glory; there were no titles, no noble attitudes, no national funeral, not even election to the Academy. After the June Days,[3] he was a candidate for Chateaubriand's seat in the Academy, but we will never read the speech he would have made on René and the youth of the century, with the first important confrontation between bourgeoisie and proletariat as background. Balzac did not end and did not die as the idol of a people or of a regime, nor even of an ardent and silent minority preparing revenge and rehabilitation in the pri-

*Translated and reprinted by permission from *Balzac. Une Mythologie réaliste* (Paris: Larousse, 1971), 231–34.

vacy of colleges and secret societies. He died in a kind of solitary night, having written for a strange and unclassifiable public, having ceased to publish and having only very partially realized his dream: to move into his fabulous house with L'Etrangère, after having published his *Complete Works* and having earned a fortune.[4] As for his career (political or journalistic), it seems that with sick and worn-out heart and mind he gave up, dreaming only of rest.

Beyond these biographical singularities, there is, in the culmination of this life, something like the image of the fatal and necessary derailment of the artist and the man of intelligence, as the century and the modern world take hold. Rising above the triumphalism of Victor Hugo, Balzac reaches toward Baudelaire, Flaubert, and Verlaine, toward the great solitary writers and the great "*maudits*."[5] Balzac dies full of illusion, owner of a house, of various collections, of paintings, but covered in debts that his widow will take years to pay, and at the cost of fully and shamelessly exploiting—as a woman of the system and well-counseled as such—the mine that had been left to her. Although he was a property owner, in the end Balzac truly possessed nothing but that extraordinary and invisible museum that the vultures would be unable to steal. Here the story of Pons, let us recall, is transparent and full of meaning: the Camusot-Popinots possess only the appearance of expensive objects, the simulacra; their beauty and spirit will always escape them.[6]

The true world of Balzac is not the one in which he sought to cut a figure and in which he rather vainly and restlessly moved. A radical scission now opens between the world of careers and real existence, and that of superior meanings. Of Balzac there remains only the *Comédie humaine,* whereas we are still discussing the importance of Jean Racine's work in the context of his career. Balzac, surely more than any other great romantic writer, has imposed this image of a literature henceforth endowed with a mission. In 1821, that was not the assumption; it was a time when the dream was to marry an English girl. But precisely because things had changed, something different occurred: literature had come of age and now signified and functioned entirely through specifically literary devices. Whence, for a long time and still today among men of our times, we find a phenomenon of rejection with respect to Balzac.

One thing, which confirms the shocking nature of Balzac, is certain: republican tradition and practice at the end of the century will not know what to do with this man for whom the main conflict had ceased being the one between Ancien Régime and Modern World to become the one that opposed Money to Life, to the need to live. The Third Republic loved Balzac no more than it loved Stendhal. For its streets, squares, pageantry, for its prize givings and departures to war, it preferred Hugo, Michelet, Gambetta, even Thiers or Châteaubriand to either of them. What could be done with Balzac in the context of modern jingoism and of honest administration? Thus arises the problem of the real meaning and usefulness of Balzac's work. This whole production, from 1820 to 1850, followed the development of the century and also went beyond it; it challenged the century's messianic ascensional values, its central postulate of the existence of a truly seamless, uninterrupted Republic of the sons of the bourgeois revolutions of 1789 and 1830, on the model of liberalism or "French" socialism. A *monstre sacré* of modern Parisian life, making no concessions to "culture," impossible to integrate, irrecuperable, Balzac was to find himself anesthetized, neutralized, placed in orbit at a respectful planetary distance by official criticism. It is surely not for nothing that progressive ideology preferred Hugo perched on his rock.

Today, however, secular and republican bourgeois messianism has lost much of its glow. Balzac has gained some. It is not without interest to note that the beneficiary in no way belongs to the race of "angelic" writers, but to that of productive and proletarian writers. Others have made their way as much by their (exemplary) lives or adventures as by their work. It has never been possible to reduce or simply to attach Balzac to this kind of subsidiary epic. Then why should we be astonished that Balzac and the Balzacian canon should have been truly recognized and correctly judged as events of civilization only by those who were one day to translate into another language what he could as yet only say through his stories and his heroes?[7] His long-misunderstood primary work, this material that challenged consecrated forms and practices, is an admirable testimony to the specific and invincible power of literature, at a moment when analysis and ideology were still stammering.

Notes

1. [Ed. note: The reference is to Hugo's poem "En Plein Ciel," in which progress in aviation is taken as a metaphor for an eventual human liberation.]

2. [Ed. note: The references are to Victor Hugo's exile after 1852, part of which he spent on the Channel Islands; to Alfred de Vigny's poem "La Maison du Berger"; and to the expulsion of Ernest Renan from the Collège de France in 1864. All are dramatic symbols of political or intellectual opposition.]

3. [Ed. note: The reference is to the Revolution of 1848. "René" is a familiar reference to the poet Châteaubriand.]

4. [Ed. note: Mme Hanska, who was to become Mme Balzac shortly before the novelist's death, first wrote to him using the pseudonym "L'Etrangère"—an epithet that has clung to her to this day.]

5. [Ed. note: A group of poets of the midcentury (including Verlaine and Rimbaud) were popularly known as the "Poètes maudits" or "Poets of Damnation" because of their difficult and depressing relationship with the society in which they lived.]

6. [Ed. note: The reference is to the virtual theft of Cousin Pons's art collection in the novel that bears his name.]

7. [Ed. note: The allusion is to Marx's and Engels's sympathetic reading of Balzac's work.]

[Balzac's Metaphors]

Lucienne Frappier-Mazur*

Every day sees the publication of a new study of metaphor.[1] Any theo-retical conclusion can represent only a step in present-day research.[2]

At least we now know more about the possible relationships between image and fictional form. We also see more clearly the various mental mecha-nisms that underpin metaphor, metonymy, and synecdoche, and that deter-mine their appearance, their superposition, and their connections, whether they refer to the cultural code, to their context, or to an extralinguistic referent.

An important theoretical consequence results from this. Thanks to the explanatory function of the image, its all-encompassing development, and the recurrence of the same categories in the novel, our study confirms the fact that many metaphors of our discourse belong to the language of psycho-analysis; more generally, it confirms the identical nature of associative mecha-nisms that come into play in these two modes of expression. We have seen that associations of similarity, contiguity, and inclusion, and the processes of displacement and of condensation that they entail, are common to the inter-nal structure of the image in texts as well as dreams. Metaphors of money and of food, which refer to a physiological domain, illustrate this phenome-non to the point of self-evidence, by bringing together the very categories that the unconscious associates and identifies: money-phallus, food-sexuality, and others. The sadomasochistic pairing is continued in the complementarity of the weapon and the wound. These associations are not unique to Balzac, nor indeed to literature. They can be found in other systems of representa-tion such as mythology or the visual arts.

Another omnipresent factor, exceptionally developed in Balzac even outside the physiological domain, contributes to tightening the links be-tween the metaphoric text and the psychoanaltyical point of view: this is the theory of unitary energy that is expressed throughout the *Comédie humaine*. Most of the categories of images that we have studied end up by representing that centralizing energy and its ramifications in Thought. The monetary metaphor analyzes in detail the quantitative character of that energy, but the same economic point of view also pervades the other categories. Balzac did not invent this theory. It has ancient and composite sources, as Moïse Le Yaouanc has shown, and it was defended by the greatest names in contempo-rary medicine.[3] But the *Comédie humaine* provides an interpretation and demonstration that gives Balzac a place among the precursors of the Freud-ian conception of psychic energy. The conjunction with psychoanalysis

*Translated and reprinted by permission from *L'Expression métaphorique dans la Comédie humaine. Domaine social et physiologique* (Paris: Klincksieck, 1976), 343–47. © Lucienne Frappier-Mazur, 1976.

corresponds to an internal principle of Balzac's work that goes beyond the domain of the image.

The expression of the quantitative point of view endows the problem of metaphor in the *Comédie humaine* with certain particularities. First of all, we wonder if the image can contribute to the elaboration of character as a definite identity. The response varies according to the categories. The multiple images for which the name of a character serves as a point of encounter carry semantic features that, drawn together, do not constitute a truly integrated totality. To this it is now possible to add that character is seen, at least through the image, as the locus of a conflict or of an exchange of energy. Is this always the case? Among the categories studied in this book, only the theatrical metaphor approaches the question of self-consciousness—without resolving it—since it shows the subject to be uncertain of his own identity and of the nature of truth. The metaphor of gambling, which presupposes the identification between character and real individual, is deflected towards an "energetical" interpretation. And yet, the situation is different in categories we have not studied here. The larger part of the religious metaphor, that of mystical and erotic experience, is devoted to the birth of awareness and to the establishment (or loss) of the self. Other categories gravitate, entirely or in part, around the question of the identity of the subject.[4] In fact, the ensemble of the metaphorical text assigns equal importance to the quantitative and qualitative aspects of personality. But the economic point of view almost entirely monopolizes the domain of social and physiological metaphors, because the latter lends itself to such a monopoly, and because that corresponds to Balzac's overall undertaking.

In the second place, the unitary principle that governs Balzac's world also crystallizes a tension inherent in the implementation of metaphor in the *Comédie humaine*. On the one hand, the metaphorical procedure is atemporal, at least traditionally so, and its fundamental categories use language as a means of creating an image of eternal man: from this point of view, the conception of a quantifiable and centralizing energy, whose operations are described by the metaphor, refers us to the idea of an immutable human nature. On the other hand, many of the metaphors describe a society determined by the historical moment to which it belongs: certain critics establish an absolute interdependency between the theme of the depletion of strength implied by the unitary theory and the type of society that Balzac undertook to describe. Pierre Barbéris agrees with the remark of one of Balzac's contemporaries, according to whom "the electrical and galvanic qualities in the author of *La Peau de chagrin* can be explained by society, by its absurd and crazy pace." And he finds the explanation of the "self-destructive life force" in the then-current state of society.[5]

To a certain extent, the study of social and physiological metaphors confirms this point of view, without allowing us to consider the universe of the *Comédie humaine* as a simple replica of contemporary reality, which, in fact, Barbéris does not claim. It is difficult to assert, moreover, that under the July Monarchy the acquisitive bourgeois property owner and the lazy or ambitious aristocrat really burned more energy than the serf attached to the soil (as Balzac would say) in the medieval system of production. The same remark must be made apropos of a Rastignac or of a Mme Camusot straining toward success, as compared to their literary ancestors who are victims of passion, and this in spite of Balzac's affirmations to the contrary. Furthermore, Balzac himself does not always limit to the new society the broader opposition that, coming back to "eternal" mankind, he establishes between the social relations that consume and the withdrawn life that preserves. In both cases, his work explains this contrast by the thesis of the destructive superiority of desire over the act.

That being said, it is correct to see a correlation between contemporary upheavals and the "self-destructive life force" of the Balzacian creature—which doesn't mean that Racine's heroes or those of *La Princesse de Clèves* are not also consumed with passion. There is no need to postulate a perfect referential correspondence between the universe of the *Comédie humaine* and the society of 1830. But the analysis in terms of energy coincides with a conception of man inscribed in History, in its encounter with the cannibalistically desirous Balzac. It is true that the theory of the harmful consequences of intellectual and affective expenditure—of the idea that kills—was adopted by contemporary medicine. Its widespread acceptance at the time had several causes. One of them was certainly the progress of materialistic thought during the preceding two centuries. But the metaphorical Balzacian text offers us a second one, in the connection it establishes between the emergence of money—the generalized equivalent that enormously extends the range of desire—and the supremacy of desire over the act as a consumer of energy. In this way, the metaphor presents that *type* of economy in which notions of quantification and autodestructive desire dominate as the product of the *types* of forces that characterize that period. That does not imply that the "energetical" hypothesis is less appropriate in other periods: even if it is ultimately impossible to define the nature of energy, it represents an irreducible substratum. But it undergoes a unique development in the *Comédie humaine,* because its action, which is creative as well as destructive, can reflect the functioning of money and speculation.

But this only partially clarifies the ambiguous position of the metaphor between eternal man and historical man. It is possible to make it somewhat more precise by examining more closely the meaning of the image, according to the domains that are compared. In the description of social struggle, the image establishes an obvious correlation between the power relationships and the period in which they are exercised. This point can be verified even in the group of cannibalistic metaphors devoted to money, and in spite of its strongly physiological character. We have studied in detail, in connection with the stereotypes of social situations, the process of "temporalization" that affects the relationship of the vehicle to the tenor. This process is the same in the other categories, but it has a less-critical function to the extent that other categories escape more easily from the rigidity of the stereotype. This correlation, however, expressed by the image, between the "energetical" point of view and the historical moment, does not automatically assign to the society the responsibility for the depletion of strength. We have seen, on the contrary, that the metaphor tends sometimes to make "human nature" the primary cause of the social situation, and that this point of view does not contradict certain political views expressed by Balzac. In the same way, his historical vision and his mythology are extensions of each other.

In addition, there is no contradiction between generalizing metaphorical strategy and the tenor of the metaphor, when the metaphor shows the mechanism of exchange and of combustion directly at work in inter- and intrasubjective relationships. On the contrary, both come together to trace the picture of a human nature in which the only determinations are biological, in which the passions move in a closed space outside of time: "Passion is humanity," said Balzac. "Without it religion, history, the novel, and art would be useless."[6]

To sum up, we find on the one hand whole groups of metaphors that do not distinguish the economy from the existence of the historical moment, but that at the same time depend on an infrastructure that refers us to an eternal conception of man; on the other hand, we find no less important groups that refer directly to this archetypical vision of humanity. One might say that the theater, play, and the patriarchate illustrate the first case, and that physiological metaphors distribute themselves more or less evenly between the two.

As for the very important categories that are not considered in this study, and that endlessly reopen the question of self-consciousness, these introduce a different perspective. Placing themselves outside of historical contingencies, they contribute also to the definition of an atemporal being. But by expressing a qualitative point of view, they also show that this being carries within itself its own principle of development.

The ability to evolve thus conferred upon the subject at the very center of atemporal strategy has its equivalent, in all categories, in the semantic distance that Balzac cultivates between vehicle and tenor, the new meanings that he introduces revealing the same attempt to move beyond familiar references. There is no subversion in this undertaking, merely a desire for progress. Balzac does not anticipate Lautréamont.[7] In his case, every new relationship, once verbalized, becomes eternal.

For the modern reader, the metaphorical Balzacian text outlines with astonishing force the myths of a historical period, certain of which are still our own; it sheds light on truths that seem fundamental; it sometimes sketches out new relationships. If it reflects the tension between historical man and eternal man, it can also, as we have just indicated, sketch a synthesis between the two. There is nothing surprising in that, since Balzac dreamed of this synthesis in other contexts, not in the case of social man. In 1842, while asserting that society improves mankind, he still claims not to believe in social progress. But, as in 1832, he asserts his belief "in the progress of mankind over itself," and he hopes for the emergence of "the total being." He believes that man is "a finite creature, but one endowed with perfectible faculties," thanks to the action of his *interior self*, which expresses itself through prodigious expenditures of *Willpower*—always a question of energy. The present is sombre, but Balzac does not abandon the hope that the evolutionist hypothesis implies. If thought kills, it also gives life. In other words, the development of man is not social, it is biological.

In Balzac's work, Being must eternally create itself. The metaphor defines human nature, deepens our understanding of it, and participates in its progress.

Notes

1. [Ed. note: The author analyzes a large number of metaphors in the *Comédie humaine*, which she classifies as those of Games (Theater and Gambling), Patriarchy (Primitive Man, Criminal-Victim-Executioner, Courtesan, King-Master-Slave, Army, Church, Law, Money), and The Human Body (Cannibalism and Nutrition, Internal and Organic Sensations, Illness, Weapons and Wounds). Her terms *comparé* and *comparant* correspond roughly to the English terms "tenor" and "vehicle."]

2. I must cite the book by Paul Ricœur, *La Métaphore vive* (The living metaphor) (Paris: Seuil, 1975), which appeared too late for consultation.

3. By Cabanis and Broussais among others. The influence of the latter on Balzac has been noted in my discussion of metaphors of illness. See M. Le Yaouanc, *Nosographie de l'humanité balzacienne* (The nosography of Balzac's characters) (Paris: Maloine, 1959), 35–61, 153–75.

4. One group of plant and aquatic metaphors, according to our preliminary analyses, evokes, as do certain religious metaphors, the pantheistic fusion of the self. On the other hand, the metaphor of light closely identifies light and energy. See our article "Balzac et les images reparaissantes: Lumière et flamme dans *La Comédie humaine*," *Revue d'histoire littéraire de la France*, January–March 1966, 45–80.

5. Pierre Barbéris, *Balzac. Une Mythologie réaliste* (Balzac, a realistic mythology) (Paris: Larousse, 1971), 279–80.

6. *Avant-Propos* of 1842, 1, 16.

7. [Ed. note: The reference is to a later nineteenth-century poet, precursor of the surrealists.]

Metadiscourse and Aesthetic Commentary in Balzac: A Few Problems

Françoise Van Rossum-Guyon*

The importance of ideological commentary in *La Comédie humaine* is well known, as is the fact that Balzac ceaselessly expounds the theory of his

*Translated and reprinted by permission from "Texte et idéologie," *Degrés* 24/25 (1980–81), B-1–B-12.

practice.[1] It seems then possible to extract from the *Comédie humaine* an ensemble of propositions that—connected to analagous texts scattered through the prefaces, the critical essays, or the correspondence—would constitute a representative ensemble of what one might consider the Balzacian theory of the novel.[2]

Just limiting ourselves to the novels, it seems possible, and even legitimate, to isolate—among the many and diverse procedures of self-representation and self-reflection that are at work there—a specific and pertinent level of novelistic metadiscourse: that of the narrator. The latter, in effect, explicitly describes his role in narration, control, communication, and ideological commentary,[3] and moreover furnishes indications of the nature, the functioning, and the scope of the novel in general, of the *Comédie humaine*, of the literary work, as well as their links with literature, the other arts, and general knowledge. These interventions are, further, identifiable on the basis of certain distinctive formal characteristics: changes in tense, strong modalization ("it is necessary to"), the use of a lexicon marked by reference to cognitive codes ("explain," "understand"), mimetic codes ("paint," "sketch"), or generic codes ("scene," "tableau," "story"), and so forth.

A systematic count of these interventions in a group of novels, established according to criteria of date of composition, inclusion in the *Comédie humaine*, and the novelistic theme selected, ought to permit us to isolate on the one hand a particular vocabulary, to establish the lexical field according to the paradigms of author, work, and reader, to study its frequency and distribution, and to indicate its particularities, taking account of the contexts of occurrence; and furthermore it should permit us to classify these interventions and study their functions.

As we have noted elsewhere, the analysis of these interventions displays both the variety of their modalities and the multiplicity and complexity of their functions.[4] But it is at the level of the very creation of a corpus made up of such utterances that a certain number of problems present themselves. These problems are, as I will try to show, an index to the specific way in which the relationships between the novelistic text and its metatext are realized in the *Comédie humaine;* but it will also surely be seen that the specific problems raised by the resistance of a particular text to an attempt of this sort do not fail to raise, in their turn, more general problems of a theoretical as well as a critical nature.

A first problem: delimiting the corpus. Metanovelistic utterances are identifiable, as we have said, because—among other things—of the presence of a linguistic metavocabulary: *drama, tale, scene, to explain, to paint,* and so on. These terms seem in effect to refer explicitly to codes or models of reference according to which (or against which) the novel is constituted. But alongside such utterances there are an infinite number of others that imply a reference to the same codes without making them explicit—for example, the innumerable and celebrated examples of *here is how* and *this is reason . . .*

The interventions relating to the control of the text do not bear solely on the modes of presentation and construction of the narrative, but just as much—if not more—on the organization and the modalities of the story: relationships between past and present in "the story of a life," relationships among characters, the role of places and objects. In some cases the narrator plays on both registers: "Such are the minor events that were to introduce *one more character into this domestic scene, contrary to the laws of Aristotle and Horace*." (MM, 614).

One characteristic aspect of Balzacian metalanguage is, moreover, constituted by the incursion of metalanguage into the diegesis in order to describe facts ("the history of the husband" [PG, 106], "the drama of the son-in-law" [PG, 113]), or to describe characters (the characters of "this domestic scene" [MM, 614], "that old man is a veritable poem or, as the romantics say, a drama" [CP, 1145]), and it sometimes happens that the narrator himself underscores the diegetic use of the term: "Old Goriot had left the door open, so that the student would not forget to *recite his daughter*, as he used to say" (PG, 176).[5]

Metadiscourse develops, indeed, into a veritable commentary that can designate what the novel is or is not ("Ah! take note: this drama is neither a fiction nor a novel" [PG, 50]); specify its mode of construction and its nature ("Where the end of ordinary novels is in the middle of this only-too-true story, rather anacreontic and terribly moral" [CB, 131]); enumerate its constituting elements, for example description, dialogue, and even language ("for our language must be violated for a moment in order to describe new whims that a few women share" [IP, 157]); justify the presence (or omission) of an element of the narrative ("The hungry mechanical presses have by now so completely erased the memory of this obsolete machine that it is necessary to mention the old tools here . . . for they play their role in this minor epic" [IP, 124]); or again to indicate its possible or desired effects ("Here is the succinct story of this honeymoon; its retelling will perhaps not be lost on artists" [CB, 241]).

In these cases, metadiscourse assumes the diverse functions of naming, communicating, structuring, evaluating, rendering likely, on the basis of which one could try to classify such interventions. But an examination of these few examples suffices for us to realize that each of them assumes several functions at once. This functional polyvalence increases when the commentary is more elaborate. Additionally, the latter often develops an ideological commentary that can bear on all the elements of the "reality" evoked by the novel, and without our being able to establish boundaries between what belongs to theorizing on the art of the novel or to a meditation on other aspects of reality. This is the case, for example, of the famous tirade in *La Cousine Bette* on the pleasures of artistic conception and the difficulties of its execution.

As Gérard Genette, has shown,[6] finally, ideological commentary in Balzac is generally subordinated to the necessities of the story. This is also the case in esthetic pronouncements. The intervention of the narrator in *Le Cousin Pons* ("Here begins the drama, or, if you wish, the terrible comedy of the death of a bachelor" [CP, 630]), has the immediate and local function of introducing the "drama" and of warning us of its gravity; the explanations of the psychological conditions of artistic creation in *La Cousine Bette* without any doubt illuminate the destiny of Steinbock.[7] One can then wonder to what extent these esthetic statements would be more separable than the others from the novelistic text that includes them.

Beyond these problems posed by the delimitation and classification of a corpus constituted by the pronouncements of the narrator, there is the problem of the relationship between the metadiscourse of the narrator and other devices of self-representation by which and thanks to which the novel takes itself as object and refers to its own codes. It happens, in fact, that the characters also make references to the novel, to literature, and to art in general. Of course it is important to distinguish these interventions from those of the narrator. The very fact that in *Illusions perdues* Lousteau's statements on the conditions of the production and reception of literary works are opposed to those of d'Arthez (as, in *Modeste Mignon*, those of Butscha are opposed to those of Canalis or La Brière) suffices to show the importance that must be attached to the integration of the discourses of the characters into the novels. Lousteau's advice to Lucien in *Illusions perdues* serves, for example, to characterize Lousteau and to prepare the moral decline of Lucien. But these discourses contain terms analagous, if not often identical, to those used by the narrator, and they develop analogous themes. In certain cases they even oddly resemble those that the "author" or his substitutes (such as Félix Davin) conduct in his prefaces or correspondence, or even those of certain critics—Gérard de Mollènes, for example.[8]

These shifting frontiers between the metadiscourse of the narrator and other procedures of self-representation can also be found in connection with titles, typography, or the *mise en abyme* (Story within a story). A characteristic example in this regard is that of "Olympia ou les Vengeances romaines" in *La Muse du département*. This fragment of a gothic novel integrated into the novel announces via its subject the adulterous affair of Dinah and Lousteau, as well as their tragic (although quite different) end; it reflects through its presentation (pagination, fragmentation, title, and typography) the material conditions of reading and, by the effects that the reading produces, its psychological and social conditions. Lousteau's and Bianchon's commentary on it ("It is impossible for me not to call to your attention the extent to which the literature of the Empire went straight to the heart of things without stopping for any details" [MD, 713]; "In the old days novels were only expected to engage the reader . . . Little by little the reader came to want style, interest, pathos, positive facts: he demanded the five literary senses: invention, style, thought, knowledge, and sentiment" [MD, 714]), as well as the titles of the chapters in which their commentary is inserted (for example: "The Novel

Belongs to the Days of Anne Radcliffe") show—a contrario—the model against which Balzac's novel was written.

This example, which offers by itself all the elements that we have just indicated, could give rise to much commentary,[9] but I think it suffices to indicate the complexity of the problems raised by the delimitation and the classification of a body of metanovelistic statements. Undoubtedly, these problems are not specific as such to Balzac. They refer back to a more general theoretical problem, that of the status that must be granted to the metalinguistic function within the literary text, as a text "with incorporated metalanguage." As Philippe Hamon has shown, at a maximum one could include under the aegis of this function all "cognitive space of the text, consisting of all the interpretations of the narrator and the characters," and it is quite certain that "if one extends the notion of metalinguistic apparatus too far, one risks diluting the concept."[10]

But this example and most of those that we have mentioned above have also allowed us to clarify the different forms taken by procedures of self-representation in the novels of Balzac, certain modalities of their functioning, and the need to consider their integration into their various contexts. A somewhat more detailed analysis will permit us to show to what extent the resistance of the novelistic text to attempts at delimiting a metatext reveals the particular way in which that text takes itself as object.

The examination of such explicit interventions by the narrator in three novels—*Le Père Goriot, Illusions perdues,* and *Splendeurs et misères des courtisanes*—will permit us to make a few observations about the particularities of the lexicon used by Balzac, as well as about certain functions of these interventions.

One notices, to begin with, the frequency of certain words used to designate respectively the author, the narration, the work (the novel), and its reception; that is, *painter* or *historian* for "novelist," *explain* and *paint* for "tell," *drama* and *narrative* for "novel," *observe* and *understand* for "read." It is important to note that the word "novel" is never used to designate the novel one is in the process of reading, and that "novelist" never designates the narrator either. The use of these terms in other contexts to designate either older novels ("fireside novels" [SM, 541], "Empire novels" [MD, 713]), or other novelists either real (Walter Scott and Cooper [SM, 673], Hoffmann [IP, 507]) or fictional (Lucien de Rubempré [IP, 302]), underscores by contrast the importance of this omission, which can be explained not by the desire to create verisimilitude ("All is true . . ." [PG, 50]), but rather by the rejection of a certain code: that of the "ordinary novel." The reference to the novelistic code is, in effect, very frequent when it is a question of describing actions or characters that, contrary to those of Balzac, are "novelistic." Inversely, the word "study" refers exclusively to one of these three novels or to another novel of the *Comédie humaine* (SM 813, 735), and the narrator does not hesitate in this case to break the novelistic illusion: *"This study, already lengthy, would seem unfinished if . . ."* (SM, 813); or: "but it will find its place in the Study that will paint the lawyers of Paris" (SM, 735).

The frequency of the substitutes *explain* and *paint* to designate narration (and correlatively of *understand* and *see* to designate reception) surely corresponds to the two great systems of cognitive and mimetic reference based on which and in view of which the *Comédie humaine* constitutes itself as an explanatory history of society and a portrait of social mores. But a more precise examination of contexts of occurrence makes obvious the complexity of the connections between the novelistic text and the systems that it seems to designate explicitly. Each of these terms enters in fact into a system of both equivalencies and differences that manifests the ambiguity and the paradoxical character of the relationships between text and metatext. Let us begin, for example, with a few occurrences of the words *paint* and *picture:* "These details paint the entire province" (IP, 237); "The negligence of David Séchard had causes that will paint this young man" (IP, 139); "This prudence paints the customs . . . of these families" (IP, 152); "The spectacle of these miseries and the appearance of this room were horrible to him [Rastignac] . . . on the one hand images of the most elegant social setting . . . on the other sinister pictures edged with slime" (PG, 118). In these examples, the use of these terms seems to postulate an equivalence between the real and its representation. This equivalence, which can also be found in the use of terms such as *scene, novel,* or *type,* is sometimes quite explicit, as in this famous passage: "But Paris is a veritable ocean. . . . Explore it, describe it! However careful you may be in exploring it, in describing it, however numerous and devoted the explorers of this sea, there will always be virgin zones . . . something unheard-of, forgotten by literary divers" (PG, 59).

In other cases the use of these terms seems to establish an equivalency between the different modes of representation and their codes of reference. *Paint* thus equals *describe, show, tell, explain:* "The familiar style of conversation gives us an expression that can paint this young man in two words" (IP, 586); "No expression, no painting can render the rage that seizes writers when their pride suffers" (IP, 518); "Old Goriot, on whose head a painter, like a historian, would have focused all the light in the picture" (PG, 63).

The fact that the interventions of the narrator bear on the plot as much as on the narrative, and that the vocabulary of metalanguage invades the diegesis, creates an equivalency between the novel and the reality it is supposed to represent. But one must note that this equivalency is reversible to the extent that, if the novel is given as "real," the "real" in its turn is to be seen as a picture: "Although they had come from Fougères, where the landscape they were contemplating can also be seen, with the differences produced by changes in perspective, they could not resist admiring it one last time . . . The view of this countryside was animated by the fleeting brilliance with which nature sometimes enjoys enhancing its imperishable creations" (CH, 14–15); or as a text to be deciphered, as Mme de Beauséant declares: "I have read the book of the world, and I found in it pages that were unknown to me" (PG, 116). These equivalencies underscore rather than suppress the ambiguity of the novel as a representation of reality.

Opposing these series of equivalencies there is, however, a whole series of differences that underscore the distinction between reality and its modes of representation:

- difficulties of representation: "No figure of rhetoric could paint . . ." (SM, 549).

- possibilities offered by recourse to certain models: "In order accurately to paint the physiognomy of this Christ of Paternity, one would have to seek comparisons with the images that the Princes of the palette have invented . . . (PG, 231).

- effects produced: "If he were well painted in his struggle with Paris, the poor student would provide one of the most dramatic subjects of our modern civilization" (PG, 152).

- specification of different methods of constructing the narrative: "This last act of the drama can, however, complete the picture of the customs that constitute this study" (SM, 798).

- need for an explanatory analysis: "Mme de Bargeton loved arts and letters—an extravagant taste, a mania highly deplored in Angoulême, but which we must justify by sketching the life of this lady . . . whose influence determined Lucien's destiny" (IP, 157).

In other interventions, the use of these terms underscores the differences among the genres and the subgenres—*poetry* and *prose, theater* and *novel, tragedy* and *comedy*—or the differences between the modalities of narration and of representation—*scene* versus *tableau, drama* versus *narrative, description* versus *narration, digression* versus *action, anecdote* versus *story, type* versus *spectacle,* and so forth.

Now the differences created by the opposition of terms acquire meaning from their integration into the various novels. A more elaborate analysis of other novels would show, for example, that in *Les Chouans* a systematic opposition is created between neighboring terms such as *description* and *painting, color* and *emotion;* or in *La Bourse,* between the terms *artist* and *painter;* or again in *Illusions perdues* between *poem, poet,* and *poetry.* The narrator plays with these oppositions and constructs his own system of connotations. Only by establishing the relationship of the terms in each novel and in the ensemble of the *Comédie humaine* can we grasp the importance of this apparent paradox according to which Vautrin, a novelistic character par excellence, can define himself as a poet: "I am a great poet. I do not write my poems: they consist of actions and feelings" (PG, 141); and that on the contrary Maître Petit-Claud can say of Lucien, "That young man isn't a poet; he is an unending novel" (IP, 717). One would have to uncover all the series of substitutes linked by comparisons and analogies in order to discover common denominators in the case of equivalencies, or conversely the system of oppositions and their hierarchy, in each novel and in the ensemble of the entire work.

This serialization of the differences underscores the importance in these passages of references to genres and the various arts. The recourse to a code of nonnarrative reference such as the theater, or to a code of nonliterary reference such as painting, accentuates the difference between one or another mode of representation, dramatic or descriptive; but Balzac also uses the pertinent qualities of these codes to the advantage of his text. This is also the case for references to the drama or the comedy and more generally to the other arts and creations of thought, in particular scientific systems.[11] Let us limit ourselves to painting. Raphaël, for example, is not invoked simply to signify Beauty, as Roland Barthes claims,[12] but as a function of the necessities of representation. Likewise it is not by chance that Christ and the Virgin figure respectively in *La Peau de chagrin* and in *Le Curé de village*, nor that it is a Watteau fan and not a Christ by Girardon that Cousin Pons offers to the Chief Judge's wife in the final version of the novel.[13] The esthetic and historical values that are attached to painting or theater are taken advantage of, as are their compositional values: the contrast between light and dark or foreground and background, the play of colors for portraits and landscapes, the concentration of characters and dialogue in "scenes," and so on.[14] A whole series of novels, from *La Maison du Chat-qui-pelote* to *Le Cousin Pons*, including *Pierre Grassou* and *Le Chef d'oeuvre inconnu*, thematize and problematize to the extreme the relationships of the painter to painting, as many other novels thematize relationships with art or science.[15] And in these cases, the text not only englobes and moves beyond its metatext but radically transforms it.

Balzac's metadiscourse, therefore, occupies a particularly paradoxical status. On the one hand, it constitutes itself as an autonomous discourse that has even been isolated and developed into "Balzac's ideas about the novel."[16] On the other hand it segments, organizes, and rationalizes its language-object, since it designates it and displays the models according to which it functions, as well as the codes of reference on the basis of which it is constituted.

Does there then remain a privileged area of knowledge in the text? The overcoding established by the metadiscourse could imply this, but we have just seen that it suffices to follow a single thread for the entire web, fictional and textual, to follow: if on the one hand the metadiscourse parallels the text, explains it, consolidates it and assures its readability, it is on the other hand engulfed, integrated, and transformed by it. One can then wonder if for the idea of a novelistic metadiscourse suggesting a knowledge of the text, one ought not substitute the idea of the production of knowledge by the texts— by this novelistic text with the particular arrangements and strategies of which we have just noted a few, but also by other texts, or rather other discourses, with which it competes. But this implies, obviously, the use of other concepts and the placement of other analytical grids that would take into account, in addition, the pragmatic dimension of all these discourses, including of course that of the narrator or of the "characters" of the *Comédie humaine*.

Notes

1. This text is a very reworked version of a paper delivered in Toronto in November 1977 (the proceedings of that colloquium will appear shortly with Didier-Canada). This is one stage of work in progress on aspects and functions of metadiscourse in the works of Balzac, a project supported by the Dutch Organization for the Development of Scientific Research (ZWO). Pagination refers to the [second] Pléiade edition, published under the direction of P. G. Castex.

2. According to the formula of Gérard Genette in "Vraisemblance et motivation," *Communication* 11 (1968): 10.

3. See Gérard Genette, "Le Discours du récit," *Figures III* (Paris: Seuil, 1972), 261ff.

4. See Françoise Van Rossum-Guyon, "Des nécessités d'une digression: sur une figure du métadiscours chez Balzac," *Revue des sciences humaines* 3 (1979): 99–110; and "Redondance et discordances. Sur le métadiscours dans *Les Parents pauvres*," in Françoise Van Rossum-Guyon and Michiel van Brederode, ed., *Balzac et Les Parents pauvres* (Paris: SEDES, 1980).

5. [Ed. note: "Diegesis" refers to elements of pure plot in narration, theoretically separated from descriptive elements.]

6. Genette, "Vraisemblance et motivation," 13.

7. [Ed. note: Steinbock, a sculptor, is one of the principal characters in *La Cousine Bette*.]

8. But this is another problem—that of the relationships among different types of texts, which I will leave to one side for the moment.

9. See, for example, Lucien Dallenbach, "Du fragment au Cosmos," *Poétique* 40, (November 1979).

10. Philippe Hamon, "Texte littéraire et métalangage," *Poétique* 31, (September 1977): 284.

11. See, for example, Rainer Warning, "Chaos und Kosmos: Kontingenzbewältigung in Balzacs *Comédie humaine* (Chaos and cosmos: the control of contingency in Balzac's Human Comedy)," in H. Gumbrecht, K. Stierle, R. Warning, ed., *Balzac* (Munich: Fink Verlag, UTB, 1980).

12. Roland Barthes, *S/Z* (Paris: Seuil, 1970), 40.

13. As Balzac had at first intended, on the proofs prior to correction. See the commentary by Maurice Ménard, *Le Cousin Pons* (Paris: Livre de poche, 1973), 380.

14. See Lucienne Frappier-Mazur, *L'Expression métaphorique dans La Comédie humaine* (Metaphoric expression in the *Human Comedy*) (Paris, Klincksieck, 1976); and Jean-Loup Bourget, "Ni du roman ni du théâtre," *Poétique*, no. 32 (November 1977): 459–567.

15. See Madeleine Fargeaud, *Balzac et La Recherche de l'Absolu* (Paris: Hachette, 1968); Jacques Neef, "La Localisation des sciences," in Claude Duchet, ed., *Balzac et La Peau de chagrin* (Paris: SEDES, 1979), 127–42. The same holds true for generic codes; see, for example, [also in Duchet] Ruth Amossy, "La Confession de Raphaël: Contradiction et interférences," 43–60; and Elisheva Rosen, "Le Festin de Taillefer ou les saturnales de la Monarchie de Juillet" ("Taillefer's feast or the saturnalia of the July Monarchy"), 115–26.

16. See P. Laubriet, *L'Intelligence de l'art chez Balzac* (The understanding of art in Balzac) (Paris: Didier, 1961), and G. Delattre, *Les Opinions littéraires de Balzac* (Balzac's literary opinions) (Paris: PUF, 1950).

The Ideology of Form: Partial Systems in *La Vieille Fille*

Fredric Jameson*

Whatever else it may mean, the term ideology may be taken as a *sign* designating the agreement of those who use it on a common field of study or problematics, if not a common solution to the latter's problems: those who consent to pronounce it, or who insist on doing so, may indeed be supposed to share at least a minimal conviction that the forms of consciousness are shaped or at least influenced by their social or historical ground, and that this "determining" relationship is worth studying in its own right. On the other hand, the analyst of ideology ought always to take into account the possiblity that, once raised, the concept of ideology may ultimately prove more troublesome than it is worth: in it, indeed, two contradictory tendencies are at war—the one, a promise, held out by the very application of the name itself to so many diverse social phenomena, that it will be possible to elaborate a model of the relationship in question; the other, a pressure from the historical side of the same concept which, by insisting not only on the variations in the nature of ideology from moment to moment within a given social system, but above all on the immense changes in the structure of power from one type of system to another,[1] begins to make us feel that there is something misleading about using the same word for all of them.

Nowhere do the antinomies of the concept of ideology manifest themselves more dramatically than in what is practically a *locus classicus* of such study, the novels of Balzac: socially and politically polyvalent enough to make the construction of an ideological model an exciting task, they ultimately inspire the feeling that they are too exceptional, owing to the unique transitionality of the age which they reflect, to be of any use in understanding the literary and ideological structures of other periods.

The ambiguities in Balzac have frequently been rehearsed, generally in an attempt to do away with them in one way or another and thereby to have peace, as the Brechtian character said; but most recently, one has the impression that it is the Left that has won out, and this partly because of the disappearance of the old classical and monarchist Right, and partly because the reigning liberal intellectual establishment (with its ideology of *modernism*) has been less well able to assimilate Balzac than other, more individualistic or stylized writers of the same period, such as Stendhal or Hugo. So the

*Reprinted by permission from *SubStance* 15 (1976): 29–39. © The University of Wisconsin Press.

very choice of Balzac as object of study has come itself to have the value of a sign, and to function a little like a declaration of Marxism (and let the present essay be no exception). Not that the Marxist solution to the "problem" of Balzac is without substance in its own right: on the contrary, the recent *Mythes balzaciens* of Pierre Barbéris has demonstrated, with an overwhelming fullness of detail, the truth of Lukács's canonical assertion that there is a narrative logic in Balzac's novels which is in direct contradiction to his professed political convictions. Barbéris shows that Balzac's conservatism and royalism can only be considered an "abstract" or "ideal" position—his concrete judgements on the *ancien régime* and the historical Restoration being as severe as any passed on the bourgeoisie itself—the abstractness of which alone, however, affords the novelist the distance he needs to register the raw material of his society as a whole, and in that respect this imaginary standpoint enables a "politique du réel" beyond the perceptual capacities of later novelists, more progressive or even realistic though they may have been in their social views.

Yet in literature there is a reality of the appearance just as much as an appearance that distorts a more fundamental reality: in the case of Balzac, we cannot completely ignore what he said he was, and what he thought he was, if only for the reason that at certain moments in history, readers *believed* him. So we tend to forget that the great rediscovery of Balzac in the Third Republic was essentially a conservative operation; just as the discovery of Stendhal by the same people—Taine, the positivists, Bourget—was that of a preeminently aristocratic and anti-bourgeois writer. Bourget's essay on Balzac is eloquent testimony to the fact that there was a time when Balzac's ideas were taken seriously, and when he was thought of as a social and ideological prophet not unlike, say, a Dostoevsky or a Nietzsche in our own time (and with similar results). Even the novels must have looked different: rather like those of Barbey d'Aurevilly, I would imagine, all romance and lost causes with a little whiff of "Blut und Boden" to come. Yet Taine's own study of Balzac suggests something else as well: that the greatness of the novelist was to have been himself the first to make a systematic study of the problem we raised above, namely the relationship of consciousness to its social ground. Is it possible indeed that the ideology of Balzac fascinates us precisely because Balzac was himself fascinated by ideology?

ANATOMY OF A *PHYSIOLOGIE*

The ambiguity of the term "code" becomes manifest when, deciding whether to use it in the singular or the plural, you suddenly realize that these alternatives designate two very different types of communication. In an everyday interpersonal situation, for instance, it would be misleading to speak about "codes," for the good reason that if more than one are involved, the message itself will only be imperfectly transmitted: your code, in other words, is Morse, or English, or deaf-and-dumb, but the whole point of the operation is to use but one at a time, and to make sure that your opposite number is aware which one it is. And clearly enough, this literal use of the concept of the code, in the singular, will not be very suggestive for literary analysis.

But literature is precisely not an instance of direct face-to-face communication: on the contrary, it is something like deferred or mediated communication in which certain of the Jakobsonian "factors"[2] (the addresser, for example, or the context) have been suppressed, those factors then being replaced by a relatively unnatural and artifical compensatory reenforcement of some of the remaining ones. (The other historical development which must be held accountable for the new pluralization of the phenomenon of the linguistic code is, of course, the emergence of a secular society itself, in which the hegemony of a single overall code—what we call religion—has been broken and given way to a host of private languages, codes agreed upon only by small sub-groups within the new *Gesellschaft*.)

Under these circumstances, it may become interesting to speak in terms of codes in the plural, provided we understand the consequences that spring from this new and extra-linguistic, relatively metaphorical use of the word. For one thing, our subject will then always implicitly or explicitly be that of an inconsistency or a contradiction between one or more of the codes in question: for if there were not so much as a latent incompatibility between two or more of our plural codes, there would clearly be no need to ascribe independent existence to them, and the one would automatically fall into place as a simple sub-group of the other.

Then too, I think that as a methodological fact of life we will find that as our attention to the plurality of codes increases, along with our emphasis on their mutual contradictions, our awareness of the correlated factor of the message will decrease proportionately. But how can one speak meaningfully of a code, even in the plural, without taking into account the message or messages which it was designed to transmit? The tendency, I am afraid, will be towards some MacLuhanite resolution, in which it is the codes themselves, or rather their contradiction, which become the message, a formula that seems to me to raise more problems than it solves.

We are thus led to ask ourselves whether the conflicts between the various codes at work in a given literary text are to be understood as virtual only, or whether, indeed, we can isolate certain key moments in which those conflicts become actualized, moments in which the foregrounding of some kind of interference between the various literary codes then momentarily constitutes something like a narrative event in its own right. For ordinarily, surely, the codes of a given narrative function in a relatively secondary and semantic way, and their study is little more than a kind of object- or value-oriented lexicology. This is to say that for the most part such codes are called upon to furnish the raw material of what are termed the "indices" of a given text: thus, the drumming of the fingers, in one cultural code a graphic shorthand for impatience, might in some wholly different one function as the sign of some dawning musical reverie, if not simply a way of getting your waiter's attention. The principal interest of such a lexicology of codes will then lie in the realm of comparative culture.

Yet there are other moments, in certain narrative forms, in which codes are foregrounded in such a way as to suggest what the Hegelians would call a virtual coming to consciousness of their existence and functioning in and for itself: such, for instance, are those long descriptive passages in Balzac, from which—portrait or interior—the characters and their acts recede, and in which the properties of a given object—a human being, or a house, or a particular district in a city—come to lead something like an autonomous narrative life of their own, thereby at the same time making themselves accessible to the watchful reader in the form of so many organized codes or systems which are perhaps—in the fragmentary and secular context of the modern middle-class world—not without their similarity to those primitive classification schemes described by Lévi-Strauss in his study of archaic thought or *pensée sauvage*.

The opening section of *La Vieille Fille*, the portrait of the Chevalier de Valois, a bravura piece which for wit and high spirits, and a manic and irrepressible volubility has no equal anywhere else in Balzac, may serve as a useful illustration of this process. It falls into three main sections, each of which reveals the Chevalier through the lens of a different topic, showing him now in his social deportment, now in terms of gallantry, now finally as he struggles with his own penury and invents ingenious stategems to make ends meet in some less than humiliating manner. These three groups of data about the Chevalier we will characterize as so many different codes, and the interest of the portrait will then lie in the relationship of the three codes to one another and the manner in which their alternation may be said to consti-tute something like a protonarrative in its own right, one which presumably, in something more fundamental than the simple establishment of the neces-sary preliminary information, sets the stage for the narrative proper which follows.

The first code, that of *manners*, might no doubt itself be resolved into a host of sub-codes such as that of clothing, storytelling, table manners, per-sonal hygiene, and the like. For the moment it is enough to observe that this particular code is organized around a historical—or rather, more properly, a generational—opposition between the manners of the *ancien régime* and of the authentic pre-revolutionary nobility, and those, henceforth secularized and bourgeois, of the imperfectly named Restoration itself. The Chevalier, as a kind of complete social microcosm in his own right, is something like a *sign* in which the two regimes mingle in unstable temporal coexistence: witness his "costume de transition qui unissait deux siècles l'un à l'autre",[3] a compromise which shows a good deal more realism than the intransigeant loyalty to the past of the mummified inhabitants of the companion *Cabinet des antiques*, but which nonetheless shares at least some of the absurdity of Scott's Knockdunder, who, uniting a Highlands outfit with the "fierce cocked hat deeply guarded with gold lace" of the civilized Lowlands, looks, "as someone said who had seen the executions of the insurgent prisoners in 1715 . . . as if some Jacobite enchanter, having recalled the sufferers to life, had clapped in his haste, an Englishman's head on a Highlander's body."[4]

Yet the juxtaposition with Scott and the national oppositions at work in the latter suggest that Balzac's sequence of historical moments must also be ultimately rooted in the more basic sociological reality of a *synchronic* opposition, although in his case the polarization is not that of social *forms* (the *barbaric* Highlanders versus the *civilized* Lowlanders or Sassenachs), but rather that—henceforth determinant in the post-revolutionary countries—of social *class*. For obviously, what is meant but what is not said, is that the Chevalier's attire combines modern *bourgeois* features ("habit marron à boutons dorés . . . culotte à demi juste en peau-de-soie et à boucles d'or . . . gilet blanc sans broderie" (212)) with vestiges of the old aristocratic finery in the form of the "cravate serrée sans col de chemise," the "boucles d'or carrées" of his shoes, and not least the "deux chaînes de montre qui pendaient parallèlement de chacun de ses goussets" (212–213) and which echo the "deux petites boucles représentant des têtes de nègre en diamants" (211) in the lobes of his ears. The point is, however, that the class content of this particular code, that of the Chevalier's clothing, is systematically underplayed: its modern, or Romantic, early-nineteenth-century features are for instance attributed, not to Restoration middle-class fashion, but rather to that "haute élégance anglaise" (212) associated with the British aristocracy and Beau Brummel. For the moment, in other words, Balzac passes that open conflict between aristocrat and bourgeois, which is the deepest subject of his novel, off as an internal inconsistency *within* the aristocracy itself, whether it be a question of successive generations or a distinction between national styles. We will suggest therefore that at this stage the initial class opposition is for whatever reason *repressed,* so that at the outset we are not confronted with two terms which define themselves in some stark antagonism to each other, but rather merely two separate and autonomous historical or stylistic phenomena, each of which—that of the *ancien régime,* and that of the Restoration—enjoys some plenitude of existence in its own right.

Meanwhile, in the course of the articulation of this initial code of manners, we find the account interrupted by considerations of a rather different sort. It is, indeed, as though the logic of the first code, carried to its conclusion, suddenly produced quite a different effect than that initially desired, suggesting the need, if not to call it into question, then at least to establish some new and hitherto unexpected dimension to the portrait under construction. Here is the first discordant note in the account of the Chevalier's appearance: "Seulement, cet Adonis en retraite n'avait rien de mâle dans son air, et semblait employer le fard de la toilette pour cacher les ruines occasionnées par le service militaire de la galanterie . . ." (212). What this reversal suggests is that a positive feature of one code may not turn out to be nearly so desirable in the terms of a different one: thus the very completeness with which the Chevalier is able to embody the spirit of the *ancien régime*, with all its elegance and sophistication, sets unwanted vibrations going in the wholly different area of *sexuality*, in which it proves merely to signify effeminacy.

The new code, of course, is a system in its own right, and its signals— the "ruines" of the description already quoted, but also the meaning of Du Bousquier's gaze, "fin comme celui de M. de Talleyrand, mais *un peu éteint*" (226)—ultimately derive from a whole metaphysic of energy-expense and longevity the monument to which is of course *La Peau de chagrin*, but which draws its social value from the deepest superstitions about the effects of sexual activity, and seems, indeed, in this relatively systematic form, to have been Balzac's legacy from his father.[5]

Yet this semantic value of the sexual code, the content it is able to supply to the various narrative "indices," is overshadowed by its demarcation from the preceding one, and from the heightened antitheses at work in the new context. At this point then the fundamental conflict in the novel— systematically concealed by the code of manners—seems much closer to making its appearance on the very surface of the text: the new code creates a situation in which contradiction seems unavoidable, what is positive in the first code (elegance) proving negative in the second (effeminacy). And indeed at a later stage in the narrative, the Chevalier's rival, Du Bousquier, will step into the empty slot which has been waiting for him in this new opposition, and lend it all the substance of his Herculean physique, so fascinating, in spite of herself, to Mlle Cormon: "de moyenne taille, gras comme un fournisseur, faisant parade de ses mollets de procureur égrillard. . . . Ses mains, enrichies de petits bouquets de poils à chaque phalange, offraient la preuve d'une riche musculature par de grosses veines bleues, saillantes. Enfin, il avait le poitrail de l'Hercule-Farnèse, et des épaules à soutenir la rente" (226). The mocking clink of the metaphor of opulence, however, reminds us that by the time we reach this second portrait the sexual code has already proved somewhat inadequate, at least as far as Du Bousquier is concerned.

The shift from one code to another does not, however, involve a complete abandonment of the earlier data; rather, the continuity between the two sections, between the account of the Chevalier's behavior in society and those euphemisms (transparent for Balzac's audience) which supply the appropriate sexual information, is preserved by the persistence of certain common features of both descriptions, features which are then reorganized into what, following Tynianov or Althusser, we might call new hierarchies of dominance and subordination. Take for example the Chevalier's nose ("au nombre des propriétés du chevalier, il faut compter le nez prodigieux dont l'avait doué la Nature. Ce nez partageait vigoureusement une figure pale en deux sections qui semblaient ne pas se connaître et dont une seule rougissait pendant le travail de la digestion," etc., [210]), a relatively secondary feature of the first section of the portrait, which, metonymically proving him, if not wholly worthy of his name, then at least emblematically akin to the dynastic spirit of the Bourbons as well as their predecessors, at best strikes a faintly discordant note in the general roll-call of his physical graces (blond, slender, youthful, and so forth).

Yet when this same nose reappears in an overtly sexual context, from subordinate and negative it becomes at once the "fundamental signifying trait" in terms of which all the rest are interpreted: "Le chevalier avait la voix de son nez, son organe vous eût surpris par des sons amples et redondants" (212). The symbolism of the Chevalier's nose, which the new context makes it impossible to overlook, derives of course from the oldest sexual folklore of the human race, and thus—to anticipate a methodological concept to which we will return in the second part of this essay—functions as much as a *connotation* of the narrator's social role itself (identification with some "genuinely" national and no doubt imaginary peasant background and culture), as it does as a sign in its own right.

Yet at the same time the revaluation of this sign system throws the whole message of the portrait into some confusion. The new sexual code had allowed us to glimpse, for the first time, some genuine opposition in the antithesis of the blond and ageing Adonis of the salons of the *ancien régime* to the robust Farnese Hercules of the Directory, seen now as something like an athletic champion of the rising industrial bourgeoisie. Yet the Chevalier's nose is there to remind us pointedly that this antithesis will prove itself to be a misleading and indeed erroneous one: the real opposition subsequently turning out to be, not that between elegance but effeminacy on the one hand, and crude and muscular energy on the other, but rather simply that which holds between sexuality and outright impotence. At this point, then, we begin to understand that the inconsistency between the two basic codes of the portrait, that of manners and that of sexuality, raises the even more fundamental problem of their mutual adequacy in accounting for reality itself: thus our attention shifts from the object being coded (the Chevalier) to the very nature of the picture of reality suggested by the codes themselves, and the contradiction between them—better still, the antinomy to which they give rise—is not without its analogies to those basic contradictions which according to Lévi-Strauss it was the function of the mythic narrative to resolve in the first place, contradictions to which we may equally well apply his striking formulation of the content of ritual: "Ce qu'en définitive le rituel cherche à surmonter, n'est pas la résistance du monde à l'homme mais la résistance, à l'homme, de sa pensée."[6] In these terms, we may suggest that the subsequent narrative may be seen as an attempt not merely to answer the basic question: How is it possible for the graceful, effeminate, elderly Chevalier to be more potent than the rough-and-ready bourgeois banker Du Bousquier? but also and above all, by so doing, to resolve the ultimate social contradictions (aristocracy versus bourgeoisie) of which the incompatibility of the two codes is something like a symptom.

Yet the final ironic twist of the description of Du Bousquier's physique ("des épaules à soutenir la rent") reminds us that we have not yet come to terms with the code in which the third and final section of the Chevalier's portrait is expressed, namely that of *money* itself. At this point, also, we must evaluate a formal pattern of the micro-narrative which becomes more and more insistent in the final section, even though it is present in the very first words of the novel (who *is* the so-called Chevalier de Valois, really?), and this is, of course, the indication of the presence of a *secret* and the rhetorical organization of the reader's anticipations around the breathless promise of a revelation to come. This anecdotal structure (Enigma/Revelation) is something like an empty form which in principle ought to be serviceable in the articulation of any code;[7] yet in practice, for reasons yet to be determined, it would seem to entertain a privileged relationship with the final account of the Chevalier's finances, where as in a kind of preview of the narrative proper, Balzac organizes a bewildering and virtually Proustian series of reversals around the termini of Mystery/Solution and Appearance/Reality, and the progressive generation, at each step, of some wholly unexpected result which serves to perpetuate the process on a higher plane. Thus, the fact is that the Chevalier (whoever he is, secret) is wholly destitute (secret), having but a modest pension; however (revelation), by allowing everyone to learn this fact, he gets himself invited to dinner every night of the week, thus making ends meet (unexpected denouement). Yet the real point of getting invited out is in reality (secret revealed) to earn money at whist, money which he then (further revelation!) sends himself so as to perpetuate the impression that he is receiving a modest pension which indeed he is not (a revelation which is transformed a posteriori back into a deep secret), etc.

The ultimate secret of this otherwise infinite series is that of *desire:* the Chevalier has the project of marrying Mlle Common, and ironically, it is the very success with which this ultimate secret has been kept which ensures the failure of the project: for Mlle Cormon finally ends up accepting Du Bousquier at least partly because she has failed to detect any signs that the Chevalier, whom in some ways she prefers, is interested in her. Her "stupidity" is thus only too systematically complementary to the Chevalier's deviousness: his secret is as frustrating for her in its own way as is that of Du Bousquier himself. For we must juxtapose this positive secret, of desire, with the latter's negative and indeed wholly physical secret of impotence, symbolized throughout the book by the baldness beneath his wig. Here, indeed, the reader's efforts to discover the key to the mystery is mocked by a curious formal echo-chamber: we think we get the point about Du Bousquier ("il ne pouvait plus être qu'ambitieux" [230]), but if so, then Suzanne's accusation does not make much sense. But when Du Bousquier seems himself in doubt as to whether he might or might not be responsible for the (false) pregnancy, the reader begins to wonder whether he has understood the joke properly in the first place, and indeed, in a very real sense, his own impotence becomes the textual *analogon* of that of Du Bousquier in the narrative: a secret which is not a presence, not a positive phenomenon, but rather mere absence, frustration, incomprehensibility, and so forth. Not that the Chevalier's secret fares any better, for as so often in Balzac it is as though the truth of desire were associated with unfulfillment—"Now a little fire in a wild field were like an old lecher's heart—a small spark, all the rest on's body cold." And the sudden deterioration of the Chevalier's appearance, the abrupt on-set of genuine old age after the failure of his dynastic hopes, dramatically underscores the deep underground affinity Balzac senses between desire, the timeless eternity of the unconscious, and the month-by-month and year-by-year decline of the human organism through time and history.

But the ultimate explanation for the predominance of the rhetorical figure of the secret in this final section of the portrait devoted to money lies in the peculiar and distinctive kind of opposition governed by the latter and inherent in its code. For in terms of money, there can be no genuine opposing term of any real substance: the opposite of having money is simple privation, and the "decent" poverty of the Gransons is simply a half-way house to suicide and not, as the conclusions to books like *Illusions perdues* might suggest, some positive and honest virtue in its own right. In this light, the successive oppositions generated by the successive codes of the portrait seem to fall into a pattern of increasing negativity but also increasing impoverishment as well: in the code of manners, for instance, it was still possible to be an aristocrat if one was not a bourgeois, to be a bourgeois if one was not an aristocrat: the two terms were felt to be not so much contradictions as rather simple contraries; and even here, as we saw, their mutual exclusiveness was systematically muffled and weakened by the text itself. In the second code, also, that of sexuality, it seemed as though one could either be effeminate or be masculine, and that each mode of being still retained some positive content in its own right. Already here, however, the reader begins to suspect that the antithesis is simpler than this, the mere either/or of sexuality or impotence, and it is this stark alternative of simple affirmation or negation which will become dominant in the operation of the final code of money.

Nor does the latter leave the former codes unaffected by its new structure: on the contrary, it may be said that like the money economy itself, the money code operates something like a demystification (Deleuze and Guattari call it a *decoding* in their terminology[8]) of the earlier codes, whose illusions are thereby unmasked. These demystifications are, of course, simply the effects of fresh restructurations of the type we have already described in connection with the Chevalier's nose: elements persisting through all three sections here finding yet a third position in yet a third signifying system. So, for instance, the extraordinary whiteness of the Chevalier's linen is in the first section of the portrait clearly enough a sign or *index* of the elegance with which he moves in social life as in his very element. But this same feature, persisting into the force field of the second, overtly sexual code, now gives off overtones of a somewhat different and much stronger kind: now the "blancheur" extends to the Chevalier's underlinen as well, and is set in opposition, not to the unfashionableness of bourgeois dress in general, but rather specifically to the food-spotted and urine-stained garments of other elderly people, in contrast to which the Chevalier's dazzling cleanliness becomes an explicit sign of youth and of constant preparedness for amorous encounter. From one interchangeable sign among others, therefore, this *datum* has become dominant (one which is indeed relatively conventionalized in the novels of this and the preceding period).

This element now continues to emit signals from well into the third section of the portrait, where however they are once again transformed, this time almost beyond recognition. For what we discover in the third section, dealing with the Chevalier's finances, is something like an overdetermination of the first two: better still, the readings suggested by the earlier codes were simply *wrong*, and it turns out that the spotlessness of the Chevalier's linen is neither proof of his elegance nor testimony of his erotic triumphs. On the contrary, there is another, far simpler explanation, which like Occam's razor slices across the earlier two and makes the reader wonder why it never occurred to anyone before: the Chevalier's clothes are as clean as they are for a much more basic reason than any already given, namely that he boards with a *laundress!* (gros rire, etc.)

Thus the new code is not simply another, equivalent one in a long series, but rather comes with a kind of etiological finality, and has the result of effectively discrediting all of the earlier ones and of supplanting them with a new type of thinking about their objects. The illusory richness of the older codes is demystified, and stripped of its capacity to mislead, but at the same time nothing replaces it but the abstract system of financial cause and effect itself: the object's value as a sign or a symbol is here systematically deleted, and we witness something like that passage from *quality* to *quantity* which for Marx and Engels, but also for Hegel himself, characterizes the coming into being of capitalism, and the replacement by the market system and its measurable equivalencies of the older qualitative values of pre-capitalist societies. In *Capital* this process is described in terms of the shift from production based on *use value* (in which each object is somehow unique, and carries its own properly incomparable charge of libidinal energy) to that on the basis of *exchange value*, where objects are related through the neutral medium of money itself, which, by rendering them indifferently equivalent, reduces their former qualities to the grey tastelessness of sheer number.

But information theory has given us another terminology in which to see this process, which we may then also usefully describe in terms of the passage from *analog* to *digital* systems: in the analog machine, indeed, "there is no true zero (at "zero" the machine is "off"). All the quantities involved are positive; there are no minus quantities."[9] An analog world (or an analog representation) would thus be, following Wilden's terminology, one of sheer qualitative *difference*, in which each term—fact or object—knows a kind of autonomy in its own right. Digitalization now replaces that plenitude with a network of simple *distinctions* or off/on oppositions: its data undergo a kind of rationalization and standardization which reduces the older, relatively dialectical relationships between them to the newer relatively more static type of the binary opposition. From the point of view of information theory, of course, all communication is a mixture of these two modes of thought, which may be characterized as the *iconic* (the analog) and the *metalingual* (the digital) respectively; but the thrust of the theory seems to me to retain the historical implications of the older Hegelian terminology outlined above, insofar as the "fall" into digitalization is felt to constitute both an advance in man's capacity to control the world and, at one and the same time, an impoverishment of the preceding modes of existence. The information model has the additional benefit, in the context of narrative analysis, of directing our attention to other key features of the process of digitalization, namely the appearance of the subject or shifter, the capacity for metalanguage, and the emergence of negation or of the zero.

The progression of codes in the Balzacian portrait can now be understood, therefore, as a way of *programming* the reader for the narrative to come; and the final money or digital code must now be understood in connection with the most fundamental rhythm of Balzacian plot as a whole, whose breath-taking and monotonous alternations must be understood as one gigantic off/on system in which the characters are systematically lifted on the crest of success and just as systematically dashed to the ground again. Indeed, it is in this light that the fundamental problem of Balzac's aesthetic can be understood: how, in a world of simplified digital oppositions, in which the hero can only win or lose, the predictability of these outcomes can be disguised. Balzac must preserve his system of expectations (the semantic content of his heroes' quests being varied along broad spectrum that runs from money and power and social status through invention, art, "gloire," to sex and love) while systematically sowing false clues and monitory intimations ("ce geste fatal," "comme la suite le montrera," etc.) which can then be contradicted by the immediate results of a given episode, even though they will be confirmed in the long run. There thus comes into being a unique temporal structure—something like a meta-melodrama—in which the reader's most characteristic reactions are neither hope nor fear but rather something like "hope against hope," a negation of some already present temporal perspective, which, as soon as expectation has ratified it in its turn, will be itself the object of some new reversal "beyond all expectations." So it is that the final and most unexpected reversal of all will be that in which *both* success *and* failure are cancelled out, in that desolate transcendence of which the conclusion of *La Vieille Fille* furnishes a triumphant and intolerable realization (married *and* an old maid all at once!).

Balzacian plot is thus profoundly compromised by these rhythms of appetite and acquisition which are only too clearly those of the nascent capitalist system, and it is too easy to suggest—even though it is *also* true—that Balzac thematizes the new digital and decoded forms, thus making them available to us in a critical way, his own novels furnishing something like a formal commentary on their own content. The trouble is that the reader must find it in himself to share the appetencies that drive the plot along: his very excitement is the sign of his own symbolic participation, and there is no disengaged, ironic position provided for him (as in Flaubert) so that he can survey the narrative without being compromised by it. It is more honest, with Lucien Goldmann,[10] to recognize that Balzac is in this respect also unique among the great nineteenth century writers and that to him alone the Lukácsian concept of the "problematic hero" does not apply. His real descendency is not Flaubert or naturalism, but rather the best-seller, with its thinly disguised wish-fulfillments and its cult of success and consumption. The most corrupt of all the great nineteenth century novelists, Balzac is also the most lucid and realistic, because the peculiar elements that make up his form do not only stem from personal choices and psychological attitudes, but also and above all from a unique transitional situation in the history of the novel, and in the development of the novel's raw materials, or in other words, capitalism, as well: and to say so is to recall that Balzac is also anti-capitalist, and that the other side of his ideology functions precisely as an accusation and a judgement on what we have seen to be the deepest rhythms of Balzacian narrative.

Notes

1. Louis Althusser, "Ideology and Ideological State Apparatuses," In *Lenin and Philosophy* (London: New Left Books, 1971).

2.
$$
\begin{array}{c}
\text{Context} \\
\text{Message} \\
\text{Addresser} \quad \cdots\cdots\cdots\cdots\cdots\cdots\cdots\cdots\cdots \quad \text{Addressee} \\
\text{Contact} \\
\text{Code}
\end{array}
$$

Roman Jakobson, "Closing Statement," in Thomas Sebeok, ed., *Style in Languages* (Cambridge, Mass.: MIT Press, 1960), 353.

3. Balzac, *La Comédie humaine,* Editions de la Pléiade (Paris: Gallimard, 1952), vol. 4, 213 (all future page references to this edition will be given parenthetically).

4. Sir Walter Scott, *The Heart of Midlothian* (London: Collins, 1967), chapter 44, 456.

5. See for example the letter quoted by Bernard Guyon, in *La Pensée politique et sociale de Balzac* (Balzac's political and social thought) (Paris: Armand Colin, 1967), 75.

6. Claude Lévi-Strauss, *L'Homme nu* (Naked man) (Paris: Plon, 1967), 609.

7. It does not seem appropriate to call this a "hermeneutic code," as does Roland Barthes in S/Z (Paris: Seuil, 1970), 24–28, which see, however, for a quite different approach to the codes of a text than that proposed here.

8. Gilles Deleuze and Félix Guattari, *L'Anti-Oedipe* (Anti-oedipus) (Paris: Minuit, 1972), 263–84.

9. A. G. Wilden, "Analog and Digital Communication," in *System and Structure* (London: Tavistock, 1972), 161.

10. Lucien Goldmann, *Pour une sociologie du roman* (Toward a sociology of the novel) (Paris: Gallimard, 1964), 54: "The only exception we see for the moment is precisely Balzac's own work; he was able to create a grand, structured, literary universe out of purely individualistic values, at a moment in history when men motivated by these a-historical values were in the very process of carrying out a considerable historical upheaval."

Reflections on Balzacian Models of Representation

Roland Le Huenen and
Paul Perron*

In a letter to Mme Hanska dated January 1833, Balzac announces a new project for a novel entitled *La Bataille* which he sets out in the following terms:

> I tell you that *La Bataille* is an impossible book. In it, I undertake to make you aware of all the horrors and all the beauties of a battlefield; my battle is Essling, Essling with all its consequences. A cold man sitting in his armchair must see the countryside, the irregularities of the ground, the masses of men, the strategic events, the Danube, the bridges; must admire the details and the whole of that combat; must hear the artillery; must be interested in these chess moves; must see everything. In every joint of that great body, he must feel Napoleon whom I will not show or whom I will allow to be seen in the evening crossing the Danube in a boat. Not a single female, cannons, horses, two armies, uniforms; on the first page, the cannon roars, it is silent on the last; you will read through the smoke and, when the book is closed, you must have seen everything intuitively and must recall the battle as if you had been [there].
>
> For three months now I have wrestled with this work, this ode in two volumes which everyone cries out is impossible to write[1] (28)

This fragment of a letter, which serves to fix a first approximation of the Balzacian process of representation, and hence that of the realistic novel, appears more spontaneously revealing on the whole than the prefaces, and less suspect than the narrative generally devoted to naturalizing its own procedures of figuration. It is from this perspective that our analysis will be organized.

The disclosure that "*La Bataille* is an impossible book" has a two-fold significance: it indicates the ends, and inscribes in filigree the difficulty of the means. Ideally, to narrate is necessarily to produce an effect of presence through recourse to the senses, to sight in particular. "A cold man sitting in his armchair must see the countryside . . . admire the details . . . hear the artillery . . . see everything . . . In every joint of that great body, he must

*First published in *Poetics Today* 5, no. 4 (1984): 711–29. Reprinted by permission. Translated by Barbara Benavie.

feel Napoleon . . . You will read through the smoke." In short, to narrate is to make one see as if one were there or, more precisely, as if one had been there, for the end of the passage seems to suggest a displacement of effect from presence to reminiscence: "and when the book is closed, you must have seen everything intuitively and must recall the battle as if you had been there." "Seen everything intuitively," a correction *in extremis* that resituates language in its semiotic context, for the word is neither the thing nor its stand-in, but an index that points and that causes to point, a signal that releases, as in those cases of paramnesia, an impression of déjà vu, which revives an imprint woven into memory by knowledge and experience. To represent is always to resort to the antecedence of a trace, to invoke a reference; that is, through the intermediary of the sign, to establish a topological translation affecting the space of reading. "A cold man sitting in his armchair must see . . ." Balzacian description often uses such strategies of interpellation addressed to the reader or narratee, strategies which are like summations to be represented through the mediation of an image or a memory. Thus, in *Un Drame au bord de la mer*, the beginning of Cambremer's portrait: "Try to call up before you, dear uncle, some gnarled oak stump, with all its branches lately lopped away, rearing its head, like a strange apparition, by the side of a lonely road, and you will have a clear idea of this man that we saw" (10, 1169). Or, in *Le Chef d'oeuvre inconnu*, the setting of Frenhofer's portrait: "Picture that face. A bald high forehead and rugged jutting brows above a small flat nose turned up at the end, as in the portraits of Socrates and Rabelais . . . Set this head on a spare and feeble frame, place it in a frame of lace wrought like an engraved silver fish-slice, imagine a heavy gold chain over the old man's black doublet, and you will have some dim idea of this strange personnage" (10, 414–415). Thus, the illusion of a presence, the very nature of representation, is created by the order of language itself.

Yet, "*La Bataille* is an impossible book" and we know that Balzac did not complete his project, did not even write a first draft, despite the important documentation gathered and numerous notices of impending release. Though it is not important here and now to speculate on the objective reasons that led Balzac to abandon his project, it is nevertheless possible to raise questions about the general significance of the opinion expressed concerning this aborted plan. Assessments of the respective merits of painting and literature are frequently found in Balzac's writings. The preface to *La Peau de chagrin* comes out strongly in favor of literature, "the most complicated of all the arts" (10, 51). Now this preeminence granted to writing has less to do with the techniques of expression than with the capacity of narrative to manipulate ideas, to make itself the instrument of visionary thought, a fact which, in any case, does not prejudice the outcome raised by the problematics of representation. Moreover, after the preface comes to a close, the novel is set in motion by an image: Sterne's drawing which, as we know, in *Tristram Shandy* was ironically substituted for the verbal description of Corporal Trim's whirling stick.

As can be seen from Balzac's text itself, the sign is certainly not an image and cannot in any way claim to rival the visual. Nonetheless, the temptation remains, and fascination with the pictorial appears especially powerful in the writing of portraits. As a figure of rhetoric, the aim of the portrait is to show the body and face, to create an impression of life, to render the dynamism inherent in the supposed animate model through phrasing and the choice of images. The exemplary figure of this is hypotyposis. The Balzacian portrait remains essentially faithful to these precepts, and is established along the lines of the pictorial portrait.[2] As we know, its lexicon is saturated with borrowings from the language of painters, even in the case of prefaces and letters. An example is this quotation from the preface of *Illusions perdues:* "Only once did M. Scribe attempt to do this [denounce journalism] in his light play, *Charlatanism*, which is more a portrait than a scene. The pleasure caused by that witty draft made the author aware of the need to attempt a more ample painting" (5, 113). We should also recall that a pictorial metaphor is the structuring matrix of Davin-Balzac's two prefaces describing the project for writing *Etudes de moeurs au XIXe siècle:* ". . . in this rich picture gallery, whose great halls stretch to infinity, does one not find frames of a rather remarkable size, such as those of *Eugénie Grandet*, of the *Médecin de campagne* and of *Les Chouans*, which obviously belong to the *Scènes de la vie militaire?*" (10, 1207).

Moreover, concerned with producing visual illusion, novelistic description calls upon the mediation of the image, either by evoking the memory of famous paintings to ground the written portrait,[3] or, less obviously, by the use of the citational relay of an Epinal engraving,[4] or by weighting the verbal signifier with the materiality of the chromatic: Adeline Fischer has "a complexion mingled in the unknown laboratory where good luck presides" (7, 74). Another characteristic of Balzacian writing is to relate the written face to a specific painter's technique and aesthetic. Thus the portrait of Esther van Gobseck at the beginning of *Splendeurs et misères:* "Esther, excessively strong though apparently fragile, arrested attention by one feature that is conspicuous in the faces in which Raphaël has shown his most artistic feeling, for Raphaël is the painter who has most and best rendered Jewish beauty. This remarkable effect was produced by the depth of the eye-socket, under which the eye moved free from its setting; the arch of the brow was so accurate as to resemble the groining of a vault" (6, 464). Here, the language of the portrait indexes less the reality of an image than borrowings from a critical metalanguage, that of art. Not only does this language copy the value judgments of art critics, but it also somehow guarantees the possibility of semiotic collaboration and an homogenization of signs. To account for a picture by means of writing is to assume implicitly the compatibility of languages and the admissibility of their mutual transcoding.[5] But, on closer inspection, figurative description is most often reduced to the doxastic declension of semantic fields; for example, the divine, angelic, sublime, virginal grace of Raphaël; the serious and thoughtful integrity or the ingenuous and seraphic candor of Titian.

One could further examine this type of pictorialization of the written portrait. To evoke a picture or to cite the name of a painter is to urge the reader to substitute for the graphics of sentences and the succession of verbal signs a representation belonging to the realm of figures, of simultaneity and of the whole. It is also to posit the ineffectiveness of writing or at least its inferiority vis-à-vis painting, since, in order to describe, writing must resort to the suggestion of the image. It is, finally, to recognize the inevitability of the sign, for if description evokes the character of the object represented, it also evokes its own literariness as well as the constraints inherent in its descriptive status by the very verbal discontinuity which, through sequencing, deconstructs the original unity of the object. Hence the search for palliatives, for stylistic techniques, which are various means of semiotic correlation, striving to simulate, through forced harmony of discourse, the "natural" harmony of the model.[6] Hence the admiration for Walter Scott whose work, all things considered, is praised less (in the terms of the *Avant-propos* of *La Comédie humaine*) for its historical significance than for its aesthetic qualities. Hence Balzac's enthusiasm for Cooper's novel, *Lake Ontario*, whose craftsmanship inspired this comment: "Never has the printed word encroached more on painting."[7] And hence his nostalgia for the image and fascination with the pictorial.

La Bataille really is an impossible book, even more so since the style of the sketch (as reported in the letter to Mme Hanska) seems to suggest a purely visual treatment of subject, which tends to render the description autonomous and to liberate it from explanatory commentary that invariably accompanies so many Balzacian descriptions. This scopic treatment would involve, in sum, focusing on one image, on one setting in the name of and in the search for the irreducibility of figuration. Such an hypothesis is even more probable since, in the wording of the project itself, through a determinative turn of phrase ("*my* battle is Essling"), a sort of intertextuality-effect comes to the fore, tending to limit this battle to the role of representing battles already represented against the background of other battles, which, in this specific instance, could only be the frescoes of the Napoleonic era. It is perhaps helpful to note that Balzac had a precise knowledge of Imperial iconography,[8] as can be attested from close examination of the postface of *Les Paysans* or the military scene which opens *La Femme de trente ans*. In addition, Olivier Bonnard has shown that the description of the battle of Eylau in *Colonel Chabert* presents striking analogies with Gros's painting of the scene.[9] This provides useful insights into the generative function of visual images in Balzacian creation and, more particularly, into the importance the novelist attached to iconographic documentation.[10] Yet, it is at the very moment he undertakes, and expeditiously finishes, *Colonel Chabert* that Balzac gets inextricably entangled in the descriptive aporias of *La Bataille*. Beyond the trite hypothesis concerning the intermittent nature of Balzac's genius, to what can this success and this failure be attributed if not to the formal difference between two descriptive methods?

The first method attempts to create pure effects of figures and inevitably comes up against the insurmountable literariness of the sign; the second assumes representation as a mediating necessity, and ends up designating more the absence of the object than the object itself. The summoning up of a picture, or its allusive citation, has no other goal than to further the verbal sign's indexical dimension, its transcendent functionality and its ostensory capacity. However, at one and the same time this capacity to represent imposes itself and is experienced in the unbridgeable distance separating sign from object, a distance which can be bridged only by mirror effects producing the image as presence/absence. "Thus," writes Barthes "realism (badly named, at any rate often badly interpreted) consists not in copying the real but in copying a (depicted) copy of the real: this famous *reality*, as though suffering from a fearfulness which keeps it from being touched directly, is *set farther away*, postponed, or at least captured through the pictorial matrix in which it has been steeped before being put into words . . . This is why realism cannot be designated a 'copier' but rather a 'pasticheur.' "[11] And so descriptive gesture can only "de-pict" its copy, detach it from its illusorily figural frame, by putting it into the frame of language and rendering it through discourse, the task of which will be to make it signify. The indefinitely renewed configuration of meaning settles in the very gap created between the object and its representation by the gestural nature of the sign. Originally to represent is to show, yet, as was mentioned before, this visualization is reduced to an evocation; that is, to the reiteration of a trace, an imprint left in memory through the imposition of knowledge.

But what is the nature of knowledge? The *Avant-propos* to *La Comédie humaine* and the prefaces, particularly the two prefaces by Davin-Balzac, provide the possibility for a first systematization. Davin's prefaces present the two-fold descriptive metaphor of a picture gallery designating *Les Etudes de moeurs*, and of a monument built stone by stone, the architectural pyramid of which simulates the successive staging of the *Comédie humaine* in its entirety. The *Etudes de moeurs* thus form its base, the *Etudes analytiques* its apex, and the *Etudes philosophiques* its median transition. This schematization, which Balzac summarizes in similar terms in the *Avant-propos* and the *Lettres à Madame Hanska*, as well as considerations on the unity of composition borrowed from Geoffroy Saint-Hilaire, would suggest an idealized conception of knowledge moving from effects to causes, then to principles; that is, to the entirety of a form. From this perspective, the place of representation *stricto sensu* in which the novelist's talent to become a "painter who is more or less faithful, more or less fortunate," a "teller of the dramas of intimate life," an "archaeologist of the social scene," a "classifier of professions" is, strictly speaking, only the place of accident, chance, contingency which enfolds knowledge within the common limits of observation. Accordingly, true knowledge would be elsewhere, in the elucidation of the "hidden meaning" and in meditation "on natural principles" based on "the eternal rule of truth and beauty" (1, 11–12). There is no doubt that this pseudo-scientific theory of knowledge is inscribed as a belief, as an act of faith whose ideological (that is, imaginary)[12] character is more apparent in the spontaneous and less circumspect formulation found in this letter to Mme Hanska: "Then, after the *effects* and the causes, will come the *Etudes analytiques* of which the *Physiologie du mariage* is a part; for, after the *effects* and the *causes*, the principles must be sought. The *customs* are the spectacle, the *causes* are *the wings and the machinery*. Principles, that's the *author*."[13] Nonetheless, taken literally, this theoretical fiction postulates a sharp dissociation between the realm of representation and the realm of knowledge; that is, if it is true that "as the work spirals up to the heights of thought, it becomes more compact and more dense" (p. 270). It remains to be seen if this purely thetic apprehension of knowledge is really the one that the novels set into place. It would seem, rather, that Balzacian practice actually reverses the preceding theoretical viewpoint and constitutes knowledge as a modelling activity *of* and *on* representation.

As was suggested, the relationship between language and the pictorial is infinite insofar as the sign and the image are irreducible to one another. If "*La Bataille* is an impossible book," it is, as was seen, because the place, the topos, the domain from which it emerges—despite the images, comparisons, and metaphors—are not the ones perceived by sight and the other senses, but those evoked in and through the order of syntax. It is also impossible to write because, from the vantage point occupied by "the cold man sitting in his armchair," the cycle of representation, as focalized space, is presented in its entirety.

Consequently, writing *La Bataille* consists of organizing a determined space for an observer so that he "admires the details and the whole," and the following two series of problems involving composition and structure arise. In order to represent, a framework is required, one which mediates the transition from the formless to the formed, from the indefinite to the finite, from the unlimited to the limited, from "*a* battlefield" to "*my* battle." This process of delimitation leaves traces in the actual linguistic material itself; for example, the accumulation of such deictic determinants as: "*the* countryside," "*the* irregularities" or "*that* combat," "*those* movements." It thus becomes a question of circumscribing, delimiting, assigning a place to all constitutive elements, arranging characters, squaring or gridding space to make the spectator sense the moves of the pieces on the "chessboard" of the battlefield, pieces which are deployed according to rules and principles that remain to be determined.

Thus, description, that spectacle to-be-seen, is not a simple trace of the real, but an enclosed and divided scene, naturalized through the interplay of organic and anatomical metaphors—"every joint of that great body"—and from these analogies a diagram of the battle emerges, a schema of "those chess moves" which, by becoming delineated space, take on meaning. Moreover, the scene so arranged can converge on one of two figures: the chessboard and its pieces, or the absent player whose presence is sensed and felt—"Napoleon whom I will not show." Description can therefore be organized from two centers of focus: the first, an exhaustive ordering, takes the categorical form of a "table,"[14] a grid, while the second, non-represented, is occupied by the Emperor not encompassed within the framework. All lines of the diagram point to the non-circumscribed place of the one not included in the space of representation. And yet a problem comes to the fore since attention is—or must be—fixed simultaneously on the place of representation and on the imagined site where he who manipulates from afar the shifts and moves on the chessboard is thought to be.

The project of the novel unfolds both as the representation of a scene and as the unveiling of its organizational principles; in other words, as product and process. Hence the outline hesitates between two spaces, recognizes them as distinct, but, by superimposing them, attempts to bring them to a single center of focus. This impossible play of perception, fragmented and atomized, but simultaneously framed, centered, and feasible in pictorial organization, dooms the writing project to failure. To superimpose the vanishing point on the chessboard is, on the one hand, to imagine narrative in terms of pictorial representation, but, on the other, to deny the possibilty of realistic writing arising from the concatenation of a gridded space and a vanishing point. It is, also, not to recognize the need for a space proper to narrative. Thought of too much in terms of the pictorial to function as narrative, and incapable of articulating two heterogeneous spaces at the same time, *La Bataille* could not be written and remained an impossible book.

On the one hand, *La Bataille* remains an impossible book for want of a space specific to narrative; on the other, through the interplay of the descriptive and the pictorial, *La Maison du chat-qui-pelote* does, in fact, succeed in constructing a space, the exact status of which is problematical, however. The narrative initially sets into place a completed, ordered, measurable space, which, through untimely fate—that is, an accidental glimpse—is transformed into another, disturbing, unframed, and fragmented space, a vague and undecidable libidinal space where the subject, belonging to another time, another place, cannot be constituted. And, to paraphrase Michel Foucault, if the center of knowledge in the Classical Age is the table, diagrammatical classification, order, and measure which squares space, then the Balzacian text functions as a device which delineates and structures spaces, decomposes and recomposes them according to the general principle of establishing continuity and order, suddenly followed by rift and division.

This process of order and fragmentation, gridding and vanishing point is also the structuring principle of many other of Balzac's texts. Frenhofer, for example, the painter who ends up mad in *Le Chef d'oeuvre inconnu*, refuses to resort to line, drawing, sketch, and produces a formless space of "confused masses of color and a multitude of fantastical lines" (X, 436). Moreover, the narrator takes pains to stress that the painter resembles one of Rembrandt's characters out of frame, in the same way that Chabert is compared to "a portrait by Rembrandt without a frame" (III, 321). A decentered character from the point of view of society and family, Chabert ends up on the fringes of society in Bicêtre and spends his time with a stick in hand "drawing lines in the sand" (III, 372) which are uncontrolled arabesques that can in no way be converted into closed and centered geometric figures. The final picture of Chabert tracing insane and erratic lines is reminiscent of the clausula in *Ferragus* describing the former leader of the Dévorants, broken and senile, striding along the promenade of the Observatory, an open and undifferentiated space, following, with a "vacant eye" (V, 903) the unpredictable and capricious shifts of the jack of the bowlers who occasionally use the old man's stick as a derisive unit of measure. These indecisive and indeterminable comings and goings are final moments in the constitution of a new space, a new knowledge where the subject cannot find a place; they are the end terms of transformational processes that take archaic spaces and knowledge originally inscribed in the text, redistribute them, and re-present them according to an incoherent and incomprehensible logic—troubled and troubling spaces of transition to be reproduced and re-articulated in Balzac's later texts according to modalities that remain to be defined and described.[15]

Notes

1. Honoré de Balzac, *Lettres à Madame Hanska* (Paris: Bibliophiles de l'Originale, 1967–68), 27–28. [Ed. note: All citations to the *Comédie humaine* are noted in the text and refer to the new Pléiade edition (Paris: Gallimard, 1976–81)].

2. R. Le Huenen and P. Perron, *Balzac, sémiotique du personnage romanesque: l'exemple d'Eugénie Grandet* (Montréal/Paris: Didier Erudition, 1980), 37–91.

3. Or the example of Adeline Fischer's portrait: "These beautiful creatures all have something in common, Bianca Capella, whose portrait is one of Bronzino's masterpieces; Jean Goujon's Venus . . . Signora Olympia whose portrait adorns the Doria Gallery . . ." (7, 74).

4. Or the example of Montriveau's portrait: "The principal characteristic of his great, square-hewn head was the thick luxuriant-black hair that framed his face and gave him a strikingly close resemblance to General Kleber" (4, 946).

5. For example, at the beginning of *La Maison du chat-qui-pelote*, the description of the Guillaume family, initially perceived as the written transcription of a genre painting, later on becomes the subject of an actual canvas by Sommervieux.

6. B. Vannier, *L'Inscription du corps* (Paris: Klincksieck, 1972), 36–47.

7. Quoted by Mme M. Fargeaud-Ambrière in "Documents, notes et variantes de l'Avant-propos de La Comédie humaine," (1, 1110–42).

8. "You must believe that the author of *Les Paysans* was knowledgeable enough about the times he lived in to know that Cuirassiers did not belong to the Imperial Guard. He would like to indicate, here and now, that in his study he has the uniforms of the armies under the Republic, the Empire, the Restoration, as well as a collection of all the military costumes of the

countries that France had as allies or enemies. He also has more works on the wars of 1792 to 1815 than a Maréchal of France" (9, 1290).

9. O. Bonnard, *La Peinture dans la création balzacienne* (Painting in Balzac's works) (Geneva: Droz, 1969), 53 ff.

10. In August 1834, precisely with regard to *La Bataille*, Balzac asked Mme Hanska for the following information: "I really need to see Vienna. I must explore the fields of Wagram and Essling before next July. I especially need engravings representing the uniforms of the German army, which I must purchase. Be kind enough to tell me if they do exist" (*Lettres à Madame Hanska*, I, 247). He makes the same type of request in January 1844: "I forgot, I was so sorry to leave, when I think that all the uniforms of the Russian army can be found in Petersburg; please use Colmann to do some research on this for me. I need colored engravings and, especially, in French, the names of the weapons and the regiments during Russia's wars with France." (Ibid., 2, 340).

11. R. Barthes, *S/Z* (New York: Hill and Wang, 1974), 55.

12. Cf., L. Althusser, quoted by J. L. Baudry, "Ecriture, fiction, idéologie," in *Théorie d'ensemble* (Paris: Seuil, 1968).

13. Balzac, *Lettres à Madame Hanska*, 1, 270.

14. M. Foucault, *The Order of Things* (London: Tavistock, 1970), 74–75: "The sciences always carry within themselves the project, however remote it may be, of an exhaustive ordering of the world; they are always directed, too, towards the discovery of simple elements and their progressive combination; and in their center they form a table on which knowledge is displayed in a system contemporaneous with itself. The center of knowledge in the seventeenth and eighteenth centuries is the *table*. As for the great controversies that occupied men's minds, these are accommodated quite naturally in the folds of this organization."

15. Some of the ideas expressed on what could be termed "the space of knowledge" in Balzacian fiction develop points made by Fredric Jameson in a lecture entitled "The Bourgeois Revolution and the Aesthetic Text (Flaubert)," which was given at the University of Toronto in April 1982.

SELECTED BIBLIOGRAPHY

Major Editions of Balzac's Work

The complexities of the "lifetime" editions stem principally from Balzac's habit of substantially rewriting and republishing his texts in various combinations and states. The following list gives the principal editions in which he had a hand.

Scènes de la vie privée. 2 vols. Paris: Mame et Delaunay-Vallée, Levavasseur, 1830. A second, enlarged edition in four volumes appeared in 1832.

Romans et contes philosophiques. 3 vols. Paris: Gosselin, 1831.

Scènes de la vie privée. 4 vols. Paris: Mame et Delaunay, 1832.

Nouveaux Contes philosophiques. 1 vol. Paris: Gosselin, 1832.

Etudes de moeurs au XIXe siècle. 12 vols. Paris: Béchet [subsequently Werdet], 1834–37. This edition is divided into *Scènes de la vie privée*, *Scènes de la vie de province* and *Scènes de la vie parisienne*. The *Scènes* saw several later augmented separate editions.

Le Livre mystique. 2 vols. Paris: Werdet, 1835.

Etudes philosophiques. 10 vols. Paris: Werdet, Delloye et Lecou, Souverain, 1835–40. Announced as thirty volumes, it was reduced at some point to twenty; only ten actually appeared.

Oeuvres de H. de Balzac. 8 vols. Bruxelles: Meline, Cans, 1837–43. This was the first of the notorious Belgian pirate editions.

Oeuvres complètes. La Comédie humaine. 17 vols. Paris: Furne et Cie., 1842–48. This is the celebrated edition that Balzac corrected in the margins and that, known as the "Furne corrigé," has been the basis of critical editions ever since.

After Balzac's death, collected editions continued to appear, with increasingly accurate texts and increasingly useful critical apparatuses, although they reflect the uncertainties, gaps, and contradictions that remained:

Oeuvres complètes illustrées. Edition Houssiaux. 20 vols. Paris: Houssiaux, 1853–55. This was essentially the Furne edition with three additional volumes. Various reprints appeared in 1865, 1874, 1877, and 1924.

Oeuvres complètes de H. de Balzac. Edition définitive. 26 vols. (Pléiade XII says twenty-four vols.) Paris: Calmann-Lévy, 1869–76. Reprinted in 1899, 1906, and 1924.

Oeuvres complètes de Honoré de Balzac. 40 vols. Paris: Conard, 1912–40. For many years the standard edition, the Conard, reflected the Furne corrigé state of the *Comédie humaine;* it also provided two volumes of theater, two of *Contes drolatiques,* three of *oeuvres diverses,* and a minimal critical apparatus throughout.

Oeuvres complètes. La Comédie humaine. 10 vols. Paris: Gallimard, 1935–37. Edited by Marcel Bouteron. This appeared in the famous Bibliothèque de La Pléiade. In 1959 an eleventh volume was added containing the *Contes drolatiques* and various indices.

L'Oeuvre de Balzac. 16 vols. Paris: Club français du livre, 1950. Edited by Jean-A. Ducourneau and A. Béguin. Collection "Formes et Reflets." The stories are arranged in the chronological order of the plots. This is familiarly known as the "Formes et Reflets" edition.

Oeuvres complètes. 28 vols. Paris: Club de l'honnête homme, 1955–63. Prepared by Maurice Bardèche, under the patronage of the Société des Etudes Balzaciennes.

Oeuvres complètes illustrées. 30 vols. Paris: Les Bibliophiles de l'originale, 1965–76. Edited by Jean-A. Ducourneau. This is a facsimile of the "Furne corrigé" together with voluminous additional material. Volumes 27 and 28 never appeared.

La Comédie humaine, 7 vols. Paris: Seuil, 1965–1966. Introduction by Pierre-Georges Castex, edited by Pierre Citron. This edition restores the divisions into chapters that had been eliminated in the others, and includes fragmentary materials that Balzac did not use in the novels.

La Comédie humaine. 12 vols. Paris: Gallimard, 1976–1981. Edited by P. G. Castex et. al. This is a revision of the 1935 Pléiade edition.

Along the way, naturally, many individual novels have been issued in critical editions.[1] Additionally, the ever-popular Classiques Garnier series provides excellent, inexpensive, and "semischolarly" editions for those who find the price of the leather-bound Pléiade volumes rather daunting. All originally edited by Maurice Allem, the Classiques Garnier have gradually been replaced by more modern editions of all the most famous titles, prepared by scholars profiting from recent research. But it was surely Jean Pommier's edition of *L'Eglise* in 1947 that set the standard for modern critical editing.[2]

Critical Studies

The following list is highly selective, limited to works of general interest in French and English published within the past fifty years. They have been chosen as good starting points from which the reader can move to more specialized studies.

Allemand, André. *Unité et structures de l'univers balzacien.* Paris: Plon, 1965. An excellent study that views the *Comédie humaine* as a set of reciprocal internal relationships among individuals, places, and things.

Barbéris, Pierre. *Balzac et le mal du siècle.* 2 vols. Paris: Gallimard, 1970. A Marxist approach of enormous energy and persuasive power.

Bardèche. Maurice. *Balzac romancier: la formation de l'art du roman chez Balzac 1820–1835.* Paris: Plon, 1940. Very conservative but powerful analysis of Balzac's emergence as a novelist.

Béguin, Albert. *Balzac visionnaire.* Geneva: Skira, 1946. The major reading of the *Comédie humaine* as a philosophical enterprise.

Bertault, Philippe. *Balzac et la religion*. Paris: Boivin, 1939. The major study of Balzac as a Catholic writer.

Curtius, Ernst-Robert. *Balzac*. Paris: Grasset, 1933. Translated by Henri Jourdan. Philosophical in its approach, and very abstract in its categories and analytical terminology.

Delattre, Geneviève. *Les Opinions littéraires de Balzac*. Paris: PUF, 1961. Invaluable for setting the literary context in which Balzac worked.

Donnard, J. H. *Balzac: les Réalités économiques et sociales dans La Comédie humaine*. Paris: Armand Colin, 1961. The most thoroughgoing study of Balzac's portrait of the economic substratum of the July Monarchy.

Hemmings, F. W. J. *Balzac: An Interpretation of La Comédie humaine*. New York: Random House, 1967. An excellent first introduction, making no assumptions of prior knowledge of Balzac or his work.

Guyon, Bernard. *La Pensée politique et sociale de Balzac*. Paris: Armand Colin, 1947. Speculative and theoretical, provides an excellent counterpoint to Donnard.

Kanes, Martin. *Balzac's Comedy of Words*. Princeton: Princeton University Press, 1975. A study of the theme of language as one of the basic narrative mechanisms of the *Comédie humaine*.

Laubriet, Pierre. *L'Intelligence de l'art chez Balzac*. Paris: Didier, 1961. Immensely learned and detailed, deals with Balzac's treatment of the arts as well as with his general esthetic theories.

Lukács, Georg. *Balzac et le réalisme français*. Translated by Paul Laveau. Paris: Maspero, 1967. Originally published in Hungarian in 1934, one of the major Marxist statements on Balzac.

Nykrog, Per. *La Pensée de Balzac dans la Comédie humaine*. Copenhagen: Munksgaard, 1965. A magisterial account of the fundamental categories of Balzac's thought that moves beyond partial interpretations of the "visionary" or "realist" type.

Pritchett, V. S., *Balzac*. New York: Knopf, 1973. Not free of small errors and occasionally vague about dates, this is nevertheless an extremely engaging popular biography.

Wurmser, André. *La Comédie inhumaine*. Paris: Gallimard, 1964. Marxist and maverick, this acidulous book spares no one with whom the author might disagree. Provocative and often amusing.

Notes

1. One cannot fail to mention the following: M. Bouteron and J. Pommier, *Louis Lambert* (Paris: José Corti, 1954) [Only one volume of a projected two-volume publication ever appeared]; Suzanne-J. Bérard, *Illusions perdues* (Paris: Armand Colin, 1959) (Thèse complémentaire pour le Doctorat-ès-Lettres); Maurice Regard, *Gambara* (Paris: José Corti, 1964); Max Milner, *Massimilla Doni* (Paris: José Corti, 1964); François Germain, *L'Enfant maudit* (Paris: Belles Lettres, 1965).

2. Pommier, Jean, ed., *L'Eglise* (Paris: Droz, 1947). Under Pommier's direction, a series of remarkable scholarly editions have been produced, utilizing the materials preserved in the Lovenjoul collection.

INDEX

[Translated titles are cross-referenced to the French originals. Where there are multiple references to an author, titles are gathered under latter's name; single references are cited under title. Titles of paintings are enclosed in quotation marks]